GANGADHAR MEHER
SELECTED WORKS

GANGADHAR MEHER
SELECTED WORKS

Edited by
MADHUSUDAN PATI

विद्ययाऽमृतमश्नुते

SAMBALPUR UNIVERSITY
SAMBALPUR

ARYAN BOOKS INTERNATIONAL
NEW DELHI

Gangadhar Meher : Selected Works

A Translation Sponsored by Sambalpur University

ISBN-81-7305-212-3

First Published in **2001** by :
SAMBALPUR UNIVERSITY
Jyoti Vihar - 768019, Sambalpur (Orissa)

Printed and Distributed by :
ARYAN BOOKS INTERNATIONAL
Pooja Apts., 4B, Ansari Road, Darya Ganj, New Delhi-110 002 (India)
Tel. : 3287589, 3255799; Fax : 91-11-3270385; E-mail: aryanbooks@vsnl.com

CONTENTS

Order of the poems as in the first complete works: adopted here in honour of Sri Bhagaban Meher, son of Gangadhar, who published it courting immense hardship.

FOREWORD

Translation is a balance sheet of a special kind, for what it shows is both profit and loss. The profit that accrues from rendering a text from one language into another consists in its wider readability and recognition, depending on the magnitude of the currency of the target language and its cultural importance. As for the loss, it is primarily that of the 'untranslatable' cultural meaning, suggestive nuances and evocative power of the original. That trans-cultural barriers across literatures are insurmountable is common knowledge to both translators and readers, and yet both strive to overcome the barriers, notwithstanding the loss incurred in the process of translation. The need is very natural, human and an unmistakeable urge of civilization, to which translation alone can address.

For quite some time an effort has been on to properly project the excellence of Oriya literature and culture in the pan-Indian context by translating Oriya literary texts into English, Hindi and other Indian languages. Indeed, in recent years many important publishing houses in India, Central Sahitya Academy included, have released into the print-market a copious flow of English translations of texts written in Indian languages. Commercial motive is not the only factor to have caused this spate of translations. A catholic taste for literatures of different languages in translation, combined with a robust, liberal faith in the universality of human experience, have underpinned this translinguistic exercise, irrespective of all the post-Babel bickering of tongues. Subscribing to such a faith the Sambalpur University has brought out this volume of English translation of the major works of the poet Gangadhar Meher (1862 – 1924). We believe that an exchange between the 'mother tongue' and the 'other tongue' – in our case Oriya and English – through translation is worthwhile in the context of pan-Indian literary discourse, where Gangadhar should feature prominently. As this outstandingly gifted Oriya poet has still remained unknown to non-Oriya readership, it becomes imperative to project his works into literary circles outside Orissa.

The need for such a translation has been felt more acutely than ever since 1989, the year Sambalpur University instituted the Gangadhar National Award for poetry. Many of the awardees, eminent in their respective literatures, expressed their apologies for being ignorant of Gangadhar and evinced an eagerness to read his poetry. This was yet another prodding which prompted us to undertake the responsibility of translating the major works of the poet. And thus precipitated the present project. Professor Madhusudan Pati was assigned the editorship of the present volume of translation, and soon a team of competent translators comprising academicians, poets and critics was pressed into service. Some of them who initially agreed to participate in the project subsequently declined due to personal reasons, and the onus fell on the editor, who was requested to undertake the translation of the works assigned to them, in addition to his editorial burden, and meet the deadline. The translators enlisted for this project are well-known literary figures: Jayanta Mahapatra, Chandra Sekhar Rath, Prafulla Kumar Mohanty, Soubhagya Kumar Mishra, Pabitra Mohan Nayak, Tapas Kumar Chakrabarty, Ashok Kumar Mohapatra and Madhusudan Pati.

The project spanning a couple of years and more has entailed a vast body of meticulous work relating to editorial revisions, redrafting, dictionary-consulting, encyclopedia-browsing, post-scripting, typing, proof-reading, disk-formatting and the like. But what has sustained the editor, the translators as well as the supporting staff all through is the sense of importance of the work and above all their love for the great poet.

Prof. Madhusudan Pati had reluctantly agreed to shoulder the editorial responsibility. Our sincere thanks are due to him. But for his untiring efforts and dedication, this volume would not have seen the light of the day. I would like to record our sincere appreciation of the protracted engagement of the translators in producing a reliable version of Gangadhar's major poetry. Dr. Dinanath Pathy deserves our thanks for the elegant cover design. We wish to acknowledge with gratitude the financial support provided for the project by the Department of Higher Education, Government of Orissa. We are grateful to the Orissa Sahitya Academy for according permission to include a revised version of *Tapaswini* in the present volume. Sri Bharat Chandra Bagarty and Sri Rajendra Prasad Mishra deserve our thanks for their able and ungrudging secretarial assistance.

Even as we crave the readers' sympathetic and appreciative engagement with the themes, sensibilities and sentiments in Gangadhar's poetry, we would with utmost humility accept their judicious criticism, if any. We are sure yet more refined renderings of Gangadhar's poetry would be available to readers in the future.

Dhrubaraj Naik
Vice - Chancellor

A NOTE ON THE TRANSLATION

Assumptions and experiences associated with a translation are necessary to be clearly, if briefly, stated at the outset so that a reader unacquainted with the language of the original may have his literary bearings set right for a proper imaginative apprehension. A knowledge of the translation strategies at work is as much crucial as a familiarity with the language of translation, for in a vital way the former, too, negotiates idea and meaning. The underlying tone and temper, sensibility and sentiment of a text which give meaning to its meaning can be captured by a target-language-reader only if the requisite critical hint is made available to him before he embarks upon his voyage of discovery through the new poetic waters. What the translator has attempted to achieve and what he has, for whatever reason, forsworn are equally significant indices that help the reader appropriately tune his perceptive faculties – he knows then what imaginative efforts he himself has to make in order to effectively collaborate with the translator and arrive at a reliable understanding.

This critical tutoring becomes all the more essential if the text is set in a time and place at some considerable socio-cultural distance from the contemporary world. Although in the case of Gangadhar whose writings are less than a century old, it might seem one has to travel only a short such distance, it is in fact a deceptive closeness. Gangadhar's milieu, far more traditional than what obtained in educationally more developed spaces in his own time, is pretty remote to the present generation of readers; and his poetry, in certain areas moored to an ancient literary and moral sensitivity, is not easy today to adequately emote with unless one has an imaginative grasp of that life and that tradition. It is easy to misread as sentimentality what was to him an exercise in vital, healthy sentiments, and it is possible to mistake as needless quibbles or pedantic ornateness what to his generation was only delightful poeticality. Some of his relatively complex utterances that an average reader of his poetry in his time could comfortably grasp owing to a certain familiarity with Sanskritic derivations and traditional myths require for the uninitiated today some kind of a scholarly endeavour.

The reader of Gangadhar in translation in a non-Indian language must therefore be alert to seeming ambiguities or apparently unusual structures or figures as literary sign-posts that direct him to imaginatively respond to certain inscribed notations and, to the extent that he may, reconstruct the original feel. Since the translation is in a poetic form imposing constraints of space and style, and since the translator's creativity in English is likely to be of a limited reach in this context, Gangadhar's text runs the risk of a double loss in a situation where translation seeks to preserve fidelity to the original, not attempting to be some kind of a free and independent transcreation. On the one hand, where the poetry is of a superior excellence, the inability to manage in English the structured musicality of stanzaic, metrical patterns, alliterative-assonantal arrangements, and culture-specific evocations of the original would amount to a severe poetic loss; and, on the other, with the age of poetic innocence gone, in poetically less embellished portions of the long narratives where conventional poetic anticipations and assumptions no longer function, a suspicion might grow in the reader's mind that the original text at those points was prosaic and drab.

With all such attendant dangers we have still chosen to emphasise faithfulness to the original. The witty French saying that a translation when faithful is homely, and faithless when lovely, may not be apposite in the context of a poetry that both in its style and in its human appeal seeks equally to emphasise graceful but simple homeliness and a pure and elegant loveliness. Its homeliness constitutes its unique fascination, and its loveliness, relating more to the inner being than to outer trappings, a special virtue. To neglect fidelity in such a case would result more in unsavoury distortions than in opportunities for exquisite reconstruction. In the absence of that old-world faith and charm Gangadhar's verse would be dead, and the new poem that one might compose as a kind of modern substitute would have very little justification for carrying Gangadhar's name. Fidelity – a poetic one, obviously – would be an undoubted virtue in this instance. And notwithstanding all the temptations for a more readable, popular version, freedom of the Fitzgeraldian kind should be totally eschewed.

There is another reason why, even as efforts had to be made in certain new linguistic forms to make Gangadhar understood by present-day readers, a close reference to the original had also to be maintained. This translation, offering in English in a single volume almost all the poems of Gangadhar on which his large fame rests, was conceptualised as a pioneering effort where the primary intention was to capture the right interpretation of the poetry so that later such ventures could with relatively greater freedom and ease craft new varieties, effect new incarnations in their own imaginative ways. The present one is thus intended to serve as a kind of authentic, base document. Moreover, since it is an undertaking by a University and not individual renderings by some free-lance translators, each independent of the other's taste and priorities, there had to be a basic mould for several hands to work upon. Individual creative talents of each of the translators would no doubt come into play, but only upon agreed norms and shared outlooks. Granting primacy to the original text appeared to be a safe common discipline. No translator associated with this project could be accused of being, to use the well-known Italian pun on the word, a 'traitor'; nor is he at any point a spontaneous performer of Valery's 'pure poetry'.

This edition, offered to a general body of readers, is not the right place where an extended critical discussion should be assayed on translation-practice and translation-poetics. But a broad outline of the process through which it has been shaped has to be presented so that, as has already been indicated, a reader can properly judge the effort and know what to expect and what not. To start with, some senior teachers of English with known expertise in the field of Oriya language and literature who agreed to participate in the project accepted certain common norms so that, through all the dissimilarities caused by differences in text and talent, the volume would exhibit a certain unified wholeness. It was thus decided to, as far as possible :

(i) offer an authentic, faithful rendering of Gangadhar keeping in mind the socio-cultural suggestions and emotive value the original text bore for its contemporary readers;
(ii) address present-day readers, in other Indian languages as also outside, making the text as lucid as possible but without doing violence to the original sensibility;
(iii) attempt a sense-for-sense rendering, without sacrificing specificities of suggestion inscribed in the original; and
(iv) effect a poetic translation, without trying to adhere to the original rhyme-scheme, but constantly bearing in mind the importance of the stanza-patterns, the line-lengths, and the management of rhythm which ground the original on certain closely connected musical and emotive bases; seeking corresponding approximations, but guarding against a look of bizarre novelties in the context of the generally known tradition of poetry in English.

A preliminary draft translation of a portion of the text each translator first of all forwarded to the editor was examined and returned with detailed interpretive comments and sample verse-reworkings of a few pages, inviting participatory responses from each; thereafter, the poems were canto-wise translated, and reviewed by the editor, with suggested reworkings forwarded for the translator's consideration. The second draft then prepared was once again worked upon by the editor and a final form was consultatively developed. Thus the translations offered here are a product of a close, friendly collaboration, the responsibility for omissions and failures that might still remain after all this care lying at the doors, equally, of the translator and the editor.

For part of the endeavour in the early stages Dr. Govinda Chandra Udgata, doyen among Gangadhar scholars, worked as an Associate Editor. His untimely passing away was a grievous loss. Another friend, who had agreed to do the translation of *Pranaya Ballari*, withdrew at a late hour despite his goodwill for the project, and the editor was asked to urgently take up the burden to meet the deadline. *Tapaswini*, which had been earlier jointly translated by the present editor and Jayanta Mahapatra, had to be revised by the former as required by the original publishers and in the light of the governing norms of the project. In all, it has been an unbroken engagement of nearly two years. What has emerged through it may not have succeeded in doing full justice to Gangadhar, but certainly not because of any miserliness of effort and devotion.

This translation is prepared for English-knowing readers and not specifically for a western audience. There has been no endeavour to carry it close to the speech and literary habits of the present-day English society. In fact, certain earlier forms of expression are deliberately, if very sparingly, embedded so that the old-world flavour of Gangadhar's verse is not altogether missed. Again, there are occasions where the translation is allowed to retain Gangadhar's syntax in the interest of preserving the original tone. But adequate care has been taken to ensure that, in all, the translation does not sound curiously or uncomfortably archaic, and that a contemporary reader does not have to overstrain himself in building a proper empathy with the poetry. By and large, the language of the present translation, remaining sensitive to the language of the original, has been so managed that it does not depart from standard English but does not also flaunt a slick modernity. An acceptable translation, as is well-known, does not merely attempt near-equivalents of word, image and idiom, but strives to somehow carry across the very mode of thought, negotiating between different aesthetic and culture-specific assumptions that separate an earlier author from a contemporary reader. We have tried never to forget that obligation.

The kind of poetry Gangadhar on occasions wrote requires of the translator both grinding labour and elegant creativity, the former possible to ensure through devotion, the latter not possible to order into being. The translator, no doubt, is expected to be both interpreter and poet; but not all translators engaged here are basically poets, and except for one, none a practising poet in English. And yet they believe they can convey to an appreciable extent the poetry of the original in the new language; for, even though they may not themselves be writing poetry in English, as ardent readers and teachers of English poetry for many years they can justifiably claim to have acquired the necessary expertise with which to creatively mediate. And since they are not attempting new poems here either as trans-creators or in more modern terms as textual usurpers, but functioning only as a body of responsible translators, the deficiency in question would certainly not be a crippling one. Poetic loss they cannot prevent; but poetic communication at what might be called a secondary aesthetic level they can largely ensure, leaving the rest to the imaginative competence of each reader.

Some words of caution are due here, particularly for readers who are not very familiar even with poetry written in their own languages in the second half of the nineteenth century. As has been rightly remarked, one who does not understand Victorian sentiments cannot understand Victorian literature either, and one who is out of sympathy with those sentiments can hardly savour the joys of that poetry. This is true of Indian poetry of the second half of the nineteenth century as well; but, of course, there is a certain difference. The radical modernism associated with a keen distrust and sweeping rejection of Victorianism in English literature was championed upon the Indian literary scene only much later, and in substantially modified forms, allowing for Romantic-Victorian continuities long into the twentieth century. Only with the recent generation of elitist urban readers has the chasm grown wide, the socio-cultural climate in course of the last three decades having undergone such drastic change as to render many of the older expressions of sentiment – moral and emotional – effete, and even suspect, to many of them. Such a frame of mind which would make reading problematic even in the original would be totally counter-productive in the context of this translation.

Gangadhar's outlook on life, his moral beliefs and human sentiments, and his literary-cultural loyalties make him especially fond of certain expressions and certain imagery. For instance, there is in his poetry an abundance of reference to a 'honeyed sweetness' of experience and vision – in fact, one of his celebrated poems offers an exquisite elaboration of this very theme of all life being 'honeyed'. Similar is the case with the use of *'amrita' 'yagna'* etc. The cultural climate and individual creative taste governing the writing has such authenticity in the original that even a profusion of these expressions does not strike one as tiresomely mannered, but which in the English rendering, owing to a changed associative field, is likely to appear repetitious and stale to someone who does not remember that it was relished by the writer's immediate audience as something valuable and wholesome. Again, in the case of certain figures of speech – for example, those involving certain flora and fauna that proliferate in Gangadhar, but which are always handled aptly – repetition does not produce in the original a feeling of stereotyped exercise both because of the kind of culture-associated language it is embossed in, and because of the availability of a number of synonyms for many of those. In the absence of that awareness, an unjustified suspicion of insipid conventionality may cause even moving utterances to sound bathetic in the translation. In such cases the reader's emotional and critical sensitivities would be a crucial component in determining translational veracity and effectiveness.

Puns and double-entendres are always the most notorious things for a translator to handle. Since in the case of Gangadhar most uses of paronomasia are related to traditional mythology and not simply to lexical usage, the difficulty is multiplied. And on occasions when he engages upon poetic conceit using a string of associated metaphors through many stanzas, drawing upon his knowledge of traditional myth, ancient literature, astrology and so on, it causes almost an insuperable problem of communication in a non-Indian language. Over-frequent glossing in footnotes would impede reading continuity and poetic movement; hence, sometimes through such stretches of extended punning, we have desperately resorted to the device of inscribing in brackets a second meaning. But in case of mythological and other learned or literary references elucidatory gloss becomes inescapable. We may refer to one of the simplest allusions to '*chhaya*' (meaning 'shadow'; as also one of the two wives of the Sun-god) with which Gangadhar builds an interesting image of an amorous setting-sun stretching out his '*kara*' ('hands' as also 'rays') to capture the lengthening shadow, something that an average reader of Gangadhar's time would have understood without any gloss, but which needs to be expounded for the benefit of a contemporary reader. Sometimes at such places the syntax of the translation becomes somewhat clumsy, requiring the reader's forbearance and understanding.

There are culture-specific expressions which, obviously, have no synonyms in the target language, but there may be certain near-equivalent terms that need the greatest caution in using, for they can sometimes be pretty misleading. Thus, for instance, a female hermit (*Tapasi*) of ancient India should not really be called a nun, nor a male anchorite (*Tapas*) a monk. Similarly, the smear of sandal-wood paste and certain perfumed substances (*Angaraga*) women of pleasure or noble women in general wore in the past must not be converted into lotion, cream or such other stuff of modern times. Even more intransigent and unmanageable are some of the very common expressions Gangadhar makes use of time and again. A classic example is the use of the word '*sati*' which occurs, touchingly, numerous times in *Tapaswini*, for that is the primary description of Sita – a devoted wife, one of utterly impeccable chastity and lofty dignity, a virtuous soul, a tender yet heroic personality made invincible by her connubial loyalty which she preserves as a religion of her being. The poor translator would go on flitting among 'the virtuous one', 'the chaste one', and 'the pure one', conveying very little of the essence of the concept and practice associated with the term. And for a modern reader unacquainted with the usage – even if he does not commit the unspeakable horror of confusing it with 'suttee' – the repetition of 'virtuous one' may well sound unbearably pontifical and prosaic, whereas a word like 'lady', for example, used with even greater frequency may not at all similarly vex one's ears in an English text. Once again, in such cases the translator has to look for the reader's imaginative support.

Certain physical acts and gestures, similarly, that Gangadhar repeatedly introduces into his narrative may, for various different reasons, embarrass many of his modern readers. These behaviour-patterns have an old-world flavour. Gangadhar has drawn them both from his immediate social experience and from earlier literature, and introduces them frequently with no feeling of awkwardness whatever. Such, for example, is the description of senior people placing upon their laps their offsprings or loved ones. Now 'lap' could carry today an overtone much different from filial protectiveness and affection. But even otherwise, in a society where such acts are no longer in vogue, frequency of this reference may cause some discomfort to the reader; and where it involves sons who are themselves pretty advanced in age, as in the description of god Indra removing his son Jayanta from his lap and placing Dusmanta there, today's reader would wince. In this instance we have made it 'seating him by the side', knowing full well the emotive loss suffered by the original. Another such example is the word '*hulahuli*', the shrill sound women make by flapping their tongues on auspicious and celebratory occasions. This used to be a regular practice in Gangadhar's world and continues to be in vogue today. This cannot be conveyed as 'ululation'; but apart from the problem of equivalence, repeated use of this in Gangadhar might make a modern translator look for circumventing devices. We have allowed them to stay; so have we done in the case of the poetically rather ungainly expression, 'hair standing on end'. English does not have an equivalent to convey the sudden incursion of thrill that Gangadhar wishes to convey with *romancha* and *kadamba*; 'goose-flesh' and 'horripilation' carry negative associations of cold, fear and the like, not joy and excitement as intended in Oriya. Such difficulties are numerous.

In respect of poetic metre this translation has attempted a certain balance and flexibility. Where in the original the same pattern has been maintained throughout a long narrative, we have resorted to either a free-verse pattern as in *Indumati*, or retained the uniform quatrain-measure of the text without struggling for rhyming consistency, as in *Utkal-Laxmi* and *Pranaya Ballari*, but in both cases taking care to keep as close to the rhythm and narrative movements of the original as possible. In case of *Tapaswini* and *Kichakabadha*, the two long narratives that stylise metrical variation from canto to canto, an effort has been made to capture a broad metrical correspondence with the originals. In addition in the later poem, rhyme too has often been attempted despite an attendant risk of sounding at places somewhat forced or stilted. Obviously enough, exact replication of all the original stanza-patterns in English would be both imprudent and difficult; but to an extent a feel of the original poetic measures may be sought to be transmitted, taking care, however, to ensure that the translation does not wear an altogether strange look. All this has involved a highly painstaking process, but since reducing all of Gangadhar into a uniform blank-verse measure would have amounted to an aesthetic betrayal and resulted in poetic distortions of a fundamental kind, we have gone ahead to court all the trouble and represent the original meaning-evocation complex as best as we could.

Footnotes have been furnished in order to enable readers to quickly grasp the meanings of certain unfamiliar expressions and suggestions. The text in the original itself had carried a number of footnotes; they have not been retained as such. In case of geographical information offered in *Utkal-Laxmi* and elsewhere they are not significant elements for the poetry, and in respect of the other glosses in the original, related elucidatory keys have been planted in the body of the translation itself. But, of course, a translation cannot – must not – resort to critical elucidation like a book of commentaries. And so readers with different backgrounds may confront, on occasions, different kinds of textual, local obscurities – some relating to myth, some to nature, and some to cultural forms. But they are not likely to be large, and not likely to prevent a broad understanding of the text.

In respect of the translational deficiencies that in spite of our sincere care might have persisted through this version we would not like to take umbrage under apologetic axioms like 'no translation is perfect', 'each version has its own rationale', 'there is nothing called a definitive reading or rendering', and so on. We would rather wish to candidly acknowledge our own creative limitations and only hope that the constraints – personal and organisational – under which we engaged in this labour of love have not resulted in any false readings of Gangadhar. Poetic under-representation, no doubt, there might be; but misrepresentation through carelessness or casualness, hopefully, there isn't any. This is a first effort of its kind; poetically more effective mediations of Gangadhar would surely follow.

Editor

Gangadhar Meher (1862-1924)

INTRODUCTION

Sometimes a creative mind, a rare one, voices the aspirations and sentiments of a people and their socio-cultural ethos so intimately, feelingly and comprehensively that he acquires the status of an icon, a symbol, an historical force inspiring a special identity among succeeding generations in that community. A Homer, a Vyasa, a Shakespeare thus shapes into a phenomenon, a product of history which goes on to serve as a generator and marker of civilisational identity. During certain periods of cultural assertiveness he is projected as a kind of cult-figure; and even through times when in more sober terms he is discussed as a literary genius he continues to exert an extra-literary, subterranean influence on the community-psyche, as someone especially close, someone especially dear. Clearly enough, such an author's emotions and concerns are not confined to merely the local and the immediately communal. Like other creative geniuses he, too, remains tuned to universals, is moved as much by the timeless as by the temporal; but his experience, sympathies, habits and language so inscribe a certain ethnic belongingness that his writings come to be cherished as a prized community heritage, as a socio-cultural, and not simply a literary treasure. Gangadhar Meher is one such poet who unmistakeably represents a people and an ethos; who, even as he is extolled for his universal art, and for his inclusive sympathies and transcendent vision, continues to be honoured by them as a cultural patriarch and projected as a proud possession.

Neither in terms of quality of genius nor of empowerment attained by his language and its associated culture can Gangadhar be classed with the great ones mentioned earlier, but in his more circumscribed world he also has had a similar presence. In the context of the Oriya literary tradition shaping through the last decades of the nineteenth century and the early decades of the twentieth, he emerged as the most representative poet combining the best of the old and the new. He derived his poetic strength and authenticity from immediate experiences of life, and gave expression to human sympathies, moral sentiments and spiritual values with such a touching sincerity and convincing directness that his poetry has continued to speak home in the manner of classics to all kinds of readers, cutting across all the various strata of cultural refinement. Notwithstanding a clear-sighted perception of evil and injustice threatening human life, he steadily nurtured and persuasively articulated a robust faith in the essential goodness, beauty, and joy of creation. And he portrayed human nobility and love with a tenderness uniquely his own.

This, therefore, is a happy venture to get Gangadhar rendered into English despite the hazards of poetic loss that translation inevitably entails, and make it possible for his genius to travel beyond the confines of his language and history and reach out to a vaster audience. Incidentally, an unintended service might have been rendered in the process to Oriya readers as well; for, as the awareness dawned through the long and arduous engagement of the present translation, not many can possibly claim an adequate understanding of Gangadhar's poetry which is often disarmingly simple but equally often tantalisingly multi-layered and complex, manipulating linguistic, literary and cultural referents garnered from an extensive and varied territory. Unless one applies oneself with care and persistence, one is likely to miss a good deal. And thus, curiously but truly enough, the present version may serve to augment understanding of Gangadhar among English-knowing Oriya readers, too.

The life of Gangadhar constitutes a magnificent example of the triumph of creative genius over adverse circumstances. He was born on August 9, 1862, in a weaver's family at Barpali, then a zamindari, now a part of the Baragarh district in Orissa. His parents, Sri Chaitanya Meher and Srimati Sebati Meher, were a pious couple. Sri Meher had received a bit of schooling himself and was keen that his son should have a proper education, but such were the constraints of the family and the locality that subsequent to the completion of studies upto Class V in the lone primary school Barpali then boasted, which he managed just in three years' time, Gangadhar could not acquire a Middle/ Vernacular certificate even though he struggled till 1882 when he was twenty. Even during his school days he had to divide his time between the loom and the letters. And after leaving school and engaging full-time in his hereditary profession he continued to assiduously nurture his love of literature. The place had no library, but he used to borrow from the local teachers and others whatever works in Oriya, Sanskrit and Bengali were available with them, avidly studying late into the night after the day's work was done. He used to supplement his income by writing out official deeds and petitions; all the money he thus earned was religiously spent on purchase of books.

This extraordinary literary passion had a natural creative consequence. Between 1882 and 1885 he composed a long poem, *Rasa Ratnakara*, comprising eight cantos. It narrated a romance-tale of love and amour in the ornate *riti*-style perfected in Oriya by poets like Upendra, Abhimanyu and Dinakrishna. A teacher in residence at Barpali who went through the poem was delighted with Gangadhar's poetic effort, but rightly enough advised him to adopt a more modern style as popularised by leading poets of the time like Radhanath, Madhusudan and Nandakishore. But Gangadhar's fascination for the older style was persistent, as evidenced from *Ahalya Stava** he wrote in 1892. Soon enough thereafter the desired change would come, and with it a new poetic verve and exuberance that would make his contemporaries sit up and applaud the advent of a fresh genius into Oriya literature.

---

* *Rasa Ratnakara* and *Ahalya Stava* (like the titles of his other compositions, *Pranaya Ballari* and *Chandra Rajani*) are read as single words in Oriya.

Meanwhile, pleased with his character and talents, the zamindar had appointed him an ordinary *amin* on a pay of seven rupees a month. This position was held by Gangadhar till 1888, after which he was appointed to a clerical post of judicial *moharir* under the government. For the rest part of his service career Gangadhar continued to work in this capacity, getting transferred after 1902, successively, to Sambalpur, Bijepur, and finally, Padampur, where he retired in 1917. He continued to be at the last place for sometime more, working for the zamindar as an auditor, and then returned to his native place hoping to spend the last years in peaceful creativity. But the new zamindar at Barpali was insistent on having Gangadhar as his *moharir*, merely to flatter his vanity by keeping in his pay a man who was by then famous through the whole of Orissa, courted by rulers and intelligentsia alike. Not able to refuse, Gangadhar joined the post, but resigned soon after when he discovered the zamindar's scheming, tyrannical character. Now he gave his time to social reforms, inviting the wrath of various powerful men including the zamindar, but tenaciously, yet humbly, persisted with his efforts in spite of being made to suffer humiliations and provocations of the worst kind. His success was particularly noteworthy because of the grace, integrity and patience with which he conducted the campaign, winning over the hearts of many who had initially been violently hostile to his ideas. This great soul, who was born on a day of *Purnima* of the bright full-moon, passed away upon a dark new-moon night of *Amabasya* on April 4,1924, with nature herself as it were signifying what he had meant to the world.

Gangadhar was a poet of a high order; he was also a surpassingly good soul, exemplifying how virtues like purity, humility, dignity, and nobility, virtues that he so memorably elaborated in his poetry, could be cultivated unflinchingly and gracefully in one's own life. A poor weaver, then an ordinary official, his integrity was extraordinary, though maintained in ever so self-effacing a manner. For instance, even while serving as a low-paid *amin* he yet had the temerity to testify against his employer in a court of law. In the later part of his life when an influential admirer of his, coming to know of his worries over some secure source of income for his only living son, offered to employ the young man as a teacher in a school, Gangadhar politely declined, saying his son wouldn't be able to do justice to the students. Such acts of honesty were habitual with him; but his integrity ran deeper still, manifesting in other uncommon ways. For example, Gangadhar never spent on personal comforts even a mite out of the meagre sums he earned by way of royalty or literary awards – the money was consistently rolled back to the service of Mother Saraswati. To maintain through all vicissitudes of life – and he had more than a normal share of griefs, prematurely losing his wife and his elder son, and suffering pains and ordeals of various other kinds – such steady faith as his in the truth of a sweet and wholesome universal order, and in the sensitivities of the moral being, was extraordinary, indeed.

Living at a considerable distance from centres of socio-political power and modern educational enterprise, while he welcomed progress and development and even exhibited a surprising receptivity to scientific temper, all along his poetic career he nursed a deep predilection for old-world values and subjects from ancient Indian literature, articulating with great power and beauty the moral conviction, emotional tenderness and spiritual faith that still retained a vital hold in his society despite all traumas of political neglect and threats of cultural colonialism. No doubt, in more senses than one Gangadhar's was a healthy syncretic spirit combining impulses from the past with those of the present, values of culture with those of spontaneity, a lofty vision with ordinary sympathies, a profound transcendence along with a deeprootedness; but the urge to vindicate and reaffirm certain ancient Indian values pulsated constantly through his poetry and his inner being. It ran as an unbroken thread imparting to his poetic efforts a clear and decisive identity. Significantly enough, the urge does not degenerate into propaganda: it manifests itself in a natural, graceful, unostentatious – if on occasions somewhat an uncritical – manner.

For the last fifty years he has continued to be hailed as a *swabhaba kabi*, a natural poet, a born genius. The appellation has derived partly from his biographical background – the poverty and educational inadequacy despite which his genius flourished – and partly from an apparent artlessness that a good deal of his memorable poetry displayed, emphasising directness and simplicity of expression. But through his mature period of creativity Gangadhar did not really suffer penury as of his early years, and notwithstanding insufficient formal education he was pretty well-read in areas from where he drew the subjects of his poetry; and if *swabhaba kabi* is meant to insinuate, while glorifying spontaneity, a lack of poetic craftsmanship, dearth of wit, or infelicitous figures of speech, the description would be patently false and absurd. As one moves from one major narrative poem to the next, from one crop of lyrics to another, one is struck by a delightful maturing of style, a conscious refinement of utterance along with the unfoldment of a larger and profounder sensibility. And, yet, *swabhaba kabi* as a celebratory, adulatory expression has continued to be popular, possibly for want of a better alternative to designate Gangadhar's uniqueness among his peers.

When matched against the cultivated tonal and linguistic elevation of Madhusudan's poetry, or the Western tutoring and 'standard' style in evidence in Radhanath's – his senior contemporaries and arbiters of poetic taste of the day – Gangadhar's verse, which on occasions might appear less refined, demonstrates a deeper rootedness, a more inclusive poetic sympathy fusing the colloquial with the standard forms and admitting everyday sentiments and feelings into heightened moments, discarding embellishments in favour of human authenticity. Integrating the rural passion of a Nandakishore with the cultivated artistry of a Radhanath, synthesising the experience of the soil with the vision of Vedanta – rendering Madhusudan more homely, as it were – Gangadhar, as has been suggested earlier, acquired a unique poetic voice, a syncretic Oriya poeticality all his own, consanguinous with the rest, but at once more regional and individual. Gangadhar often offers a far more ornate fare than Radhanath, as also a more straightforward and plain representation than Nandakishore, thus responding to extremes of poetic-dramatic exigencies with equal competence. And he could be more compact than either, engaging in neatly structured articulations that would have been a delight of the New Critics of the last century.

Gangadhar had a large, inclusive view of the poet's calling. He composed, on the one hand, long epic-like narratives and concentrated lyrics and, on the other, all manner of occasional poems, simple and unpretentious. He wrote with devotional fervour, also with social indignation; celebrated the charms and wholesome ministration of nature, also satirised pettiness and evil in the society; composed elevated tales of noble life, also utterly plain, educative verses on agronomy. Poetry, he believed, was there to serve all man's needs – social and spiritual, mundane and mystical, emotional and intellectual; its manner and mode had to be different in different contexts and situations of life. So he did not entertain any elitist, aesthetic inhibitions, and continued to serve through his poetry a large humanity, unconcerned about personal fame. There is no poetic posturing at work, the only strain implicit being that of self-effacing humility, with nothing of a bold 'egotistical sublime'. Thus even through his richly orchestrated compositions there runs a natural simplicity and easy grace rarely encountered in other poets.

Gangadhar's poetic evolution presents a number of striking, and some astonishing, features. This poet whose soul remained so deeply immersed in ancient Indian traditions, who seemed to be so little affected in his creative imagination by rationalistic concerns that were getting increasingly vociferous through the century, whose rural-mythopoeic-religious mind could respond to socio-political issues of only a regional, provincial character, whose feudal values made him almost habitually laud British rule save for an occasional critical aside here and there, was yet the one who at the very end of his poetic career composed a long poem, *Bharati Bhavana*, in sustained paronomasia, deploring imperial exploitation, tyranny, and hypocrisy with an incisiveness and precision rarely surpassed by other poets of his time. In fact, as the years went by, the element of social concern in his poetry, deriving from immediate actualities of life and not simply involving idealised projections of stories of goodness in triumph and evil in nemesis, became increasingly sharper and more voluminous, manifesting in unexpected ways even in unanticipated contexts, such as greeting-poems written on formal occasions.

As already stated, Gangadhar began with the mannered, high-literary style of the *riti*-poets and later adopted a more contemporary style of versification; but he did not altogether discard figurative exuberance, selectively engaging in it in his long narratives whenever he found appropriate mood and occasion in the story-moments. Also he went a step beyond most of his contemporaries, inducting into his verse a number of colloquial elements, experimenting more and more with flexible, spoken forms of lexis, syntax and rhythm. By the time he composes his most famous narrative poem, *Tapaswini*, he is already versatile in handling the ornate, the standard-poetic, and the colloquial, shifting freely from one to the other, and effecting a variety of syntheses. This helps his poems acquire a rich vigour and fluency, ensuring both poetic excellence and dramatic aptness: while through some stretches the reader is carried forward on a smooth absorbing narrative journey, at others he is treated to a sumptuous, leisurely feast of poetic delights.

In matters of image and metaphor Gangadhar's poetry abounds in subtle and charming use of both conventional and novel elements. The lotus, the lily, various jasmines; river, mountain, forest, cave; the sun, the moon, the stars; the sky, the clouds, the winds; the swan, the cuckoo, the *chakora*, the *chatak*, the *chakravaka*; deer, tiger, elephant, cow, buffalo – metaphorical vehicles such as these are introduced time and again, but because of poetic judiciousness with reference to persona and experience rarely do they tire or repel. Some of these appear more frequently than the others – as, for instance, the lotus – revealing Gangadhar's own temperamental predilections that naturally colour his verse. But one should always be very cautious before hastily dismissing them as mannered repetition. His extensive knowledge of traditional lores, motifs, symbols, and myths connected with various flora and fauna generate subtle poetic variations, which if missed by an unwary reader would only unjustly breed the suspicion of stereotyped banality or obscurity. Further, there is something delightfully special about many of his similes and metaphors which relate to his own everyday surroundings, vibrant with a rooted strength and realistic power; but they might cause some discomfort to a modern reader unacquainted with the ethos. And, finally, there are similes which might appear somewhat archaic today, but which must have been particularly evocative in his own world and time.

These figures of speech indicate the character of his moral and emotional being, his deep feeling for nature, and, above all, his profound human sympathy. Indeed, the last element has so pronounced and persistent a sway over his inner self that it surfaces even in unexpected contexts and ways, imparting to his poetry an uncommon sensitivity and power. Thus, for instance, in course of a formal piece on the anniversary of a periodical, *Utkal Sevak*, Gangadhar abruptly introduces the *chher chhera* observance associated with the *Pus Puni* harvest-festival in his region. He feelingly describes the manner in which poor urchins then move from door to door, beating the ground with sticks and singing *chher chhera* alms-songs, shivering in tattered clothes that hardly cover their bosoms, and collecting handfuls of recently harvested rice; and then exhorts the periodical to imbibe the tenacity, modesty and sportive temper of those poor kids. What is, however, of interest to us today is the way the poem suddenly rises from the ordinarily formal to the highly emotive, revealing through the graphic sketch Gangadhar's tender heart that so pulsated with sympathy for the poor deprived creatures.

Human sympathy constitutes the core of all his major narratives, too; and it carries there a special thrust. It is significant that in his celebrated narrative poems Gangadhar repeatedly centralises the fate of wronged women, persecuted females who had to suffer terrible anguish not because they had done any evil, but, ironically enough, because they were noble and virtuous. Thus three of his poems, unequalled in Oriya literature in terms of multifaceted poetic excellence at the service of tender sentiments and elevated moral feelings, describe the fates of three suffering women – Draupadi, Shakuntala and Sita. Nursing an optimistic outlook Gangadhar did, of course, emphasise a happy outcome – in the case of Sita's story going beyond the *Ramayana* and contriving a happy vision all his own. But the torment the characters underwent, and through it the splendour their integrity diffused and the sympathy and admiration they thus evoked in the poet's heart, are thematically central to these poems. Incidentally, these poems also reveal how Gangadhar's sympathy extended to even birds and animals; in fact, to every plant and inanimate thing. A natural consequence of this habit of all-inclusive humanisation was the extended use of pathetic fallacy, the most memorable one being the picture of an indignant nature exploding into awesome belligerence in defence of the deserted Sita.

Gangadhar's was an idealistic vision sustained by deep belief in a beneficent cosmic order. Apart form the longer poems which variously inscribe the vision, some of his shorter lyrics, too, marvellously convey that faith in simple, compact, penetrating poetry. Charged with deep feeling and assurance, and exquisite in their neat structuring, these poems with their Upanisadic strain demonstrate how, notwithstanding a deep sensitivity to human suffering, Gangadhar's poetic imagination was ever under the sway of *ananda*. This abiding faith in a presiding spiritual order did not make him complacent or negligent of human woe; but with all the vast store of pity and compassion, of social anger and moral indignation that his poetry contains, his ultimate sense of a sweet and joyous world-order, manifesting through everything human and non-human, did not ever wilt. A superb integration of human sympathy with moral-spiritual affirmation, of pity and beauty – this was the hall-mark of Gangadhar's poetic temper.

One of the most notable elements in Gangadhar, in poetry as in personality, was his humility. He maintained till the very end of his life an extraordinary modesty of being. And yet his moral conviction and poetic assurance were monumental: no eminence, socio-political or literary, ever awed him so much as to distract him from his native taste and belief. While accepting the tutelage of certain masters he singlemindedly nurtured his own determinants of style, sensibility and vision, humbly but confidently modifying poetic tones and perspectives that he encountered not only in an eminent contemporary like Radhanath but also in classical giants like Valmiki, Vyasa and Kalidasa. Neither lured by sophistication nor deterred by fear of adverse comparision, he went ahead to build his own, erecting new wings that he thought were suitable and proper. Some of the introductory remarks he appended to *Pranaya Ballari*, which is an extended reconstruction of *Shakuntalam* and, partly, of the *Mahabharat*-story, as also the new elements he incorporated into the stories of Sita and Draupadi, bear decisive evidence of his independent judgement and poetic boldness.

Casual readers of Gangadhar sometimes assume that while his poetry excels in lyric appeal, feeling for nature, human sympathy, moral ardour, purity of sentiments and spiritual faith, it lacks in poetic wit. This, as his verse testifies, is patently untrue; it is a prejudice that seems to have derived from certain biographical elements such as Gangadhar's rural background, deficiency of formal education, inadequacy of exposure to western literary models, and so on. While it is true that Gangadhar's poetry is closely linked to his world, it is a false supposition that he lacked in artistic subtlety, or suffered from a narrow linguistic range or an absence of intellectual finesse. He marshalled a large vocabulary, possibly the widest among his contemporary poets, engaged in bold metaphors and similies, and evinced within his limited compass an assured intellectual clarity. It was not for nothing that Radhanath, the leading educational and literary authority of the time, not only bestowed handsome praise on Gangadhar's chaste style but once requested the latter to scrutinise and improve a book he had himself prepared on Oriya grammar.

Interestingly enough, Gangadhar was the only poet of his time to have evinced a curious intellectual urge to provide in footnotes significant information he had gathered from standard references like gazetteers while presenting an elaborate picture of the Orissan geography and landscape in his *Utkal-Laxmi*.

In life, as in literature, Gangadhar was a firm believer in combining healthy assimilative ability with native integrity. He welcomed good things from western civilisation, but as he so trenchantly asserted in his poem, *Utkal Bharatinka Ukti*, native character had to be preserved and cultural distortions avoided at all costs. Social reforms, where due, are good; but blindly courting cultural imperialism can be dangerous – pare the nails, if overgrown, but do not slice the nose by adopting some western scale, he said. In matters of cultural tradition, again, while Gangadhar's was a committed pan-Indianism, he remained a champion of Oriya nationalism, too, and passionately fought against official overlordship of Hindi in his region, thereby earning the title of an alert 'frontier guard' of Oriya language and culture. His image and concept of Orissa were much more extended and inclusive than those of many of his contemporaries to whom the coastal Puri-Cuttack-Balasore belt held the essence of Oriya identity. As his *Utkal-Laxmi* so memorably projected, Orissa and Orissan culture to him meant something far more spacious and multifarious. Interestingly, in the later part of his life Gangadhar was keener than ever in associating himself with *Utkal Sammilani*, a nationalist organisation which fought for liberation of Orissan territories from the administrative control of neighbouring provinces to the north, the north-east, and the south.

Gangadhar's first long poem in a contemporary idiom was *Indumati*, serialised in four instalments between November 1893 and April 1894 in the periodical *Utkal Prabha*, and brought out as a single volume in August 1894. The poem generated for Gangadhar instantaneous fame, earning him compliments from senior poets, critics and common readers alike. It develops the brief story of Aja and Indumati Gangadhar had encountered in Kalidasa's *Raghuvamsam* into an extended form unfolding the tragedy in a touching, dramatic sequence. Significantly enough, while in the original it is primarily Aja's story, with Indumati featuring as an auxiliary, in Gangadhar's poem she has the greater primacy. As the title indicates, it is *her* story. It is a tragi-comic love which the poem narrates connecting earth and heaven, and crafting a tale of romance and realism, sin and atonement, passion and pain. Gangadhar delineates the transformation of youthful love into a more steady and mature thing that not only offers personal fulfilment in conjugal life, but also serves to support a wider good, a theme he would assay in fuller form more than once in his later poems. Death comes abruptly; ironically yet suggestively enough, it is a garland of heavenly flowers that, falling on Indumati while she was strolling in the garden in Aja's company, kills her. The poem displays a number of characteristic Gangadharian features – exquisite portrayal of tender sentiments, feel for natural beauties, use of both conventional and novel similes, moral sensitivity, emphasis on destiny, and tragi-comic resolution. The promise of later years is clearly made manifest in this early creative venture.

Impelled by nationalist urge Gangadhar turned from mythology to history, composing an incomplete *Utkal-Laxmi,* and two short poems expressing his concern over the imminent administrative imposition of Hindi over the Sambalpur region. *Utkal-Laxmi,* first published in 1894, was to wait for twenty years to attain its revised, fuller version in 1914. In this later edition Gangadhar offered a fascinating picture of the natural beauties and literary-cultural glories of a larger Orissa that was to become a political actuality only in 1936, more than a decade after the poet had passed away. Oriya poetry had not known of a great many geographical high spots and scenic splendour in the western and southern belts which Gangadhar foregrounded in the poem, thereby rendering the picture of his motherland, 'goddess of affluence and elegance' as he called her, comprehensive and full. He introduced in the poem a story from his own imagination, making the moon-god and his star-beloved choose Orissa for a period of a happy sojourn, drawn to it by the natural excellence of the land and by its literary culture and historical glories. With this poetic alibi Gangadhar highlighted many prominent natural objects and legends of his own region that had so far remained ignored in Oriya literature.

For quite a few years now Gangadhar's pen was to lie idle, save for a didactic piece *Mahima* in 1897, and two short prose pieces where he raised certain fundamental issues relating to grammar and phonetics, and another prose bit speculating on the sound produced by the earth as it revolves and whirls. Domestic and official problems left him with no leisure, and the creative urge remained blocked. With the turn of the century he had to suffer terrible bereavements, first of his wife and soon after, in 1902, of his elder son. A few months later we find him turning to poetry with a new urgency, composing first of all a longish lyric on the rainy season, and thereafter getting engaged upon a long narrative, *Kichaka Badha*, a poem he finished through 1903 and brought out the subsequent year. In the later part of 1902 he happened to be going through the *Virataparva* of the *Mahabharata*; this seemed to have precipitated a creative resolve. His poetic priorities are now again made clear: he chooses the story of the lustful, power-blind Kichaka's nemesis rather than some other subject from the *Virataparva* because of the fascination for poetic justice which the tale unfolds. Tender sentiment and moral concern would continue to remain principal features of Gangadhar's poetry.

The reader of Gangadhar is at once arrested by the artistic development in evidence. In *Indumati* poetic exuberance was restrained; the effort was to craft a smooth dramatic narration that might be inset with superb figures of speech, but all in a context-controlled manner. In *Kichaka Badha*, on the other hand, there is a conscious juxtaposition, a concurrent manipulation of an exuberant poetic style and a straightforward dramatic style, of embellishment and plainness, with different cantos revealing different variations as dictated by narrative moods. While in descriptive sections there is a versatile display of poetic beauties, drawing upon a fecund imagination and large polysemic, polyphonic resources of literary language and traditional myth, in portions with greater emphasis on development of story there is a marked preference for realistic pictures and dramatically apt language contriving a fascinating, smooth narration. Each character is vividly drawn; even an ordinary one like the maid-servant Chapala, who works for Kichaka as a procuress, grows into as much of a memorable character as the noble heroine Draupadi. Unfailing psychological realism and exquisite poetic art make the poem stand out among its contemporary writings as a unique achievement. The praise Radhanath showered in its *Preface* was eminently deserved.

For about five years subsequent to the composition of *Kichaka Badha* Gangadhar's poetic imagination was forced to languish in the backyards of a troubled and awfully overworked life. But with his transfer to Sambalpur for the second time in Government employment, when regular monthly salary, and some leisure hours daily were assured, his creative spark – this time coaxed and fanned by a number of admirers – once again gathered strength and burst into leaping brilliance as on the earlier occasion. Some of the long lyrics like *Chandra Rajani* and *Basanta Basare* (later *Basanta Basara*) included in *Kabita Kallola* belong to this period; also the initial cantos of *Tapaswini*, his magnum opus, and the seedling of his longest narrative, *Pranaya Ballari*. Besides, he composed during this period two long poems, *Ajodhya Drushya* and *Padmini*, both informed by moral sentiments and tender feelings, but which, contrary to expectations, did not attain excellence of the same order as *Kichaka Badha* or *Tapaswini*, the possible reasons being, in one case, circumscribed narrative scope, and, in the other, inadequate historical imagination.

Kabita Kallola, a collection of six long lyrics, was published in 1912. Ostensibly about scenes and places of natural beauty – two of them, additionally, of religious importance – these poems once again point to certain fundamental qualities of Gangadhar's poetic mind that had already been highlighted earlier, namely, tender sensibility, social ardour, moral concern, and love of man and feeling for nature presented in a balanced, harmonious form. *Chandra Rajani* and *Somanatha Bijaya*, even as they paint some captivating scenes of human life in vibrant intimacy with nature, also capture a whole way of life, an entire community story. Interestingly enough, even *Basanta Basara*, designed to portray the time of spring, goes on to dramatise with delightful poetic wit a sequence of events and scenes that subtly project the poet's feeling of indignation and outrage over agents and systems of coercion and cruel insolence. What comes off centrally through this collection is, therefore, a rich humanity wedded to a deep feeling for nature that in a larger sense includes all of the non-human world in contact with man. As a composer of longer lyrics fusing the literary and the folk, nature and human tradition, tenderness and wit, aesthetic taste and religious ardour, Gangadhar, as it were, had sifted and synthesised all the typical, significant elements found in the lyrics of Nandakishore, Madhusudan and Radhanath.

Tapaswini, the story of Queen Sita's life among hermits in Valmiki's ashram, was completed in 1913 and published the following year. The poem marks the consummation of Gangadhar's poetic genius. Presenting a material so well-known and so often handled by literary artists of the highest calibre – Valmiki, Kalidasa, Bhababhuti to name just a few, with whose renderings Gangadhar was familiar – he yet fashions a work that indelibly and unmistakeably bears the impress of his own special genius. He introduces certain original elements of argument and interpretation to present both Sita and Rama as impeccable characters, but does so without compromising upon psychological truth and human authenticity, without getting the normal feeling of outrage over Sita's exile marginalised or muted. With the hapless Sita left alone upon the banks of Bhagirathi, Gangadhar portrays all nature roused into wrathful militancy: shows the sun – progenitor of the Raghus – hide his face in shame, and presents Rama in deep torment, full of self-criticism and anxiety after having felt obliged as king to pass the cruel order. But then, Gangadhar's Sita exonerates her husband, explaining her misery not only as a working of fate, but also as a consequence of what she thinks were some of her own indiscretions. Her voice of complaint surfaces against Rama, poignantly, only once, but only to be submerged in a tide of gratification the next moment when she comes to know of his abiding love.

The poem's structural design itself reveals creative assurance and insight of the first order. Concentrating on Sita's heart and mind it charts a moving development from sorrow to serenity, from a feeling of terrible deprivation to one of profound fulfilment. Bringing in the past into the present through Sita's narration of her life's story before an inquisitive, affectionate ashram-girl, delineating her life in the hermitage in vivid details, and projecting at the conclusion of the poem a vision of future apotheosis as revealed to her in a dream, Gangadhar offers a psychological rendering of Sita whose immediacy, range and elevation mark a distinct progress beyond the great classics that were the sources of his inspiration. He also offers some of the finest pictures of nature which functions here not only as background but also as participant, a companion-spirit and, further, as an outer projection of Sita's inner being. Mind and environ are splendidly integrated, and the poem breathes an idyllic, sacred hermitage-atmosphere all through with the inner and the outer functioning as agents of mutual enrichment.

The style Gangadhar was refining upon, beginning with *Indumati* and evolving through *Kichaka Badha* and *Kabita Kallola*, attains here a superb richness and virtuosity integrating different modes – elevated and simple, literary and conversational, high-romantic and realistic. With remarkable subtlety linguistic stylisation here complements dramatic requirements of narrative; consequently, background, emotion, characterisation and imaginative representation come off sure and strong. No wonder, the poem gained immediate high adulation and has continued to be valued by successive generations of readers as a deeply moving classic. This is particularly striking, because the poem makes its impact as high drama and compelling narrative poetry despite actions and events in it being rather sparse. For long eleven cantos, Gangadhar holds the reader's mind and ensures a sustained interest with only a bare story-line as support. In terms of poetic tone and sensibility, again, nothing radical beyond his earlier works is in evidence, and yet the poem strikes one as something unique and extraordinary in Gangadhar's repertoire. More than anything else, Gangadhar has come to be known as the poet of *Tapaswini*.

As has been suggested before, the tragi-comic romance of Shakuntala's story had long fascinated Gangadhar, and much ahead of attempting *Tapaswini* he had published a poem that was to serve later as the first canto of *Pranaya Ballari*. Completed in seven cantos and published in 1915 this was Gangadhar's longest narrative poem. In a foreword attached to the poem Gangadhar articulated both his indebtedness to and his creative departures from Vyasa and Kalidasa who had handled the story in markedly different ways. An interesting statistical study has revealed Gangadhar's borrowings from Kalidasa in two hundred and sixty-seven stanzas out of a total of nine-hundred and seventy-two, a large majority featuring in the first, fourth and seventh cantos. Elements thus consciously adopted and rejected throw into sharp relief Gangadhar's critical insight and creative preference; but what is of utmost significance is the tone and temper running through the entire poem. In numerous ways Gangadhar nativises the story, improves its moral content, and refines upon sentiments imparting to it a new identity. While at places the moral strain appears to be long-drawn-out, and the process of nativisation somewhat overfree, Gangadhar's success in realising a new Shakuntala is admirable.

The verse of *Pranaya Ballari* has a special quality; for one thing, here the entire poem is in a uniform measure, emphasising narrative flow more than poetic embellishment, it being more full of events than any of his earlier narratives, and for another, Gangadhar appears to give here a freer rein to his art, undeterred by considerations of aesthetic purity and actuated by considerations of realism and moral sentiment as appreciated in his own world. Despite an occasional flabbiness here and there – for example, the long stretch on the quarrel between a demon-princess and some divine damsels which is entirely his own imaginative contrivance, and, again, parts of the extended advice Kanva offers Shakuntala – the poem as a whole imparts an exquisite tenderness of appeal with its rich sensitivity to character and feeling, and its masterful integration of a simple, dramatic style with emotively compelling description. The presiding tenderness of tone is evident in its very title, as also the sub-titles of the cantos which go to symbolise development of theme through elaboration of the poetic metaphor of a love-creeper, its burgeoning shoot, bursting foliage, blooming flower, wafting fragrance, pest-afflicted state, sweet fruition, and refreshing shade. The idyllic grace, simplicity, and unblemished beauty associated with a tendrilled, flowering vine that Shakuntala symbolises, informs the poem as a whole, winning for it a vast popularity that was second only to *Tapaswini's*.

Interestingly enough, through the period that Gangadhar was composing *Pranaya Ballari*, he also wrote a collection of verses on agronomy – not really poems but educative pieces designed as mnemonic verse – published as *Krushaka Sangeeta* (Farmer's Songs) in 1914. And, amazingly enough, it was through the very same year that he composed a number of short lyrics, included in *Arghyathali* (Platter of Offering) of 1918, some of which are among the most prized poetic treasures of the Oriya people. Projecting a 'sweet', 'honeyed' vision of the world of man and the universe as a whole, conveying certain tender and intimate intimations of immortality, offering a hymn of surpassing humility and deep sincerity, three of them, namely '*Biswa Dekha Madhumaya*', '*Amrutmaya*' and '*Bhakti*', achieve distinction with their unostentatious poetic wit, structured compactness, emotional density and profound simplicity. In addition to these, Gangadhar also wrote a number of other occasional pieces included in the same volume as also in the later volume, *Kabitamala* (Garland of Verses), demonstrating his extensive and variegated poetic sympathies. While some of them engage in soft coaxing and appeal, some others resort to stinging satire; some are elegies, some ceremonial pieces; there is a long moral-devotional piece, '*Bidura Prajagara*', and two long poems, '*Panchayat*' and '*Gobilap*' (The Cow's Lament). Together they attest to the poet's belief that poetry must cater to all sections of people and serve all orders of human involvement – psychological, moral, cultural, economic, political, aesthetic and spiritual.

Gangadhar was thus a complete poet, comprehensively relating his poetry to the whole of man's being and society. There is as much room in it for the sophisticated aesthete as for the poor, unschooled farmer, exhibiting a spaciousness rarely found elsewhere. It is this large sympathy and not simply stylistic virtuosity that makes him at once traditional and boldly experimental in his choice of poetic language. Whether it is exquisite elegance and utter plainness with which he presents his poetic thoughts and sentiments, there is everywhere in his verse an unmistakeable ring of sincerity and authenticity, something that derives from his poetic belief, as also from truths of his own life. And, hence, whatever be the distance from Gangadhar's world of simplicity, traditional beliefs, and poetic values at which a reader might be positioned today, it is difficult for him to be totally out of sympathy with even some of those ordinary, casual verses Gangadhar wrote, for he cannot miss the impress they all bear of a pure, gentle, devoted, sympathetic soul. The utter harmony between life and word, the absolute coherence of personality and vision that Gangadhar so consistently exhibited has ensured for his poetry a certain validation not easily to be had elsewhere. His is an enduring image – that of an eminently good man, who is also an eminently good poet.

Madhusudan Pati

MAJOR NARRATIVES

TAPASWINI

CANTO - I

Who are you, O Lustrous One, dressed in white so pure
With your deep blue hair that surpasses nature's sapphire?

Your radiance bursts through white gossamer
And, vividly imaged, breathes joy in the heart.

Are you only moon-shine bodied forth intense?
Here, at your feet, as hair, rolls darkness.

Dazzling planets and stars, rare, glorious
Adorn your form as gemstones precious.

Garlands of white flowers embellish your neck
Woven together in some artistry divine.

The scent of your holy form entrances the world
Filling the soul with sheer delight.

What is it you pour with your hands
That men drink and shine as heavenly beings?

What mantra too, you give your chosen few
That they dispel darkness to create light anew?

It is not right that you be called a moon,
For at your feet hundred-petalled lotuses bloom.

The slime of poverty fills the pool of my life
Whose belly fouled with pouring vexation

Cherishes you as the season of autumn
Sparkling with a cheer all its own.

The lotus in the heart spreads out in beauty;
Is it blessed, O Goddess, with the touch of your feet?

My soul is charmed with their touch;
So now, O Goddess, do with it what you please.

To the ashram of Valmiki races my mind
Longing for a glimpse of the banished Sita.

How did she stitch her ruptured heart?
With whom, and how, fill her life?

Be merciful, gracious goddess, grant me strength
So my mind grows holy to see, my hand to write.

Through the woods runs the river Bhagirathi,
Its waves wearing down the western shores,

Coursing ahead to view the forest-scene
As though for life, with eager feet.

On the same bank, Vaidehi* stood, deep inside
Her grief, her eyes towards the east.

Ceaselessly flowed the tears from her eyes,
Ceaselessly wetting the top of her breast,

As masses of cloud, rising in the west,
Flood the sunset hills with heavy downpours

Or as an elephant's trunk lets loose a salvo
On the lake's bosom, wetting the evening's lotus.

With her tender, piteous cries of 'My Lord,'
She sank on the supporting earth.

Numb, she dropped unconscious, but
None was nearby to give her help.

She whose feet served a hundred maids,
Not one now saw her desperate straits.

---

* Sita, princess of Videha/Mithila (hence *Maithili*); also called *Janaki* (daughter of Janak).

Heaven Almighty! Who wouldn't tremble with fear
To look upon destiny in such terrible form?

The forest cried with the voices of birds,
The rush of the savage wind became its breath.

Its breathing was a susurrus in the trees
While leaves floated by in waves of anguish.

Startled, the deer, glancing this way and that,
Stood rooted to their feet in deep disquiet –

Like children who aren't able to tell why,
Yet are distressed to see their mothers cry.

The emperor-palm, sword in hand,
Roared in rage, ready to fight with Fate;

Brandished his arrows of leaves, shaking again and again,
The quiver of the weaver-bird's nest.

Droplets thrown off the waves of the quivering stream
Leapt the wave-crests to hit the sandy bed.

Did the enraged Bhagirathi battle with Fate
As it loaded its shots in the guns of waves?

Distraught lotuses grouped together on the lake,
And with their arrows of bees fought in formation.

Wild flowers left their stems and rolled on the earth,
With dust-smeared bodies then wrestled in combat.

In defiant anger the creepers tore the cobwebs
To shreds, as if they were the nets of Fate.

Broken-hearted, clouds with weakened bodies
Rushed in rage in bands of their own,

With blazing eyes and peals of thunder
Showed their fury against this act of Fate –

Then, sprinkling cool droplets on the virtuous face,
Brought her slowly back to consciousness.

At the sorrow of the sinless daughter-in-law,*
The sun hid his face in shame.

Daughters-in-law of the sky's quarters, sitting with faces pale,
Shook the waiting skies with long, drawn-out wails.

Soon, regaining her senses, the exalted Sita
Looked in all ten directions in sheer despair.

Ramachandra's presence was everywhere –
There he sat, grief in his heart,

Near him the gentle Laxmana with folded palms,
Endless streams of tears flowing from their eyes.

Rama, not able to ask how Sita was,
And Laxmana, too, choked for words.

She turned towards the sun, and there in his lap,
Was the Lord of Raghus, bowed head in his hands.

Her gaze then shifted upon Bhagirathi –
There close at Bhagiratha's heels was Raghupati.

Tears ran down Rama's eyes like the Ganga's flow,
In which at times he sank, then was afloat.

She turned to contemplate upon her womb,
Uncontrollable tears gushing from her eyes.

The sight of lush green grass made her wince,
Urging her to set herself on a rock.

---

* Since King Ramachandra, Sita's husband, was a scion of the solar race.

She drew back thinking something in her mind*
But could hold her sobs no more.

From the burnt face came a cry of despair
So strong, the whole forest lay stilled.

In agony she mourned: 'Lord of my Life!
Ocean of Mercy, you who shower clouds of love:

In what ill-omened moment you held this unlucky hand
And became a dwelling for awesome grief.'

Unaware of the boundless glory of the Lord, I had
Flaunted a bow in deep disdain.

You broke it in two like a sugarcane stem
And savoured me as its juice's sweetness.

Crown of heroes, you did not deem me a hindrance
And lovingly took me into forest depths.

The fetters of those feet you made a chain of love
And went around holy places and hermitages.

How can I, dear, forget the love and care
You poured to fill my being in the hostile woods?

For fear this poor slave suffered pangs of hunger
With what concern you brought her fruits from the woods!

That a bed of leaves would disturb her sleep,
You made for her a swing in the cradle of your arms.

For a mere woman's love you crossed the high seas;
And with the ten-headed demon waged a mighty war.

You bore the assault of colossal weapons,
And embraced your wounds as a necklace for the heart.

---

* The colour of the grass brought to her mind the light-blue complexion of Ramachandra's body, and the rock the story of Ahalya, who languished as a figure of stone because of her sexual trespass till the touch of Ramachandra's feet revived her into life.

And thought me truly worthy to be its locket,
Treasuring me as its crowning gem.

When I shuddered at the sight of those scars,
You soothed me always with nectar-like words.

You said: "This blood-sacrifice on the battlefield
Has made me achieve you, priceless *bibhuti*" *

The scars from those arrows are still quite fresh
But I, the unfortunate one, am already separate!

Wipe off my memory from the tablet of your heart
Or else you'll suffer each twinkling moment.

Forget this worthless being, may your subjects be happy
And let me die, but may your blemishes go.

Nurture in your heart the deathless form
Of the immortal fame emerging from this.

Father of your race, the Sun of days,
Always ready is He to bless this world.

Ever-flowing nurse of the earth, Bhagirathi, too
Images the eternal glory of your race.

You forsook me at the call of honour, Lord,
This deed is but worthy of you, O Noble One.

But how strange and perverse that the picture
Of this sinner should stick on glory's banner!

Cursed be my life, Lord! Untainted as you are
That you should be slandered for my sake.

Where can I live but at your pious feet?
Fire doesn't burn this body; where is my pyre then?

---

* Holy ash collected from *yagnya*, considered auspicious and potent.

Green woods here carry your splendour —
If I renounce these, where can I take shelter?

Your grace fructifies even upon stone
To sustain me then, why should it court misfortune?

You placed a precious jewel in my womb
But didn't say how I might keep it safe.

I had nourished firm hopes in my heart
That with this gem would I adorn the Lord's lap.

A mere castle in the air became all that hope.
Bravo, Fate! I bow a thousand times to you!

What hardships, Oh Destiny, do you plan for the child
Whose royal father's large fame embraces the world?

It may be right that lightning strikes the mountain face,
But alas! That the lives of hill-folk too are destroyed.

Glory to you, Lord! Your mouth is a honeyed spring
And the heart a rock of frozen nectar.

Whatever be the torments that strike that heart,
From your mouth flows only a sweet nectar.

How terrible must have been your heart's agony
When shameful talk of me suddenly reached your ears!

Yet you never spoke a single cruel word
But filled me with hope even as you abandoned.

The sins I earned myself are my own grief's cause,
Sins that now again flash through my mind.

I thought he was one like us, my glorious Lord,
Believing the shout 'Save me Laxmana!' was his.

With a petty mind suspected Laxmana of smallness
And forced him to go in search of my Lord.

Such was my sin that for my Lord's great glory
Drove this sinning woman into endless exile.

That I had railed at a blameless Laxmana
Has brought me now its fitting reward.

I struck his heart with thunderbolts of words
Forcing him to depart from me.

The same respectful Laxmana fell at my feet
And abandoned me here with humble words.

The evil, ten-headed demon brought forth
A severed head in front of my doubting eyes.

Distraught, I mistook it for my husband's head
As I wept in utter despair, floating in tears.

That I didn't drop dead at its sight
Is the very sin that now roasts me alive.

I made light of the joy of serving at your feet
And longed for the sights of an *ashram* –

That sin has taken me away from you,
And now it taunts me, "Sinner, do as you please."

Those were long days you spent with me, unmoved
By the solicitations of Ayodhya's royal goddess.

Unable to bear the separation any longer
That goddess looked for revenge in envy.

She used her companions in grief, the towns-people
To effect now my exile.

The second wife in Ayodhya has always the greater sway,
The husband's power, though potent, never a match to hers.

The royal goddess began to reign supreme there
After Kaikeyi's influence bore fruit.

Lord, never forget nor let go the vow
You made before the sage Astavakra;

"I can renounce Sita, verily my life,
If the need ever arises to please my subjects."

Unswerving you've honoured your father's word;
If, unsorrowing, thus I honour my consort's wishes.

Only then should I deserve the title of your wife –
This my heart would surely understand.

You are pledged to the duty of pleasing your subjects
And I, your religious mate, must follow in your steps.

May my exile serve to appease your people
And my Lord's devotions remain unsullied.'

The wind grew still at the virtuous Sita's weeping;
All nature grieved, spanning water and sky.

Quiet were the dancing crests of Jahnavi*
And bird-calls in the forest were hushed.

Not a single leaf shook in the trees,
And stilled were the frolicsome creepers' limbs.

On every single branch, birds pricked up their ears,
Hearts grief-stricken at the bursts of weeping.

The fawn, its mother's teat in its mouth,
Stood transfixed, forgetting to suckle.

The deer and its doe, not chewing the tufts of grass,
Craned their necks to catch the doleful notes.

Peacocks and peahens with their young
Held their play, as if painted on canvas.

And tuskers, females and baby elephants, stood still
As wooden pieces, forgetting their way to the Ganga.

---

* Another name for Ganga.

CANTO - II

Peace rules in
Valmiki's hermitage kingdom
Coffers brimming with cool shade
gifted from nature's green.

Guilelessly those trees
on their own,
Offer what they have,
each to his own measure.

They are soldiers too,
serving for nature's wars,
Armouring their bodies
with foliage thick.

They build strong, lithe limbs
with workouts in the rains
To bring in riches of light,
beating the heat of the sun.

To protect the kingdom
from onslaught of winter,
As burning logs too,
they become arrows of flame.

In time defeated nature
offers them relief,
Gifting fruiting-buds
in the hands of the trees.

Holding in its womb
the star-gemmed ocean-sky,
Each drop of dew
sucks Agastya's* glory.

Pits of water around the trees,
with an ocean's pride,
Nurture in their wombs
the halo of the moon.

Sita's piteous cries
pierced all of a sudden,
Began shaking insistently
the home of Lady-Peace.

Perturbed, the kindly Lady
looked around
For a chariot to carry her fast
to the wailing woman.

Virgin girls of the ashram
were away busy then,
Examining the wind-blown
young vines in the garden.

When a strange new note
struck their ears,
Eager to recognise
they were all eyes and ears.

In their hearts they sensed
it wasn't the cooing of a dove,
Nor was it a koel's call
or a veena's strains.

It wasn't a conch's sound
nor a peacock's cry,
But a fountain of a female voice
poignant in its flow.

---

* Sage in Indian myth famous for his exploit of having sucked an ocean dry.

And peace found her a chariot
in the hearts of those maids.
She rode on, the *anchal* of bark
streaming as a banner in the breeze.

Peace felt stunned
at the waves of her weeping,
Yet did not waste a moment
to approach her close.

The girls stopped short,
and from a distance
Saw a woman rare,
drowned in tears profuse.

Startled, one thought,
'This is strange indeed,
And incredible, that such a woman
should be here in the woods.

Is she some goddess then,
from the celestial city,
Who had directly fallen to earth
under a recent curse?

Or was it the ornament[1]
of Indra's court that had
Slipped off Airabata's[2] back
while crossing the skies?'

Another thought,
'Is the Janhavi incarnate,
Flooding the earth
with the fountain of her tears?

Or is she verily Compassion
like a hailstone slipping through heaven,
Which the heat of others' grief
slowly melts away here?

1. Sachi, the wife of Indra, chief of gods in heaven.
2. Indra's elephant.

Or else this lush-haired woman
is a star with the clouds
That spawn a spring
when it plunges down to earth.

Had the sound of her cries
broken as a startling peal
We'd have thought it was lightning
with a cloudburst come.

But how could a cricket-chirping
harsh summer day
Liken to a dew-raining moonlight night
loud with koel's trills?

If she had a veena in her hand,
we would call her Saraswati,
Agonised with Visnu's separation
sits here weeping.'

With such thoughts coursing within
the girls went near Janaki
But none felt brave enough
to speak to her consoling words.

For how could
a *nirmala** have the strength
To clean the turbid waters
of the Mahanadi in the rains?

As that very river swells
mingling with Ib, Ang, and Tel,
So did Sita's sorrow deepen
in the company of the maids.

The girls stood around her,
not daring to speak,
Love fettered their feet
and they could not leave.

---

* A fruit that makes impurities in the water settle down.

Piteously gazing alone
 at their peaceful eyes
The tormented soul set free
 a flood of anguished waves.

The virtuous Sita
 surrounded by tearful girls
Wept on in acute agony,
 floating in the waters of her grief,

Like a melodious swan
 sending out cries of pain,
Amid lotus blooms
 wet by sheldrake-spray.

Unable to bear it more
 a girl hurried to Valmiki
And reported in haste,
 her voice, poignant, upset:

'O Father, a woman,
 as if a figure of butter,
Is out there in the forest,
 weeping herself to distraction.

For her dear consort
 she calls aloud again and again,
Wistfully recalling to herself
 his graces and affection.

A vermilion mark shines
 alluringly on her forehead,
As though it's a full-moon
 to her lotus-like face.

Gem-studded bangles
 adorn her hands,
As their gleams break through
 the sands of her sea of grief.

Like the yellow seed
in a lotus in half-bloom,
She captivates
in handsome lotus-hued silks.

Her garments are wet
from her unending tears,
Whether woman or goddess,
it is hard to recognise.'

The great sage listened
in silence, then shut his eyes,
And holding his body and head erect
sat still for a while.

Then he arose, saying,
'Let's take a look,' and stepped out,
And close upon the sage's heels
followed his disciples.

Daughters of the ashram,
other sages, curious,
Accompanied their friend
who had brought the news.

The deer and their does
followed with their young,
From tree to tree darted
koels, peacocks, and herons.

Bringing joy to the eye
parakeets, mynahs and doves
Set free upon the sea of winds
the floats of their bodies.

So did march forward
an army of Peace –
A sweeping flood
to the rock-barrier of Sita's grief.

The powerful currents
of the mighty Mahanadi
Swallow up
the terrible rocks of Rameswara* –

Still the rocks would never topple;
just the flow rages
And losing direction,
falls with reeling head.

Wouldn't the same fate
befall Peace in her campaign?
Let it, intoxicated as she is
in self-conceit.

A little distance ahead
the sage came upon Janaki,
All others crowding round
on branch and ground, and in the sky.

White-haired and bearded,
the ash-smeared sage Valmiki,
And by his imposing figure,
the virtuous Sita, of gold and white,

Like Uma
deep in mediation
Under the snow-capped Himalayas,
slient, motionless.

At the sage's approach,
Janaki held back her sorrow,
And the maelstrom of apprehension
was stilled in her heart.

'Daughter,' said the sage,
'I can imagine
How your heart is in flood
with the grief of parting.

---

* A place near Sambalpur where the river-bed is full of intricate rising rocks.

The river's course is easier
because its hopes are on the sea,
As it crosses obstacles, rocks
and mountains blocking its path.

It forgets all past misfortunes
in its union with the sea;
No difference then exists
between the lives of the two.

If by an act of Fate,
a sand dune pushes upward
And tears the heart of the sea
keeping both apart,

The river does not die,
for the sea sustains the other
And holds it close,
opening its heart out like a lake.

The same fate, my child,
is yours on this earth,
Don't make of your worries then
a fearful pyre.

Your father-in-law is my friend,
and so is your father;
Take the world as distasteful
and feel free to live here.

You shall have no cares
living in this ashram,
And don't feel concerned
about the child you'll deliver.'

Janaki heard the sage's words,
fell at his feet, and then
Rose, wiping her face
with the garment she wore.

'May you be a mother of heroes,'
the revered sage said,
Blessing her, and spoke to her
sweet, consoling words.

He urged, 'Come, my dear,
let us not linger more,
Adorn my ashram,
dwelling among the young girls there.'

He asked the girls
to collect her things
And respectfully they hurried
to do his bidding.

They squabbled among themselves
to pick up her exquisite packets,
Then supporting her gently,
led her along.

His wooden sandals
striking misfortune on the head,
The sage slowly led the way,
Rama's love-goddess behind him.

Like the sun's charioteer,
the great sage in ochre robes,
And following him, Vaidehi,
like the radiance of the sun.

The rays were drowning
in the waters of a sea of sorrow,
Only Anuru, the charioteer,
shone through bright and clear.

Flocks of birds had sat still,
intently listening to the words
That passed between
the great sage and the virtuous Sita.

Seeing them walk
towards the ashram,
They burst into loud calls
in joyous abandon.

Perhaps these were victory-cries
of the hosts of peace!
The fawns danced around
in satisfaction deep.

Over and over again they gazed
at the new guest's face
As if it were a sea of love,
with longing eyes.

She entered the city of Peace
like the goddess of Victory,
Rama's beloved herself,
risen from the sea of misery.

Their moon-spangled plumes spread high,
on either side
Hundreds of peacocks moved
along the borders of the path.

Young elephants,
lotuses in their upraised trunks,
Jostled one another
to follow them with the herd.

From the trees
hung leaves massed with flowers,
While in rows sat cranes,
forming banners of white.

Koels' dulcet voices rang
with auspicious songs,
The deep chorus of their chants
as victory conches full.

Flocks of parakeets and mynahs
soared from the trees,
And with open claws showered
petals on their path again and again.

Welcome-lamps were lit,
the evening star shone too,
And the star of Rama's eyes
sparkled in the sage's ashram.

On Valmiki's orders,
a maid carried her packets inside,
Then washed clean
the virtuous woman's face.

Just when another began
to pour water on her feet,
Sita took the pitcher from her
and washed her feet herself.

Seating her on a mat
of fresh leaves, another
Placed before her
fruits in platters of leaf.

Anukampa, the aged hermit-woman,
took her in her lap,
Mopped her reddened forehead
with her lotus palm.

With the clean and bright water
of her flowing love,
She flooded and cooled
the pure woman's heart.

She gazed into Sita's eyes once and again
and spoke tender and slow:
'It's my good fortune, my dear,
you've come to me today.

Noble empress, my child,
you have filled your golden palace
With gloom, and brightened
this cottage of mine.

I know you wouldn't have had
any food all day,
And the baby in your womb
must be restive and kicking.

So eat, my child! What shyness is this
in your mother's home,
For these girls who keep watch
are but your companions!'

With these words, she peeled
an orange, offering her
A few flakes, and gave her
bananas too, bright as camphor.

And the pulp of the *Kendu,*
pieces of jackfruit,
Sweet dates
and other juicy titbits.

'Eat, my child,'
she entreated again and again,
Offering her handfuls
of pomegranate seeds.

She kept on coaxing her,
saying 'some more, some more.'
And fed the virtuous one
a dozen berries.

And Sita lived through
those joys of a mother's love
She hadn't known as a child,
here in the forest of Valmiki.

Janaki rinsed her mouth
after her repast of fruits,
Then, at Anukampa's behest,
was seated upon a wooden dais.

A girl offered
a cardamom in her hand,
Which the one of lovely face
put lovingly in her mouth.

Another brought a sheaf
of soft, dry hay
And spread a deer-skin
over it to make a bed.

Two of the girls
stayed on with Vaidehi,
While the rest departed
to their own cottages.

CANTO - III

Under clear skies sunlight poured bright over sea and earth
As Laxmana left Vaidehi on Bhagirathi's bank.
Was it that the god of day, in fear of shame, unrolled a curtain of white,
Lest the torture of Rama's wife be seen from the city of the gods?
Aware of its design, twilight soon lifted that cover from the earth
To reveal the evils of the race of the Sun.

Scores of stars appeared on the field of the sky
One after another at the call of birds; more came then, crowding together.
There, in a vast courtyard below, they saw Rama, descendant of the Sun,
Sitting all alone, with mournful face and tearful eyes.
He mused: 'Princely power was a mere pretext for slavery,
The exalted office an unending grind at subjects' feet.

A lie, spoken by hundreds of subjects gathered together,
Over and over again, in deference is declared as truth.
A king's happiness is the sacrifice in the *yagna* for his subjects' peace,
Bound to his duties with firm ropes of *dharma,* he can't move a step aside.
The coronation they perform is just a severing of the head,
And the ritual fanning a ruse to drive the flies away.

Even a god's heart would not house sadness in bliss,
So the king, called a mighty god, partakes of fame's nectar.
And for the good of his subjects is he placed high,
Like a cloud risen as vapour from the subjects' blood.
The thunderbolt isn't there in the waters of the earth, but easily lies in the clouds,
Powerful is the mace in the king's hand, but never in the hands of his subjects.

Lightning's fire might scorch its heart, yet the cloud must rain,
Renouncing all joys the king must please his subjects, and so be worshipped high.
Kingship on earth is the head of the ladder to heaven,
And a king who strays is destroyed, falling deep.
He wields a baton like a magician, looking equally on one and all,
Dancing on the tightrope of kingship, without a care for his life.
For, with his feet on the rope, if the dancer did not walk on,
Many would clap and laugh at him, and the drummer chide him too.

The people would insult me more, if this self of mine
Listless with Maithili's separation neglects the duties.
The world would deride me then as the worthless scion of Raghu's race
Who, infatuated with his wife, thoughtlessly forsook kingship.
However venerable *Vanaprastha's*[1] resort, my time is not yet come,
And Bharata too would not agree, to take upon himself my duties.

An object in one's lap seen again and again, loses its appeal day by day,
But love grows more when the lap is empty, as zero added to a number.
The gross body is not immortal, immortal only is the mind;
When the mind hasn't broken the bonds of compansionship,
That happiness is happiness alone.
Has anyone lived on earth all his days
In true affluence, a golden crown on his head?
For fame and slander, defying time, grow into contenders certain.
Bound to their natures men move towards hell or heaven,
Only the lowly mind seeks fleeting pleasures, ignoring the opinions of men.

My beloved is away, but my lotus-bud-beloved is in full bloom
In the love-pool of my heart, where my importunate mind-bee plunders her honey.
Why do you keep shedding tears in misery, O eyes of mine?
If then the pool dries up, my lotus cannot hold itself.
My heart, be a dam of stone, and seal these eyes' streams,
My breath, blow gently too, lest my heart's precious one trembles.
My ears, do not be restless, you shall hear and shed your pain,
For Laxmana would return and speak all about my life's mate.
O tormented skin! The breeze will soon be here to dry your sweat,
Carrying the pain-killing scents of her sweet body that inhabits as if the lotus.[2]
There is one other thing; come, be you all one with the mind,
And revel in life's unending joys upon the lake of the heart.
Like a fresh lotus, my life's companion, blooms there,
Where the sun of memory, ever refulgent, never sets.

But listen, my tongue; you mustn't,
Partaking your subjects' wealth, long for that joy,
And react against those whose riches you have enjoyed.
This life is mine still because of my service to men,
Or how else could I have melted a thunderbolt and drunk it as holy juice?

---

1 Third stage of life when one renounces home.
2. Suggestion of Lakshmi, the goddess of prosperity.

At daybreak I shall set free the mynah and parakeet from their cages,
So their calls of "Sita!" won't excite you more.
The fawn too, shall join the one with *alta* [1] - decorted feet,
For the silken collar around its neck glistens like an *alta* streak.
Why should the peacock and its peahen keep on calling here,
And why shouldn't the mockingbird leave too, with no voice here to mimic its call?
Enduring its ill fate, the veena would be slient now; for bereft
Of the accomplished musician's voice how can it gain applause?'

Then Rama shut his eyes for a while, and climbing the peak of anxiety,
Saw Time's spectacle, its fierce currents rushing past him.
There he saw both the moving and the still, emerge and vanish into the depths,
Like bubbles, some holding for a moment, and others afloat a few days.
In that terrible flow of water, stood upraised the mountain of fame,
Kissing the Lord's feet, the sky, looming fearless and firm.
Chaste women in bright attire walked with their consorts
In couples on the mountainside; happy, as ever,
Many kings there were, shining upon rows of gem-studded thrones,
Wearing garlands of heavenly flowers,
Vessels of whose beings held riches of virtues, acquired through arduous feats,
Whom, the poets, mountain-dwellers, came to escort by their hands.
Those evil ones who, ignoring virtue, forcibly ascended the hill,
Were struck by the bolt-like fists of the poets, to live in deep torment.
Touched by their misfortune, Rama suddenly opened his eyes.
He saw the earth's floors covered in a pall of darkness;
Adorning the deep blue sky, shone stars with luminous faces,
The moon wasn't there, but their joys hadn't lessened.

He said, 'Oh stars, you aren't confined to the love-prison of the moon;
Level-headedly at the Creator's will, to keep the starry wheel in motion,
Away from your consort, to still emit light for all the unbearable pain,
For the sake of the world, you forget your agony, and keep to the path of duty.
Visit then Valmiki's ashram, hasten, and offer your initiation there,
Where the moon of my heart, sitting alone, would be pining in tears for me.
Should on this night, the she-*chakrabaka*,[2] cry out her distraught heart,
The sensitive one might lose her hold and rid herself of life.

---

1. Alta: a red liquid.
2. A bird of the ruddy-goose family that separated from its mate sends out plaints upon the night. Kin to the shelduck.

So show her the pool, and point at the forest of lilies,
For even through the moon does not rise, they live on without being fretful.
She must not think reunion is a problem grave and deep;
Explain to her, since you know yourself, how fulfilling is the union of hearts.

She mustn't have a scope for doubt, she of the *sarasa*-eyes,
So surely convey her all my feelings, you who have witnessed all.
As the flow of my soul is joined to her womb,
When you say this to her, she wouldn't think it at all untrue.'
Could a certain lightness have touched Rama's heart in this? –
In vain did the stars peer raising a film of darkness* before them.
One who fails to understand the virtues of the good, and excels in finding fault,
He is prone to suffer at his lofty station the painful ironies of fate.
The stars had looked for the pleasure of discovering taints in Rama,
But bowed their heads in humility, when they saw his heart was so lofty.
Hesitant to see Rama's grief, the sorrow-torn moon
Rose from the ocean of milk only after night had fallen.
The *chakora* called out tauntingly to the *chakrabaka* bird,
'Do not grieve, for derision is writ on your forehead.'
So he could afford to scorn, because fate had poured neactar in his mouth,
And that is the way of the rich; always ready to clap at others' grief.

Elsewhere, Rama's spouse, deep in the sorrow of separation,
Bereft of the comforts of a scintillating palace, and couches of priceless ivory,
Sat in the familiar hut of leaves, on a seat of deer-skin,
Recalling to herself the events of the past.
Love-soaked sweet words, spoken by the Lord of her being,
Entering on their own, struck clear melodies in the gramophone of her heart.
Deep in thought, in her mind she came upon a vision brilliant,
Of emerald-bright arms – fear-dispelling, straight and graceful – beside her head;
Close by, reflected in memory's mirror, Laxmana alone with his bow,
The same way he used to, denying himself sleep, constant companion on guard.
Then, as the thought flashed that the same husband and his brother had exiled her,
Her dulled eyes, like a frost-bitten lotus, let loose streams of tears.

As the date-palm pierced by the juice-collector, still and silent
Sheds its juice; so was Sita's state, stabbed inside.
The lover recalling the beloved's grace, and the beloved her lover's ways,
So did both sit on grief's seat slicing the night with the sword of patience.

---

* Darkness; also base instincts.

Her brain and soul strained hard, sweat ran down ceaselessly,
Wetting the thick eyelashes, and drenching her cheeks.
The night took the form of an owl and hooted, but as it slowly felt faint
Flooded the sky with her blood, and found deliverance in escape.
And the stars, surrendering their pride at the lovers' feet,
Dropped to the ground in the guise of flowers, begging for refuge.
Without malice, the Lord of Raghus, Preserver of All, protected their honour,
Uttering the boon: 'Aeon upon aeon, upon my head shall you find your place.'

CANTO - IV

With eyes of a full-blown lotus came Dawn, heralding peace,[1]
For a sight of Janaki, thirst afire in her soul.
Offering pearls of dew in her foliage-hands
She waited in the courtyard of Sita's cottage,
And with the koel's voice, pleaded:
'Appear before me, Noble One, for now the night is ended.'

Saffron her apparel of light, a flowery sheen manifest,
Serene of form, these arouse in the mind a belief
That some yogic goddess is here, who soothes with words sweet,
Calling out endearingly, to ease all sorrows;
As if to gift life anew
She has alighted upon earth from the heavens high.

The breeze sang, the bee strummed the *veena*,
And the morning's scents kept dancing on Dawn's orders.
The pheasant with sombre eulogy, began her notes of praise;
In a slick attire arrived the chief herald drongo,
And with winsome sweetness said: 'Rise, Oh Empress
Of Chastity, for now the night is gone.'

Vedic chants of sages rang through the green woods;
The sonorous *Oum* rose high, piercing the skies,
As if the resonance of Saraswati's *veena*,
Entrancing Vishnu, coursed into Ananta's [2] ears.
Moment to moment the woods pulsed brighter
As if Life's force swelled with the power of mantra.

---

1. A possible variant would be – ' Auspicious emerged Dawn, a full-blown lotus.'
2. The mythical serpent Shesa whose coils form a bed for Lord Vishnu as He rests upon an ocean of milk in the upper heavens of Vaikuntha.

The celibate Anukampa, deep-set in austerities,
Came near Janaka's daughter then, and said solemnly:
'Arise, Vaidehi, for the tender-limbed Dawn
Is here: gratify her with the joy of your sight.
The river Tamasa too waits
For happiness of fondling you once in her lap.'

With Rama's heroic figure etched on the tablet
Of her grief-steeped mind, like the sun
Mirrored in a drop of dew in the lotus's heart,
The chaste Janaki rose from her bed;
Then, bowing at Anukampa's feet,
Humbly offered worship at the feet of Dawn.

She hymned her thus: 'Oh Destoryer of Darkness,
Praised be you on earth as the harbinger of the sun.
At your tender feet he collects his light,
And with full hopes I seek succour there.
Lover of fair fragrances, Oh goddess of solar race,
May you spread good fortune all around.'

At night's end, with eager heart,
The nurse of the hermitage, Tamasa, clear and pure,
Threw sprays of fragrant water and flowers in the yard;
Lighting with the morning star her auspicious lamp,
Her fish-eyes flickering, watched
Longingly for the chaste Sita's blessed advent.

From the cottage in flood with the ashram-girls' ardour,
Emerged the pure and lustrous Sita, admired the world over,
And with Anukampa by her side,
Hastened for a bath towards Tamasa's stream.
With her wave-like hands Tamasa fondly embraced
And caressed the virtuous form.

With a voice sweet as nectar, she happily said:
'My child, I had never cherished the hope
That Sita, necklace on the royal goddess's breast,
Would renounce the world and come to me here
To play upon my bosom. Only for your sake
Will the world acclaim and call me the fortunate one.

Meandering through many forests, unbeguiled in charming canyons,
Crossing numerous obstacles with a clear vision,[1]
Not counting the pain of darknesses, nor charmed
By the joy of light, I keep to my long course
With deep-bowed head, So I fulfill my life,
Pleasing with gifts of water all who live on my banks.

Mandakini and Godavari are thus just as able as me;
Yet are crowned in glory, having gained
Inexhaustible wealth in your footprints
And in your body's scents that endow godliness –
For which I had always craved,
And without which I had felt ever disgraced.

Because of my good deeds performed in the past,
And knowing my heart's desire,
Dharma[2] in time brought you down to me,
Rare riches have I found; and now, I will be fulfilled,
Drawing you to my lap and talking to you day after day;
The purity of your being
Shall wash clean the sins of my life.

Skeins of swans and geese, pairs of *chakrabakas* and cranes,
In spirited play in my lap, shall sip the water
Made pure by the touch of your sacred form
And live by my side for ever,
Singing your praise with their notes;
And to my ears gift happiness unending.

The thought they would be cleansed by Sita's touch
Would make the flowers abandon their home of vines;
Floating, dipping, hurrying along from far to approach you,
They would be circling around
As you bathe in my waters;
Do not then, Compassionate One, push them away.

---

1. Gangadhar's words here carry a double-meaning; 'clear water' and 'clean life'. We have put 'clear vision'.
2. Piety, as also Cosmic Law.

Upon my banks you shall wander,
Spreading eternal splendour in the woods,
This the trees would catch and glow with light,
Acquiring strength divine, imparting peace;
Green and rose on leaf
Forever be pellucid its exquisite beauty.'

Sita said: 'The stream is clear and sweet as coconut water,
Not mere water, but truly my mother's milk;
From the breasts of mountains it flows as a stream of nectar
Towards Sita who is so lifeless now.
Ah, in the garb of Tamasa,
Riven in the heart with my grief,
You are indeed a mother in this land to me.

A fissure tears your back, the other side visible clear;
Still, so the daughter be pleased,
You open your loving eyes, and with adoring words
One by one, you speak solicitously, fondling me.
Marvellous, Oh Mother, is your heart,
Full of sand to absorb all my sorrows' heat.

The Sita who in the eyes of the people of Rama's kingdom
Was held to be tainted, and banished,
The same one you believe firm in her *dharma* of martial devotion,
Will succeed in making sacred and pure
All that moves and rests upon this earth!
A mother truly understands her daughter's pain,
And a burnt face appears lovable
As a moon-face to her mother's eyes.

Your banks will surely be my permanent refuge
And my hopes only at your peaceful lotus-feet;
For one whose world is empty, it's just a mother's lap
That is the storehouse of love on this earth.
When one's mother has a womb full of gems,
Why should she yearn for other places?'

Tranquil, clear and cool was Tamasa's pure waters,
And in nature alike were all the ashram's girls;
Agile in affection, Tamasa,
Taking on the guise of their reflections,

Made herself their exact likenesses;
And embracing their bodies,
In deep ardour swiftly mingled in them.

Constantly thus at Sita's side to watch her grace,
Was for her an occasion propitious;
So the clever one made herself many-eyed,
And gained numerous hearts and minds, and forms various.
The heart's delights multiply
When joined to others of similar spirit and nature.

Their bath over, they came back
And offered worship at the feet of Valmiki.
The chief sage blessed them, saying: 'May you all
Persevere, and succeed in earning the riches of wisdom.'
Then, with special warmth, addressed Sita:
'May you give birth to heroes, free of hazard.

'My daughter, tend these plants of the hermitage
With labour and love, as if these be your children;
So would you naturally grow in experience and know
How precious and rare is the germ of an offspring.
Anukampa shall always be there
To attend to all your needs.'

All then left, as wished by the Chief Sage,
Carrying pitchers in their lotus-soft arms.
In beauty, Janaka's daughter outshone them all,
A scintillating diamond among bits of crystal;
And the forest's charm deepened with the invaluable find
When they reached the garden.

The goddess of the woods, thrilled to find the heavenly Sita
At her door, embellished herself with the rays of the sun.
Smiling with her leaf-lips, her teeth flashing
Like *mahua* flowers, she decked herself lovingly to steal Sita's mind,
Offering the red *salmali*, and held forth
Drifts of dew on the grass to wash her feet.

She offered a seat of ground-lotus, welcoming her
Through the mynah's melodious calls.
Made fresh lotuses to bloom in the waters of autumnal pools,

And, with the hum of bees as though greeting the she-swan,
Said: 'My night of pain is over
With the touch of your sun-bright feet.'

'A dream came true when I saw you by sheer luck,
And with a heart pulsing with infinite joy
Followed your life in Chitrakuta valley,
In Dandaka nurtured by perfect sages,
And in the *Asoka* forests of Lanka beyond the seas;
Placed you as a model before my eyes
And for fourteen years sculpted an icon of love.

As you flew back through the sky on the Puspaka,*
Flower in hand, I kept looking up sadly with eyes of the deer
And beseeching with peacock-cries went on calling out fondly,
Till you had gone past hearing's range.
Have you then come back, dear,
Recalling a friend's cries after so long a time?

Friend, unable to bear the agony of unending separation,
Thinking of the end I became an anchorite;
Seeing my own self in the mirror of your heart, flooding it in love,
I welcomed you in deep delight;
Accept now my gratitude,
That you have fulfilled my desire with so much love.

Goodwill that ensues from the company of the good,
As the unchanging blue of the sky, never dies.
With a friend who is virtuous the heart's desire goes not in vain,
So it is that I am able to see you today;
For it is fate which fulfils such things,
And it is my love for you, my friend, that has made me fortunate!'

The sweet enchantment of sylvan beauties,
Like a newly risen mass of cloud,
Suddenly surfaced in Sita's mind
To cool the burning pain of the fire of separation
In the woodlands of her heart.
The daughter of Janaka muttered:
'I am your prisoner for life.'

---

* Mythical aerial car.

CANTO - V

The one to whose shore-feet rushed the waves of beauty,
With a surf-crown of flowers on the head,
In the sea of royal gardens kissing her nails of pearl;
The ashram's plants, creepers, and blooms entire
Thrilled with joy at her auspicious visit.

As it was, it was spring time;
The warm golden rays of the morning sun,
Splattering on dew-drenched leaves,
Played in many-hued tints as they fell on the drops,
And wove a rare canopy of diamonds, pearls and rubies.

Those feet of the Virtuous One
That had robbed the glories of the ten crowns
Of the ten-headed demon, adorned with sun-bright rubies
The very same feet, as it were,
Scattered today the amassed pride
Of those very rubies in the sage's garden.

Sita's heart, stained with the many tints
Of the dark-hued Rama, was pilfered by the trees
That grew deep-green in time.
And with her mind bound to her consort alone,
The lustre of her limbs,
Were drawn to the numerous flowers,
To make them their home.

The bee took only the lustre of her hair,
The *champak* took the wealth of her body's radiance,
To the hibiscus went the elegance of her lips,
And so to the others, to its own taste each.
All were splendour-filled,
As if goddess Laxmi from heaven, come down to earth,
Had made the garden an immortal field of sport.
The charm of the Virtuous One was like nectar

That ambrosial rendered the honey in the flowers;
Thus did her tenderness and grace
Last for ever in the limbs of the garden blooms;
And the Chaste One turned anchorite,
Desiccated in heart and limb
To live on as a forest dweller.

To welcome the virtuous guest,
All night long the spiders
Wove their exquisite canopies,
Draping them with golden flowers.
Ripe oranges, spheres of gold,
Hung in hundreds in long lines.

And there the charming banana-maid stood,
Sheaves of leaf-banners in her hand;
The graceful *muchukunda, kunda* and *boula* plants,
And *niali* and *madhavi* – creepers all,
Looked on, ready with their offerings of flowers;
The young tuberose too, was there with them,
Her head ornamented with blooms.

When the daughter of Janaka
Came near with her companions,
In raptures they scattered flowers
On the chaste Sita in the soft breeze;
A few kissed her head,
Some shook her hand, some embraced her,
While some others adored her feet.

To lick the bright-red feet
The hibiscus stretched out her tongue;
Desiring to kiss the pearl-lustred nails,
With wide-open mouth waited the pomegranate;
Longing for the gift of mercy,
The *chinichampa* turned green
After Rama's form.

Here and there some pale-white, tender plants
Soft and creamy as the face of the infant moon,
Kept straining their heads above the fence,
With longing looks towards the Virtuous One.

Those that could not raise themselves
Went on peering through chinks in the fence,
Restless for a view.

The wagtails *chanchi* and *phulchuin* sat on the fence
And gazed on the virtuous Sita,
Calling out now and then,
And wagging their tails in ecstasy;
All along waiting eagerly for Sita
To water the plants, so they'd drink from the pit without fear.

The spider falls at the feet
And once again climbs the tree,
Scurrying swiftly from tree to branch
To show off its artistry;
The sun plays the painter,
In many-splendoured hues
Setting off the morning's gossamer.

A natural green the groves of trees,
And on the tree-tops the *thinthinies* emerald-hued,
Briskly grooming themselves with their beaks;
Resplendent to the eye,
Like the sun's rays
Looted by waves of a dark-blue sea.

Was it that the love-resplendent heart of Rama
Uneasy upon the royal throne,
Had rushed to this garden
To end the Virtuous One's agony -
The auspicious light of his eyes
Forming pearls of love in Sita's heart
Like drops of rain in *Swati.**

Dense jackfruit groves on one side,
Mangoes kissing the sky on another,
And like the waters of a natural lake
The sky spreads under the margins of foliage;

---

* Refers to a belief that drops of water taken in by oysters form into pearls when the star Swati is in ascendance.

As though the shoulders of hundreds of trees
Together lift up the forest with one mind.
As if a group of ascetics had taken refuge
On the secluded banks of a lake of peace;
Heavy burdens of trials on their heads, they wait,
Silent, solemn and still;
As though eager in mind
That, in the cold and the heat, Sita's agony should lessen
Under the moon and the sun.

Elsewhere stands a blue-green mansion,
Graced by woody berries, this forest of *Ingudi*;
Inside which the Shyama[1] lives, a newly-married bride,
Pouring out her mellifluous notes;
Bedecking her home with blue sapphire,
As if ordered by Indra, his wife Sachi
Invites the virtuous Sita for worship.

Bright and velvety the blue leaves,
The groves of *punnaga* greener than all,
Did they fly there perchance from Utkal
To gladden the heart of the chaste Sita?
Or was it Rama here,
Taking on the Blue Mountain's form,
To relish the waves of Sita's love-sea?

The Virtuous One with her companions
Strolled round the garden once;
Was it Bhagirathi on Aryavarta's heart,
That flowed with her tributaries!
The path glittered,
Humbling the garden of Kubera
In which *gandharva*[2]-girls revelled.

They carried then the waters of Tamasa,
And filled the pits around the roots,
As if heavenly maidens were watering

---

1. A bird of dark colour.
2. Heavenly musicians and dancers.

The gardens of Nandana* from the celestial Ganga;
Or was it the lightning-filled clouds
Lifting the water of the seas,
Were flooding the bosom of the earth?

With *anchals* drawn tight against the waists,
They walked on with quick steps,
Holding pitchers on their dishevelled heads,
As sweat ran down their foreheads,
Which they wiped with their hands,
Pausing from time to time
For the slow-moving princess.

Soon Anukampa came upon them, and said
In a voice ringing sweet and maternal
'My Sita doesn't know how to fetch water,
Let her not strain so hard on her first visit,
But merely look around the garden once.

Come dear, come into the cool shade,
We'll sit awhile, don't exert yourself more,
Let me tell you some rules of the ashram.'
With such words, fondly she took her aside.
The Virtuous One and Anukampa sat in the shade,
And the girls kept watering the plants.

Then Anukampa began, 'Sita dear,
All man's work is grounded on love.
Just as in each flower its scent,
So in each life does love reside;
And it is after the nature of each
That love bears fruits –
Divine, human or demoniac.

Many practice austerities, but as demons,
Proud and arrogant, fostering passion,
In anger, on bodily strength, inflicting on oneself pain;

---

* Garden in heaven.

These are not possible in your nature,
For you adore equally with a pure heart
Gods, brahmins, teachers and the wise,
With simplicity, purity and love.

Soothing and truthful words, pleasantly said,
Are your beloved embellishment,
Guile hasn't touched your heart,
How can *Maya*[*] then, come near you?
Your charming serene form proclaims,
You no more wish for worldly involvement.

Your ordained nature is of an ascetic,
I noticed this at once when I saw you first;
Most tender is your sanctified being,
A rare fruit of awful penance,
The blossom of the creeper of righteousness –
The customary work of novices is not for you.

Just fetch some gourdfuls of water
Along with these girls every day,
Brighten the flame of their lamp of ardour;
They would never leave you alone,
For these are my instructions to them,
And don't ever bear with thirst and hunger,
Denying your needs out of shyness.

When the girls are at work in the garden,
Be yourself at your ease;
Whenever you desire anything,
The girls will fulfill your wishes at once.
And don't hesitate at all
And pluck any fruit or flower
Of the garden that you wish.'

The day touched the seventh hour,
And the girls, with their empty pitchers,
Settled quietly near Anukampa

---

* Primal delusion.

With sweating limbs, one by one:
By a cheerful thorn-apple flower
As though a bunch of fruits; and beside,
Dew-drenched flowers in bud.

They rose, and bathing again,
Went back to their living quarters;
All together had their repast
Of fruit and roots collected by the ascetics.
In reading and discourses spent then,
As was their daily habit,
The ashram's inmates spent the noon.

The joy of affection of these forest ascetics
Dispelled the grief of the Virtuous One,
The thought of princely pleasures
Never entered, even by chance,
The pathway of her memory;
In her heart's clear pool,
Rama, the handsome royal swan,
Frolicked about for ever.

CANTO - VI

One night, the Moon with *Chitra*, rose in the sky,
And the white jasmine blossomed in abundance.
Slowly on the rambling jasmine in the ashram,
Joyous masses of blooms gave off their fragrance.
Burdened with the scents of *madhavi*, *bakula*,
Malli and *niali*, the breeze blew languid,
And moved along, embracing with abandon
The clear moonlight on the sands of Tamasa.
Near Janaki's cottage, patches of moonlight
In varied shapes under the trees,
Advancing gradually towards the east,
Shrank and lengthened, and effaced their forms.

A short distance from her cottage,
Vaidehi sat with a friend in the cool moonlight.
Moonbeams around her body
Appeared as if radiating from her haloed limbs.
On a leaf two fireflies glowed with a luminescence
More sublime than the moon's!
Looking at them, the Virtuous One thought:
'Well done, fireflies, in your insect-life!
There may be many creatures in this world
Surpassing you, but who else can match your gleams?
You were indeed fortunate to have the Creator's boon,
So is your refulgence so enchanting to every eye.'

Then the love-calls of the *chakrabaka* floated in,
Striking recurrently like showers of sorrow.
The waters of pity began spreading on their own,
In the lakes of Sita's eyes to the cheek's shores.
Swiftly Janaki hid her face from her friend,
And wiped her tears, as if they were sweat.
But the friend knew, and asked: 'Tell me, Gentle One,
Why does the *chakrabaka* call hauntingly when night comes?
Does this bird live in cities too?

And does it cry out in despair, at midnight?
If that be, what do the townspeople
Feel when they hear its plaintive cries?'

At her words Sita could not contain her tears,
And could not, too, speak with her choking voice.
Her companion then said: 'Forget my words,
Forgive my childishness; I caused you needless pain'.
Janaki rejoined: 'Dear friend, my heart is uneasy
Not having told you all about myself.
As I hope to spend these last years
Of my life in your company,
If I don't confide my feelings to you
How can you go on trusting me?
Speech, too, would lessen the burden of my grief,
And from the story of my life,
You would know what the world is like.

Friend, I am a princess. I grew up in the royal palace,
In luxury and comforts, in the cradle of joys;
Swans, peacocks, koels, parrots and mynahs
Kept the palace reverberating with delight.
The *chakrabaka* used to cry out at night,
But my child's heart was never touched by it.
My childhood was soon over, and when I attained youth,
I saw one day kings assembled from many lands.
My father had preserved a gem-studded bow,
An object of rare beauty.
One after another, the kings failed
Even to lift the bow, and returned to their seats.
Ornate crowns covering their white-haired heads,
So many kings tried to show off their might.
A few young princes too, in lion-like manner,
Tugged at the bow, but stepped back, defeated.
Seeing their arrogant gait and fruitless daring
My heart was filled with laughter.
I sat in the balcony, quietly amused,
Observing them in the company of friends.

And then came a crest-mantle of the race
Of warriors, whose radiance
Subdued the glitter of the best of emeralds.

He approached the bow in all his splendour,
As if he were the Sun himself in a prince's guise.
My heart melted of its own when I looked on him:
Such a feeling is so rare in the life of an ashramite.
The fun I was making of the kings, the light-hearted mood,
Vanished in a moment.
Oh friend, never had I imagined
That my eyes would see so handsome a form.
My pure heart began to humbly adore
His glowing crimson feet.

My father had vowed my hand only to him
Who could string and snap the bow;
I thought then, the end of his oath had come,
And I would be an anchorite by his leave;
For who would break the bow? Could anyone now?
And this hero of heroes had already won my heart.
If the heart is with one, and she weds another,
Both in life and death will suffer awful reversal.
For one whose lovable hands
Were meant to hold Cupid's bow of flowers,
It seemed an insult for him to lift that bow.
It was my good fortune that this brave youth
Broke with the mighty bow the sorrow in my heart.
So I was wed to the emperor of heroes,
Feeling blessed to have his divine love;
The jewel among heroes had three younger brothers,
They too were offered the hands of my sisters three.

On the way from my father's house to my husband's,
When I saw the great Bhargava,* a comet to the warrior race,
Placing a resplendent bow in my consort's hand again,
I was filled with fear; for I thought,
He might win some sparkling woman again
And she might become a rival to my love.
When my husband fixed an arrow to the bow,
The great glory of Bhargava at once became his.
As the sun's rays enhance the love of the lotus,
So did his heroism swell the joy in my heart.

---

* Warrior-sage Parsurama who was out to test Rama's strength.

But the heart thinks one way, results shape in another,
It is hard to know, friend, Destiny's ways in the world.

A dazzling banner of glory fluttering in the sky,
The hero of heroes cheerfully rode back home.
My father-in-law's palace was a forest of riches;
When the good news coursed as spring-breeze there,
Flowers of joy burst upon its trees of beauty,
And leaves of splendour stole the minds of men.
The four newly-married brothers,
Radiantly adorned with ornaments,
With their wives' attires even more brightly fashioned,
Entered the palace with euphoria high.
Friend, there was an old woman in the palace,
Who spoke aloud, showering happiness all around:
'The glorious pageant of all four star-spangled quarters of the sky
Beautify with their presence today the royal abode.'
I glanced and saw the fair faces of my sisters
Turn crimson with the bashfulness of new love,
And the fresh beads of sweat on them
Gleam with the finery of the ornaments they wore.
Now as I look at the moonlight on your sweating brow.
That picture, my friend, now comes to my mind.

Much is said about the riches of heaven,
Which the ears cherish as truth, and tempt the mind.
And so even a king abdicates his throne,
To perform austerities in the forests,
Living on fruits and roots.
But what I saw, dear friend, in my father-in-law's
Home, I thought I would never find
Even in the abode of the celestial Lord.
My new parents' affection, and my husband's love,
Made me view heaven as but a slight thing.
Ever-new festivities were the order of the day,
Of kinds I'd never imagined would be on earth.
The wealth of my husband's love, and the opulence
Of the palace illumined my hours,
The day passed happily on.
So full was I that I had no time or ears then
To hear the *chakrabaka's* plaintive notes.
And in this way twelve years sped by,

Appearing as only twelve days to me.
Once my husband came and said in confidence;
'Beloved, we shall spend the night in austerities;
For with the hope you would be her heart's ornament,
The Royal Goddess is crowning me tomorrow.'
I quipped: 'Lord, would that heavenly love
Which was all mine, be shared now?'
He said: 'It may seem natural a thing. But remember,
The Royal Goddess bows at the feet of a woman of virtue.
The ocean's waters rise as clouds in the sky,
Then, serving the good of the world,
Enter the womb of the sea.'
That night was spent by us in pious observance
Until day broke with loud auspicious music.

Escorted by the minister my husband went to meet the King, his father,
But returned to tell me in grief-stricken words:
'My life's partner, I leave behind my life with you,
And at father's behest, I leave for the forest today.
Bharata, my beloved brother, will be the Crown Prince;
The Royal Goddess is now engrossed in his love.
Do not, Oh Sensitive One, sulk like an elder,
But give Bharata all regard as due to a king.'
As I observed my husband's countenance,
It appeared vividly content as ever.
His mind was eager to journey to the forest,
But it seemed as if his soul was in torment for my sake.
I might have thought my husband's words were a joke,
But soon, all around went up an effusion of lament,
Shaking the palace with exclamations of pain;
Stunned, I wondered, what a strange nightmare!
In shock still, I said: 'Lord, if you leave
For the forest, what use is a palace for this slave?
I would have been queen, but happily shall be a beggar
And serve your noble feet wandering in the forest.
My mind is tethered to these holy feet,
These my refuge; apart from you
I crave not heaven's affluence.
When you leave for the forests with a smile,
Your dear brother shall be the Crown Prince,
And Queen-to-be would be my sister Mandavi;
Why shouldn't I then follow your footsteps?

Sita could never live on, bereft of that happiness.
Of bitter taste all the world
If she cannot serve the feet of her lord.'

Whatever sorrow was there in my husband's heart,
Was quickly dispelled by my words.
Leaving behind parents, brothers, friends, servants,
My husband took me along to the forests.
Only my brother-in-law, Laxmana,
Joined us as my husband's companion in exile.

We consigned royal pleasures into the river
Of forgetfulness, and roamed through
Thickly forested hills with new-found delight.
The daughters of sages became my friends;
My mind remained submerged in the waters of their affection.
Many days we stayed in the Panchabati forest,
Leading a cheerful life on Godavari's holy banks.

Towards the end of night, the wind
Would steal the scents of wild flowers,
Then come floating in and fill the cottage.
The koel would come as a royal eulogist,
And pour its mellifluous notes into our ears.
Absorbed in their dancing, peafowl
Adorned at dawn the courtyard of our cottage.
Frolicking fawns would come up curious,
To eat of the wild rice from my hands.
And baby elephants would leave their mothers
To play near me, whisking food from my hands.
I wove attractive garlands from many-hued flowers
And draped my husband's neck as gifts of love.
He would embellish my braids with various blossoms,
And take me around thickets of wild flowers.
He'd say: 'My dear, you are the living image
Of my love, my soul's companion.
Precious as heavenly bliss.'
And I would answer: 'Lord of my heart,
With the claims on your love, nothing compares,
Even divine pleasures seem trite.'

One day I built columns and a canopy with flowers,
Made also a throne of *kadamba* blooms,
An umbrella and a plume, all of flowers,
And crafted an exotic fan from exquisite petals;
With the leaves of *ketaki* designed a crown,
Lining the most attractive flowers as if they were gems;
And begged him: 'I'ld like to worship you, Lord,
So be gracious, please be seated on this throne.'
The magnanimous one, my husband, smiled, saying:
'Forbidden me, dear, are all royal trappings,
But I'll make you today the goddess of wild flowers.'
With these words, he forcibly held me by the hand,
And with many endearments decked me with flowers,
Overriding my protests with oaths; and then
Stood before me, his gaze deep and unwavering.
My eyes dropped to the ground in sheer shyness,
I stayed transfixed, melting upon the seat of flowers.
Then my husband, the king among lovers,
Said with pleasure: 'Oh Goddess of Flowers,
Do grant me a look of your pity!'
I stole a glance at his blissful, smiling face
And said: 'Conscientious Lord, this is indeed improper!
Can a common serving-maid be ever held worthy
Of something which is not permitted
Even at the worship of the master's feet?'
He answered: 'This is always the way with lovers,
One gains delight by enhancing the other's glory'.
Hearing such words of love from my husband's lips,
I praised my stars and fell silent, greatly content.

Evening came, and the moon rose in the sky,
My hand in his, we walked in the woods.
He was commending the pleasures of exile,
So my mind would be joyful.
On hearing then the cries of a nearby *chakrabaka*,
He kissed me all of a sudden, the lord of my being.
Amused, I asked him the reason for this,
To which his answer comes now to my mind.

He said: 'Beloved, this *chakrabaka,* away
From his mate, burns now in the fire of grief.
All day he stays besotted with his beloved,
And now, away from her, feels life to be bitter.
If you weren't here as my companion in the forest,
I'd be wandering around singed in grief.
Whatever I describe as the joys of exile,
All those would then be desiccating my life.
Without his beloved the lover's heart
Is naturally in torment,
And for a tortured being the world seems futile.
One who floats upon the sea of life
Only hopes to cross it in the skiff of a beloved.'
I hadn't experienced till then
The pangs of separation. It made me laugh,
As I bowed my head in shyness.
Ah, me! That after some years its intolerable pain
Should have occupied my entire being!
Only the one who suffers knows another's sorrow,
So the *chakrabaka's* cry today unleashed my tears.'

The novice said: 'Friend, now I surely know,
Your husband's heart is a storehouse
Of nectarous love. That jewel among kings
Must be crying out like the *chakrabaka;*
May the night of your misfortunes soon end.
A golden family life has been laid waste,
Why had this terrible injustice to take place?
The one whom the king had made his life's love,
How could he be moved to renounce her?
Shame on the judgement of Providence!
How foul its choice –
To bring some poison and pour upon the nectar that was there.'

CANTO - VII

The Virtuous One in mourning voice said, 'Friend,
My ill luck alone has caused me all this grief;
Providence is not to blame for my fate,
And my husband by nature is a sea of kindness.
My heart hadn't believed for a moment, dear,
That, away from him, I could still remain alive;
Friend, I endured pain unbearable and deep,
So I might see my noble Lord's face.
Into my ears then, hope would whisper
Mantras of solace, and my death-wish disappear;
But that hope now dies of its own,
And my heart gets seared as I think of it.'

Her companion said: 'Friend, I can't comprehend,
How was the hope, and why did it die?
Pious as you are, your grief has been intense,
Yet you do not fault Providence; this is strange indeed!'
The Pure One answered: 'After you hear, my friend,
The tale of my sorrow, you will understand:
The way I invited the most frightful suffering,
And the manner my hopes met with death.

One day, near our cottage in Panchabati,
A deer of gold cavorted in sheer delight,
A graceful sheen on his embellished limbs,
Glittering vividly in the rays of the sun!
The splendour of painted spots on the golden body,
Brought into my eyes a fantasy of sparkling gems;
Never had I seen a deer of that kind,
Neither in the city, nor palace nor woods!

I thought: When I would return to the city
I shall bring along that exquisite deer with me
And astound the city folk, describing together
The abundant beauty of the forest!

I offered some grass in the hope of holding him;
Startled, this emperor-deer wouldn't come near;
Tempting my heart, delighting my eyes,
Again and again he ran off into the woods!
Noticing the anxiety in my heart,
My husband then said fondly:
'Soon I'll bring back that lovely deer,
My love, and satisfy your longing.'
With his arrows and bow, nimble on his feet,
My lord raced away in swift pursuit;
Very soon, O friend, hot on the deer's chase,
He moved past the range of my sight!

Then a cry, 'Save me, Laxmana!' rang through the woods,
My heart was distraught at the shout for help.
I pricked up my ears and listened intently;
Once again the cry rose: 'Save me, Laxmana!'
The valiant Laxmana was by my side;
I urged, 'Go forth Laxmana, there be some danger.'
To put my mind at rest, he said,
'Do not fear, for this voice is not Rama's!'
Only heroes, Friend, understand heroic nature;
I saw Laxmana all serene and grave.
But frail indeed is a woman's heart,
And I, more agitated at his calm answer,
Pleaded, then spoke to him stinging words,
Forcing him to go in search of my husband.
All my wealth of happiness and good fortune then
Was swept away in Laxmana's course.
And here came danger incarnate,
In a great yogi's guise, calling for alms at the gate.

Refusing to wait till my husband's return, the Evil One,
Was persistent, bearing upon me for alms,
Which when I offered him he pulled my hand
And forced me quickly into a flying chariot;
Oh how I begged, how protested hard,
But the Wicked One, unmoved, didn't pay heed.
I learnt then, attire is no sign of virtue;
A holy exterior his, yet so perverse inside!

People think *dharma* is all-auspicious,
But few know Yama too bears the name of *dharma*![1]

The Evil One flew the chariot towards the South,
The skiey path shaking in reverberation.
Howsomuch loud my screams as I went on wailing,
It was all lost in the roar of the speeding chariot.
I looked at the wild peacocks below,
Their eyes were on me, as they wept;
Herds of deer with their gazes turned upward,
Kept their startled eyes upon the chariot.
A bird [2] blocked the path and gave fight,
But the despicable one severed its wings;
Even the wind, blowing fiercely against the craft,
Could not prevent the evil-minded one.
On the way the hills soared up their heads
But couldn't block the aerial car;
With sorrowful eyes I kept looking below,
Hoping to send a message to those on earth.
I knew words wouldn't carry through the noise
Of the chariot, so I flung my jewellery down.
I watched the rivers in their anguish
Go lean, and become still and listless.
Saw giant trees shrink their forms,
Holding onto one another in fear of that one;
The deer and the birds all went into hiding
And the earth slowly lapsed into silence.

East, West and South, the sky's three quarters,
Gradually took on a deep blue hue,
No sign of earth was visible anywhere –
The Wicked One flew his chariot in there.
Ahead, the horizon gave off a vivid glare,
I wondered if it were some forest fire;
As the chariot went closer and closer,
Numerous clusters of light began to appear.
I thought they were stars that forsook the sky,

---

1. In Indian mythology Dharma is one of the names of Yama, the god of death.
2. Jatayu, king of vultures.

And huddled there together in groups during the day,
Spurning the sky's dome, on parting from the moon,
Lighting in their hearts the fires of separation.
Or was it that my earthly sport was over
And I was entering the realm of the Lord of Death?
Now I could see tiers of ornate towers
Looking exquisite with golden pitchers on their tops.
Soon, the city, its palaces and streets
Came to view, shining in the refulgent Sun,
Who, with his rays flooding the cupolas,
Brought on a splendour on the mansion-roofs.
A thought then crossed my mind:
The yogi was surely a messenger of Death's,
And I shall fearlessly approach the Lord of Death
Raising in hand my blazing sword of marital devotion.

The yogi brought his chariot down in the suburbs,
And drove it along a garden path;
The path had been laid with elaborate marble,
And the garden looked glorious with fruit and flower.
Of those, an *asoka* tree stood unsurpassed in beauty,
With its clusters of flowers in full bloom.
A glittering mansion occupied the garden,
Made marvellous with many-spangled gems.
The yogi said: 'Stay in there, and worry not
About your separation from your husband;
At an end are the hardships of your forest-life,
Enjoy here heavenly pleasures and adorn this land.
For all that is rare in the three worlds,
Instantly at your wish will now be yours;
A thousand soft-limbed virgins shall serve
Fondly as slaves at your lotus-feet.'
There he summoned a thousand maids, decked in gems,
And spoke to them in words of firm command:
'Remember she is the Empress of my heart,
So serve her well with hearts of devotion,
Fulfil her wishes, night and day,
And expound at large my glories before her;
Take all good care, so that her mind
Becomes ensnared in my opulence.'

With these words, the yogi left,
My heart filling with amazement;
Who could the yogi be, and why had he
Brought me here, and what was this land of his –
I could guess nothing at all.
How was I the heart's empress to this yogi?
I still retained the body of Rama's spouse,
I had not died, nor had my wits all gone –
My sole refuge the son of Kausalya, O friend.
Then, I resolved firmly in my heart,
Whoever the yogi might be, what had I to fear?
So long my being held consciousness,
Only Kausalya's son was my refuge, dear.
Be this death's world or heaven's kingdom
Even though the gods kept revelling here,
Who could succeed in stealing my heart? –
Kausalya's son was my only heaven.
Why would I need a thousand maids?
Food and toilette were no more my needs;
My being's master would be roaming the forest,
And only at his feet would my mind be.
Even if a hundred *Saraswatis* with elegant *veenas*
Trilled their music for me,
Could it ever equal the single word
My husband's regal lips uttered?

Brooding thus, and with my mind fixed upon
His venerable feet, I soon lost consciousness.
I knew not what days I spent there and how,
Only I knew my mind held thoughts of my husband alone.
Nights and days in that world
Seemed long as the time of the gods.*
I thought it was some heavenly abode,
And imbued my being with divine courage.
I prayed to the Lord for heavenly strength,
And for devotion to my husband worthy of a goddess's heart;
I pinned my hopes upon the nectar of my husband's feet,
And paid no heed to hunger and thirst.

---

* A day for the gods equals six months for men.

Various anointments, numerous ornaments,
Delicacies of all kinds were brought in by the maids;
Fawning upon me, they said many flattering words,
But my mind felt moved with none of these.

In time I learnt from the talk of the maids
That Ravana was a conqueror of all three worlds
And Lanka the sea-moated kingdom his realm,
At whose name quailed the chief of gods.
I had been carried to that world
By that wicked one in a yogi's attire.
His city and palace were of peerless splendour,
Inaccessible to both men and demi-gods.
Whatever his heart wished for,
Was fulfilled by the gods out of fear.
Whenever the red tint spread in his eyes
The god Brahma began quailing in fear.
I recalled then, hearing the name of Ravana,
How his pride had been humbled by Siva's bow,
And I wondered how the dog had the audacity
To wish for the holy drink of sacrifice.

True enough, the evilhearted one came one day
And stood near me in his fiery form,
With evil design the impudent sinner
Kept on ranting his sinful words.
When he saw tears streaming down the massed clouds
Of my misfortune, he withdrew with pride-darkened mind;
And in that cloud-mass burned
The terrible lightning-flash of his hope!

O friend, from the day that I knew
The sinful demon had touched my hand,
An unbearable fire would course through me
From that point to torment my entire being.
All the hair over my body
Seemed poisoned arrow-heads to me;
And I thought, what pain indeed, did the does suffer
When hunters' arrows pierced them!
I bore in my heart this intolerable agony,
And held my mind firm in righteousness.

Only I had kept the faith firm in my heart,
That *dharma* was ever the weak female's support.
Just once in ignorance I had stretched out my hand,
Offering alms to the evil demon in disguise;
If he forced himself on me, I thought,
Either I should kill, or be killed by him.
If truly *dharma* prevails upon this earth,
The world will witness my amazing act:
Even if mountain-high be the cotton-heap of sin,
A single spark of piety can burn it down.

Look, dear friend, how *dharma* came true,
Pouring nectar into my being, as it were.
A monkey brought me news of my husband,
And returned after defying the might of Ravana.
Soon the jewel of Raghus with an army of monkeys,
Building a bridge across the waters of the sea,
Crossed the impassable ocean, attacked Lanka
And implanted terror in the demon-chief's heart.
Began he an arduous sacrifice of war,
And Lanka trembled to piercing simian shouts;
All the mighty warriors of Ravana's clan
Became living sacrifices of this *yagna*.
Only one* was on the righteous path,
Taking refuge at the feet of the Lord of Raghus;
He stood, a firm column in that great sacrifice,
A garland of salvation around his neck.
Those streams of tears my eyes had shed,
A billion times flowed the demon's blood;
Ravana, floating in terror on a sea of misery,
Fell into the crocodile-jaws of my master's arrows.

The Lord of Raghus then called me near,
And with a look devoid of affection, said;
'There is no sin greater on earth than evil company,
Contact of an evil man only brings intense torment.
You lived in the sinful palace of the lust-blind demon

---

* Bibhisana, Ravana's youngest brother, an ally and devotee of Rama, compared here with the pillar to which sacrificial animals are tied.

And your mind could have been touched by sin;
No more can I receive you back
For to do that would bring on a social scandal.
When the cloud's water once begins to fall
Can the same cloud any more draw it in?
Flame-like, only when it burns in the fire,
Will the water again rise to merge with the cloud!'
I thought: 'I had just kept myself alive
So I might serve my master's lotus-feet;
If I am not fit now to touch those feet,
Of what use, any more, is that life to me?
With my eyes on his noble face I'll destroy this body;
What greater happiness could I have than this?
When this body is burnt out, surely would my soul
Find a home in the noble being of my Lord!
And if, by the power of *dharma,* this body is kept whole,
I will regain my Lord's love two times over.'

I said then, 'May the holy fire be lit,
So this servant-maid may bathe in it.'
The obedient, ever-ungrudging Laxmana
Most grudgingly lit a pyre soon;
The flames swaying in the wind
Grew eager and quick to soar into the sky.
With thirsting eyes on his lotus-face,
I approached the fire, and with a strong will
Said aloud: 'Oh Sun and Moon, Wind, Sky and Fire!
You know well the hearts of all living creatures.
If my heart had been lured even a whit
Towards any but the scion of the Raghus,
Then you, O Fire, who consume all,
Burn me to ashes this moment!
It's true I was captive in the demon-city,
But if he ever ensnared me in sin,
The bliss of seeing the lotus-feet of my lord
Be not mine for a billion births; burn me, O Fire!
You care not for the pious nor the sinner,
And by your *dharma*, consume each one's life;
If *dharma* in this world is for ever true,
Then save me from the slander against my *dharma*!
Oh *Dharma*! Inhabit my being in your natural virtue,

And enter this fire fearlessly with me.
If not in life, then oh, in death at least,
Make me a serving-maid at my lord's feet!
When that my body is burnt, and it turns into ash –
Make that ash manure a plant,
And giving the wood of the tree to a carpenter,
Shape me into sandals for the feet of my Lord!'

Looking up, again and again, at my master's noble face,
I entered fearlessly into the fire.
The gem of Raghus wept at the sight, wept Laxmana,
And a loud wail of weeping rose from the army.
Tears gushed unending from countless eyes,
Drowning my being in the waters of pity,
And the fire seemed strangely cool inside;
The sky was filled with exclamations of grief.
A voice from the heavens then declared in my favour,
And my Lord knew I was pure and chaste;
The fire went out under *dharma*'s sway,
And by *dharma*'s power was my life saved.
All my sorrows were burnt to ash,
And I was a maid again, luckily at my lord's feet;
I thought: 'Only since I had kept my life through pain,
Now I could gain the lotus-feet of my Lord.'

My Lord seated me in a regal chariot,
And with his select band of monkey-warriors,
Commenced his return journey for Ayodhya,
Rejoicing in victory on his path through the skies.
And I having crossed the desert-country of separation,
Found in my shrivelled heart an ocean of love;
An unparalleled joy rising through my being,
The world seemed to fill with sheer delight.
When there is unhappiness in one's life,
No pleasure is seen in the entire universe,
But when the time of happiness comes,
The world appears to overflow with bliss.

The chariot which had thrust me into a well of danger,
I stepped on it now upon a mound of glory.
Those scenes which had only left me wailing
Those very ones now swelled my cheer.

The gem-lit chariot, its versatile movements,
The clouds overhead, and below,
The Lord of Waters, the Sea,
Lakes, mountains, and trees
Became a love-maze for my eyes.
All those forests, places where we stayed before,
Dense groves of creepers, beautiful hills,
Smoke-palled hermitages of sages,
Kept calling my heart as we flew past above.
Sages' daughters with dishevelled hair,
Hearing the chariot's roar from afar,
Looked on with astonished, upturned faces,
Arousing memories of past pleasures in me.
Their pure love, their warm friendliness,
Their lips that made sweet and gentle talk,
Their simple, serene eyes, full of tenderness,
Rained nectar on the meadows of my memory.

Slowly the names of all those virgins
Began opening up like lucent lotuses
In my mind's pool, as a day of happiness
Dawned after the dark deep night of absence.
The profuse fragrance of their old love
Stirred my heart with delirious delight;
But my desire to see the forest barely satisfied
The chariot coursed ahead speedily.
My mind could not shake off
The enchanting woods, a storehouse of nature's loveliness ·
The mind, too, was on the chariot in the skies,
Then again, if flitted to my mother-in-law's feet;
As it revelled by my dark-hued handsome husband,
My mind playing upon all three planes,
Acquired a semicircular form,
Of a rainbow on new clouds.

The king of Ayodhya, my father-in-law,
With his son, his very soul, gone into the forests,
Had sped to Indra in the land of the gods,
The lamp of his life extinguished in sorrow.
When Bharata found the kingdom without a king,
He rushed to my husband in the forest,
And with folded palms poured out his griefs;

We were then living in Chitrakuta.
The prince begged and entreated
My husband to return as the Lord of the world,
But the Lord of Raghus turned down the appeals
Rousing his parental devotion intenser still.
He said: 'The word that father would not break,
But rather shed his own body for,
How can I wring the neck of *dharma's* crane
My parent nurtured, banishing my conscience?'
Bharata fell weeping at his feet,
And begged, 'Keep me then here to serve your feet;
For when the sun leaves the earth,
Moving to the mountain where it sets,
Can his rays then abandon him?'
My Lord rejoined: 'The cool rays of the moon
Dispel at night the sorrows of the earth.'
And Bharata answered with deep humility:
'The moon only receives the rays of the sun.
As the serpent Shesa bears the earth's burden,
So will your precious sandals on my head
Sustain the kingdom;
When the gems on the sandals shine on my head,
Enemy-hordes would then fear me as a cobra!'
My Lord put his sandals in Bharata's hands,
Which Bharata then placed upon his head;
Returning from the forest with tearful eyes,
The noble hero engaged himself
To relieve the sufferings of the royal goddess.
He was there, at the end of fourteen years,
Watching the road for our return,
And there did our chariot touch the earth.
Alighting from the car, I bowed, taking on my head
The dust of the feet of my three mothers-in-law.
When he saw my Lord along with Laxmana and me
Bharata lost himself in a river of ecstasy;
Returning the sandals in reverence to the feet of my Lord,
He took up a royal umbrella and a silk-plumed fan,
And offered his worship.

My beloved husband became king, and I his queen,
I served my Lord's feet in keeping with his wish;
And whatever I wished for, and whenever,

Was fulfilled always in quick time.
Seated in a skiff of love, we, a royal couple,
Used to cruise around in a sea of bliss;
We drowned thus many years sporting in joyous abandon
Upon the waves of prosperity and good fortune.
Who knew then, that Fate had inscribed
An endless hieroglyph of sorrow on my brow;
That, the calamity of a terrible *badaba*-fire,*
Would rise and destroy all!
As the sky is coloured at the end of the day's grace,
So at the end of my good fortune I was with child;
More solicitous than ever grew my life's master,
Fulfilling every desire of mine with fondness and love.
One day I said: 'I long to sport in the forest
In the company of my friends of the woods;'
Before the night had gone, friend, before the new day dawned,
My husband sent me off with Laxmana into the forest!
Helping me down from the boat on Ganga's bank,
The words that Laxmana gently spoke' –

There she broke off, the Virtuous One, her voice choked,
And with her eye on the terrible suffering ahead,
She wept, cast upon an endless river of tears;
Quickly the sage's daughter held her close,
And wailed, her face touching the Virtuous One's,
When the lady ascetics came running at the sound of their cries.
They led them both into the cottage,
And spoke things various, pleasantly diverting their minds;
They talked too of the morning's chores,
Of watering the plants, picking the flowers,
And lay down to sleep.

* Mythical fire smouldering underneath the sea.

CANTO - VIII

As youth is augmented in the human frame,
So did spring unfold into summer in the forest;
Just as its lustihood gets stronger by day,
So did the summer heat grow more intense.
Like the longings for earthly pleasures,
The enchanting mirage stretched out her limbs.
Wisps of cotton flew from the silk-cotton tree,
As the miser's wealth slips away from his crypt in time.
No more had the *palasa* her scarlet brilliance,
For all worldly things be evanescent.
The jasmine bloomed in profusion with the heat,
And the scents were richer from its limbs.
The good heart remains firm through the heat of suffering,
And the fame of serenity grows opulent.
The vine-jasmine watched her with delight –
The good one for sure savours the company of the good.
With one mind both then parleyed together:
'Let us give off our scents throughout the summer,
And when the earth cools during the rains,
All creatures would have a peaceful respite.
The *kadamba* and *ketaki* too, are never mean
In gifting fragrance; they would keep men content.
We shall hand them the task of delighting the people,
And, smiling, renounce the world of trees.'

The upright lotus raised her head,
And cheerfully endorsing what they had said,
Joined in, saying: 'With you too, I will be,
And plunge into the high waves of the sea of Time.'
The jasmine asked unconvinced: 'How can you do it,
Since the sun, your husband, will not release you?'
The lotus answered: 'When the clouds gather,
My husband cannot see my face.

Suffering then a few days of sorrow,
I shall end my earthly ritual;
For he would not pierce the clouds,
And rather suffer pain for the world's good.
How can I then, enjoy my husband's tender love
For long? It is not written in my fate;
My heart would always cherish his feet,
And thus would death escort me away.
If in this life I bear some days of pain,
My husband's noble face will be mine in the next.'

As the words fell in Janaki's inner ears,
She acknowledged them as her own life's ideal,
And said: 'Lotus dear, indeed you are virtuous,
And the path of piety is clear before you;
I happen to be your sister in a sense
And more, for I too share your fate.
I also enjoyed my husband's love in the forest
In a sweet,* clean house of happiness.
The bright sun, your husband, is the Lord of the day,
And my husband, the earth's lord, comes of the same race.
Whatever you say of the future course of your life,
Is already mine; I travel that very same path.
Blessed be your heart. Praise to you, Chaste One,
Fill my being with your unblemished mind.
My husband did wince under people's slander,
And sorrowfully abandoned me.
Tell me whether my fate will grant me later
The sight of my husband! Speak, oh you of divine sight!'

Under the cool of hundred-petalled lotuses,
In the deep-azure bosom of the pool's waters,
The *chakrabaka* pair spent the noon,
As did the royal swan with his mate.
The shrimp, dodging the arrow-like beaks of ducks,
With long leaps across the clumps of lotus,
Lost its way in the jungle of umbrella-huge leaves,
And ended up as the repast of the crane.
Into the upraised womb of the lotus leaf,

---

* Gangadhar's word carries two meanings- 'nectarous' and 'watery'.

Fell the tiny minnow, and leapt away upon the water;
Hardly would the frog sit upon the bent lotus-stem,
But take a sudden leap in fear of the water-snake.
Upon the mango branch the mournful koel sat
Behind a screen of leaves near the crow's nest;
She suffered her thirst, not pouring out her nectar,
As though in hiding, afraid of the hateful one.
The *champa** did not spread his tail to dance,
Nor quiver the roots of his bright-red feathers;
Not even ruffling his wings with defiant cries,
Angered at the sight of his own kind.
It is only hunger that pushes him to fight,
Why else should a brother turn into a foe?
He sits with his slender frame and full belly,
Content, on a branch of a towering sal.
Flocks of parakeets in *mahua* groves
Peeled the *mahua* fruits in a show of eating;
With the habits of Brahmins they went on drawing
A subtle almanac, presaging future rains.

In the cool shade of dense, tender leaves
Of a banyan tree on the Tamasa's bank, where
The cottage spills with scents of the wild jasmine,
Surrenders summer at the feet of Peace –
Valmiki was there seated, opening his eyes
Of wisdom, envisioning the holy *Ramayana*.
Some monks were busy with their studies,
Others with chanting the Vedas.
Sita, lethargic, heavy with child,
Surrounded by a group of hermit-women
On seats of leaves under lush bowers,
Savoured the peace with a tranquil gaze;
Was it the moon's orb, with its halo,
Upon the setting hill, at the departure of night?
A swathe of sweat on Sita's pallid cheeks,
And like cold dew, the misty liquid in her eyes.

There, among the holy women, the queen of noble Rama,
Recalling the ways of Lanka's she-ogres,

---

* A fighting bird that also sings; the bulbul.

Sat comparing in her mind the divine spirit of those around her
With the diabolical nature of the demonesses.
When thoughts of the heroic son of the Wind-God [1]
Came to her mind, she paid homage to the god,
And gracefully fanning with a palm-leaf fan,
Received cool swirls of air as *prasad* [2]
The lovely thought-dame came at that time
And spoke with humble words:
'Noble one, at the door are gathered some
Who are longingly waiting for a sight of you.
It appears they have come a long way;
Singular is their desire,
That makes light of this summer heat!
When one sees their charming forms,
The heart turns into an abode of love.'
The noble Sita said: 'Friend, bring them in at once,
Praised be my fortune that they bear me such love!
Seeing them, both my eyes
Shall surely assuage their heat of sin.'

At the Virtuous Lady's wish, one came in first
And spoke with a soft smile wreathed on her lips,
Sprinkling the nectar of loving words
As would an intimate relation of long years;
'Dear and noble one, do you recall the past,
When you had set feet in my house?
Then, my limbs gained the riches of divine splendour
From the effulgence of your noble form.
My springs, reflecting that radiance,
Run down thrilled with joy.
My host of flowers with joyous faces
Shame the heavenly garden with taunting laughter.
Ever fragrant, the waters of my stream
Animate all who live upon my banks.
The flocks of peafowl, reared by you with love,
Sing your praises each day with loud calls.
Unshaken in their faith of seeing you,
The massed clouds come again and again;

1. Hanuman, the monkey-god, celebrated for his valour and his devotion to Rama.
2. Sacred food that had been offered to God.

Moving from cave to cave in their search for you,
Question me with solemn, rolling voices,
To know where the lovely Sita is.
They never take my answers of 'No' –
And with the torch of lightning, search on still,
Certain that the exquisite Sita would be there.
Do you recognise, my lady, this luckless one?
After long years I have come to your royal presence;
Fortunate have been, I, Chitrakuta,[1] to have
Adorned my crown with the dust of your feet.'

A woman resplendent in vivid colours appeared then,
With elegant limbs of a clear, bright silkiness,
Eternal companion of Sylvan Beauty,
The one who humbled the pride of the scorching sun;
Her neck bedecked with a garland of wild jasmine,
Mahua blossoms emblazoning the wide forehead,
Blackberries like blue gems for her eartops,
And oyster shells designed for her precious girdle;
Stealer of the hearts of forest-dwelling ascetics,
Exquisite with her comely, well-braided blue plaits;
With cheerful face and soft and flowing words,
Said sweetly to the Virtuous One:
'Gentle One, accept my gratitude,
For I remain ever indebted to you for your love.
How can I repay you? I haven't the strength:
Make me fulfilled and blessed, Oh Virtuous One,
By accepting my total devotion.
Are there not many like me on this earth,
But who else has received so much of your grace?
Blessed with your holy sight,
My sands have changed to dust of gold.
Since my sport delighted your divine eyes,
You turned my bosom into a field of diamonds;
Even though there is the mountain-king's daughter,
The river that issues from Vishnu's feet,[2]

1. Mountain-range where Rama, Sita and Laxmana spent a part of the period of their exile.
2. Ganga, the daughter of the Himalayas, celebrated in myth as flowing from the feet of Vishnu.

I am still known as the Mahanadi*
After the title you have bestowed on me.'

Then Godavari, wide-limbed, stepped forward,
The shadow of sorrow on her face,
Shedding tears in inconsolable grief
And wiping her lotus-eyes with her *anchal* again.
She had brought with her marvellous pictures,
Painted in many brilliant colours;
With the Virtuous One's consent she opened these
And hastened to display them one by one.
One showed flowers fallen from creepers
Wilting in the harsh heat of the sun,
Trees on beds of dry, parched leaves
Standing lifeless in wan attire.
Some tree's broken branch, that hadn't still
Severed clean from the limbs of the tree,
Begged a little succour of the spread of grass,
Kissing one's head, clinging to another's feet;
Another tree appeared strangely white
With the droppings of birds all over;
Still another had given up its good cheer,
Hiding its face in the dirty linen of spiders' webs.
The toads, observing the cranes' might,
And leaping again and again, felt exhausted;
Some others kept hiding under the rocks,
Sitting still and filling their bellies.
Elsewhere, herds of wild buffalo
Went on muddying the waters of a pond;
Smeared with slime, the lotuses were tossed about
By the feet of the wallowing buffaloes.

Somewhere, a python waited in hope of prey
Near the water, motionless like a log of wood.
Close by, on the lookout on a deer-path,
A tiger hid, smacking its lips.
In one painting, she saw too,
Furiously burning wild fires
Filling the forest with murky smoke.

---

* Literally : the Great River.

Fearful tongues of flame rose from countless branches,
Leaping upward to merge with the sky;
Piles of flaming leaves rising in the air
Were carried away on floats of smoke,
Descending on distant trees to convey the news,
They soon set the trees ablaze with their heat.
Numerous leaves blackened as they rose
And soon disappeared in the skies.
A number of birds flew off to safety
While others fell into the wombs of fire.
Herds of deer, buffalo, elephant,
Rabbits, boar, jackals and bears,
Were engulfed in the pall of smoke, and stood
Transfixed in alarm, not knowing where to flee.
Bewildered, terrified, hordes of monkeys
Raced away scampering from tree to tree;
With their young on their backs or in their arms,
They sped through the smoke towards the water.
Right up to the bank of the flowing river,
The animals crowded thick, agitated, and in fear.
Godavari put in: 'You have just seen, child,
The misery of Dandaka after you left.'
The Virtuous One, never able
To bear the pain of others, lamented:
'Alas! Dandaka, my treasure-trove of sport,
I would feel gratified to alleviate your miseries
And cool you with the tears from my eyes.'

Ayodhya came then to the Virtuous One's presence,
And in a voice hoarse with choked anguish,
Read out a letter from the goddess of royalty
With trembling lips, bowed in embarrassment deep:
'Friend, I was the night and you were the moon;
You left then, shutting the lilies of my eyes.
Without you I haven't now a moment's happiness
And am dressed as a bride without ornaments.
The royal palace has become a forest today,
And your absence, raging in there
Like a burning fire, has destroyed all.
Nothing is left of its festival of beauty
The tall trees and their dense, blithe foliage –
Trees so large-hearted and noble – all are burnt.

Ah me; so helplessly has been destroyed there
The sweet-scented, smiling race of flowers.
Deer-herds of Peace and elephants of Patience
With restless beings in the smoke of sadness,
Have run to the center of the lake of fortitude,
And drowned their bodies neck-deep.
The evil-hearted, powerful carnivores,
Even they haven't escaped.
Only the fathomless deep of Rama's noble heart
Has held it burning as a *badaba* fire.
As the moon with its middle in Rahu's* mouth,
Without you, the king is merely a shape;
His bejewelled palace a thick darkness fills,
Like a mass of cloud a starry sky.
The mothers sit brooding with shattered hearts
Like ponds with their waters dried up;
For they cherish you as more precious
Than the she-cobra her ruby.
The gates are all shut in the garden of delight,
Who can then catch a glimpse of the flowers inside?
Clump-grasses rise up as traders of perfume,
Spreading out the fallen flowers to dry.
Rows of creepers and trees are sunk in grief,
And with thoughts of you slowly withering away.

The splendid walks of conch-white marble,
Only dry leaves have made their seats.
The brothers, obedient to the Lord's words,
Go about with bowed heads in their misery,
Like serpents deadened by magical mantras
Or elephants in fear of the sharp prod.
The shapely cheeks of your sisters
Rest sadly against their lotus-palms,
And their bodies languish day by day,
As the moon wanes through the dark fortnight.
Your companions in music never touch the face

---

* Mythical demon, supposed to periodically swallow (and disgorge) the Sun and the Moon, causing eclipses.

Of the *mridanga,** going mute themselves.
And like flowers of the day before,
Your maids too keep their own lives going
In deep despair.'

The pale, beautiful Ayodhya sank into her seat,
Exhausted, unable to finish her reading.
The kindly Janaki noticed her condition,
And was overwhelmed with grief herself.
The day now approached its end,
And the guests returned to their places;
While the women hermits sweetly escorted the virtuous Sita
And then repaired to their separate duties.

* Percussion instrument played on two sides.

CANTO - IX

With each passing day, heavier and heavier
Grew the womb of the virtuous Sita;
It became hard for her to rise from her seat
And then, standing, to hold herself erect.
Lest it cause her pain in her state,
The rains came to break down the heat.
Throngs of clouds rose in the sky's four quarters
To impart strength into her tired being.
They raised a dark cover across in the sky,
Shutting out the heat of the sun above.
In the bat of an eyelid a flash of lightning
Startled the eyes with the splendour of the canopy;
Damsels of the sky's quarters tidied their blue plaits
And decked them with strings of pearl-like cranes.
Scooping up gem-dust from the ocean's bottom,
The guardians of the skies adorned an archway.
But selfishly giving up all thought of shame,
Indra[1] claimed the bow as his own.
Defiant, the lord of the seas[2] declared
It'ld remain with him, since made with his gems.
Other guardians, observing the duties of the righteous,
Allotted them the right by turns.

The rains poured down on Earth's head,
Which was burning with her daughter's heat of pain[3].
Upon rivers, ponds, forests and hills,
It went on raining indiscriminately.
The earth's exhilaration showed up everywhere
With sprouting grass and plants, and flourishing *kadambas*.
Earth's bosom was flooded with water
And Tamasa ran overflowing her banks,

---

1. Indra, chief of the gods, is the Lord of the Eastern quarters.
2. Varuna, the Sea-god, is the Lord of the Western quarters.
3. Sita was Earth's daughter.

As if her joys had brimmed over,
Rejoicing in Janaki's childbirth, so close at hand.
Hills and forests gave up the fire in their hearts,
And scrubbed their bodies, looking fresh and cheerful.
Living in her fortress of thorns, the *ketaki*,
Of sweet laughter in her prickly frame,
Said as it were, 'Impaled as you are, O Vaidehi,
In this forest of misfortune, have no fear.
I am myself pierced in a jungle of thorns,
Yet my perfume makes me adored the world over.
Living as an ascetic among all these hermits,
You, of sterling mind, will be worshipped by all.
If one's own virtues are a divine ornament,
Will the stain the world's eyes cause ever matter?
If the bees feel repelled at the sight of my spines,
Should I sacrifice the promise of my fragrance?'

The attractive gulmohar bloomed and charmed
Both heart and eye with her colourful attire.
The queen-of-the-night had been waiting all spring
To send her flowery epistle to the monsoon rains.
Most delightfully narrated therein were
The tales of lotus, jasmine and *kutaja*.*
The rain cared for them as if they were precious gems,
But who can break the laws of Providence?
It couldn't save them by all its efforts
And all three fell into the clutches of Time.
Thus the Virtuous One came to learn
That one mustn't neglect the pious all one's life.
Creepers of jasmine with a profusion of flowers
Celebrated together their yearly festival.
As though for the entertainment of the Virtuous One,
A palace of the sweetest blooms was fashioned.
The July-rain-night in cerulean apparel,
Jasmine in hand, crowned with the queen-of-the-night,
Stood in the courtyard of Sita's cottage
And kept vigil, to steal away her pain.

---

* A wild jasmine.

Vaidehi's labour pains
Soon began to appear in quick succession; close by,
The frogs, sharing the painful spasms of the Virtuous One,
Croaked in outbursts of deep despair;
In the skies the *chataka*-bird,[1] bearing Sita's thirst,
Begged rain of the clouds again and again.
Aged female ascetics surrounding the Virtuous One
Were engaged in the needful chores.
At night the Virtuous One gave birth to twins,
Sons who rendered pale the moon's lustre.
The princes' radiance mingled with lightning
To illumine all ten quarters of the sky.
In a surge of joy, Indra fired his cannons:
The ignorant thought it was just the roll of thunder.
The *hulahuli* of celestial ladies
Merged delightfully with the rumble of clouds.
Forests and hills began showering flowers,
And rivers, lakes, and pools danced in joy.
Longing for a sight of the Virtuous One's sons,
The clouds came down in the form of torrents.
And the rivers, their hearts frantic to see them,
Swiftly overflowed their banks.
The fish abandoned the ocean,
And joined the rivers in dancing.
Fishes too rose to the surfaces of fields, lakes
And pools to dance in jubilation;
While the mudskipper slid up the palm tree
Eager beyond all others for a sight of the twins.

Then, hurried the great sage Valmiki,
To behold the twin princes.
He thought the planets of Jupiter and Venus[2]
Had risen together in the sky of the ashram.
The heart of the great sage, like the dawn,
Was filled with the scents of flowers of delight.
The great sage took a blade of *kusa* grass in his hand,
And with sacred chants nipped it fore and rear;
Then, handing them over to Anukampa, said:

---

1. Which is supposed to wait for the rain to slake its thirst.
2. *Sukra*, in Indian tradition, a male figure.

'Perform the purificatory rites of the infants;
Use the upper half for the first born,
And the lower half for the younger son.'
Anukampa did as instructed by the sage,
Observing too the rites against evil spirits.
Touched ritually with the *kusa* and *lava* parts of the grass,
Their bodies shone brighter than well-cut gems;
As fire does, when held to the dry grass
Or the dawn's new sun freed from the sea's waves.
When Janaki looked at the faces of her sons,
Happiness and sorrow, both entered her heart.
Happiness exclaimed: 'Praised she be, and blessed,
That she held in her womb twin princes
Like the sun and moon, so praise be hers a hundred times;
For no greater glory is there upon this earth.'
And Sorrow said: 'These sons of a king
Should have adorned today a jewelled palace,
Would have been the delight of the royal heart,
And removed the penury of the lowly and the poor;
In what rich measure would the people this day
Have got gifts of coins, jewels, clothes and ornaments!
Auspicious music would have resounded in the city
And felicitous tunes filled the sky.
Alas, that they should take shelter in an ashram,
As if they be children of ascetics!'

Stealing two tear-streams from the Virtuous One's eyes,
Sorrow left, leaving her to her filial love.
And the heart of the chaste Sita was filled
With pure happiness, moved by the princes's beauty.
Even for a moment she was not inclined
To shift her gaze away from the princes.
Love-lustrous colours from the mother's eyes
Dyed the figures of the princes all the while,
Reflecting in those eyes a wonderful belief,
That they must be the Sun and Moon incarnate.
And a throne was placed in her mind
For happiness to manifest her sovereign power.
The rejoicing Anukampa then severed
The umbilical cords of the infants.
She bathed them in sanctified water
And performed other desired rites.

At the sight of the princes the circle of hermit-women
Broke into loud exclamations of joy,
And groups of young sons of the sages began chanting
The glories of Rama to the rhythms of dancing.

It was by chance that on that night
Had halted in the holy ashram of Valmiki,
The great hero Shatrughna, leading an expedition
To kill a terrible demon, the invincible Lavana;
In the tumult of joy in the ashram he, too
Was drowned in the river of celebration.
Exultant, he sang praises of the Virtuous One:
'You, O Mother, you are the sanctifier of Raghu's race,
Just as your own mother, herself Mother Earth,
You too, Mother, are all-enduring;
Daughter of the Earth, it's our good fortune
That you had borne the earth's finest gems in your womb,
Those gems that you gifted the race of Raghus today
Shall embellish the head of Ayodhya's royal goddess.'
In the cheer and rejoicing of the young acolytes
Joined herds of deer and flocks of birds.
In a moment, as it were, the fearful dark night
Of tempestuous July was at an end.
Sumitra's son offered his obeisance to the sage
And then left in the direction of Lavana.

The Virtuous One's heart felt naturally inclined
To please the ashram's ascetics with presents;
But where had she the riches after her heart,
Having herself taken shelter in the forest?
The moonlight longs to please the world,
But then banks of cloud blanket the skies.
When the Virtuous One left her palace,
She had thought she would get back soon;
Just a few ornaments and clothes she had brought along,
To offer as gifts for the girls of the hermitage.
Embarrassed, she humbly handed these over,
And pleased the hearts of the ashram's ascetics.
Accepting those as if they were moonbeams,
Their hearts' ocean opened up in waves of joy.
Whatever fruits and wild rice they had stored,
They doled out to the birds and the deer.

Who fell on the food, scrambling for it.
Some birds flew off with the food in their bills;
The chicks were in their nests with wide open mouths,
The mother-birds shared the food equally among them.
The peacock and peahen, with rapturous outbursts
Put up a *tandava*-dance on a tree,
And the koel spread the good news
From land to land near and far.
The royal swan flew off with cackles of delight
To convey the joyous tidings at Kailasha.
And to secure Gauri's trust,
She had held up as a letter a fresh lotus leaf.

Full of rejoicing in her heart at the news,
Gauri left Kailasha with Hara's consent;
Through the skies she flew, in the form of Goddess *Sasthi*,[1]
Longing to be worshipped at the hands of the Virtuous Sita.
Under lightning's guise, with resplendent clouds,
She hastened to the hermitage of Valmiki.
Her radiance shone like the *Mothers Seven*[2]
Through the figures of the ashram's seven virgin girls.
On the sixth day, having accepted worship
Fervently from the Virtuous One's hands,
She whose hands granted all boons,
Destroyed the future afflictions of the royal twins
And left, blessing them with the strength of lions.

Soon it was the twenty-first day after their birth:
The auspicious time for the naming of the twins.
To hear the naming of the Virtuous One's sons,
The gods came down, leaving their celestial abode.
Curious about the forthcoming events,
The goddesses followed the gods, in various groups.
The clouds were then making way in the sky
For the blessed advent of autumn;
So all of them travelled easily on that path
In radiant chariots, along with the rays of the sun.
In the guise of enchanting fragrances

1. Presiding deity of infants.
2. The Sapta-matrika, or Seven Mothers, worshipped for the protection of a child.

They settled upon the flowers in the ashram.
With half-smiles, as though to bloom,
They spread their divine charm.
And some, in great jubilation,
Entered the hearts of the ascetics.

Ascetics, both men and women, on Valmiki's urging,
Went into the garden with two-fold joy;
Then, collecting different leaves and flowers,
Erected an elaborate floral altar.
At the first hour of night
The hermitage shone with strings of oil lamps.
And there, the lamps pillaged profusely
The *ingudi* oil from the hands of the ascetics.
All around, flowering trees and creepers
Revelled at the touch of ripples of light.
Surely the hour belonged to the flowers,
And prouder and prouder grew the tuberose.
Sitting among the ascetics on the many-petalled dais
Shone the sage of great austerities;
As the Ocean of Milk among the seas,
Or as Indra among gods in their grandeur,
Or amid lofty Himalayan peaks,
The towering summit of Gaurishankar.

The Virtuous One and Anukampa came onto the dais,
Holding the two princes in their lotus-arms;
Like *Chhaya* and *Sangyan* carrying the *Aswinis*,*
Grace stood triumphant there.
As if it were the East with her morning star,
Close to the waning moon of the thirteenth
Dark night, holding their images
In the lake of her womb, ensconced in pride.
Companions of the Virtuous Sita, the ashram virgins,
Of innocent heart, and with cheerful faces,
Attired in the clothes she had gifted them,
Settled down happily beside the Chaste One –
Resembling a forest of lotuses by the side of Dawn,
Having won her gift of the fresh, tender rays of the sun.

---

* The offsprings of the Sun-god and His two consorts are named in the line.

The gods were worshipped in Vedic rites
To the blowing of conches and horns.
Then bestowing his benediction upon the elder child,
The chief of the sages declared with satisfaction:
'He has been sanctified with the tips of *kusa* grass,
And so as Kusa would be a goad to elephant-like foes.'
The younger one was named in the same manner,
The wise and mighty sage calling him Lava.
The ascetics sang together in praise of Rama
To the rhythms of percussion instruments.
And the girls of the ashram played on the veena,
Pouring out songs sweeter than nectar.

Gods and goddesses in the shapes of flowers,
Danced on, happily spreading their perfume.
Herds of deer and doe stood around them,
Watching with wonder-struck eyes.
The forest joined in the din of the celebrations
Under the pretext of sending echoes.
And trees and creepers, all engaged in music,
Felt proud as celestial musicians;
In joy the ashram gleamed and shone,
But upon the lily of the Virtuous One's face,
Rested still a darkness in the absence of Rama –
Her festival-day was but the dark night of the moon,
Yet the darkness enhanced her splendour,
For it is darkness that makes the moonshine so sought after.
Jewel-bright glittered the two handsome princes,
Like deep caverns in a hill of precious stones.
Gods and sages together in joyous festivity
Enhanced the glory of the Virtuous One.
A godly way is this of the world's noble ones:
Their delight is in honouring worthy beings.

Closing the ceremony then, the magnanimous sage
Pronounced his blessing upon the princes.
The gods, seated on the lotus-hearts
Of the ascetics, intoned: 'So be it.'
Trees and creepers together in the forest
Uttered in solemn tones: 'So be it.'
And from all ten quarters of the sky,
The guardians voiced in unison: 'So be it.'

CANTO - X

Blessed with the twins the Virtuous One
Busied herself in cares of raising them,
Cherishing them more than her own life.
As the ties of love fastened her fast,
She wouldn't leave their side a moment
And began to feel her life's burden lighten.

Though she would leave them behind only once
In a day, when she went out for her bath,
She would rush back in trepidation,
Her clothes soaked, dripping with water,
Her soul quickening at the thought
Of seeing the lotus-faces of her sons.

Trampling over the pride of the moon-digits,
The limbs of the princes became bigger and bigger.
Like the full moon, their faces day by day
Became edifices of loveliness.
Slowly they knew their mother's face,
And grew eager to climb into her lap.

They would smile, looking up at their mother's face
But cry aloud at once to be taken into her lap.
And when the mother held them fondly there,
They would play on happily as if on swings of joy;
As they looked at her face again and again,
They would smile, making her smile with them.

Even in her wildest dreams she hadn't thought,
A smile would ever sprout on her burnt-out face.
But the rare laughter of a rare happiness
Came to manifest on its own.
And every day the Virtuous One would curse her fate
That her husband wasn't there to share this delight.

In the form of teeth on their lotus-faces
The goddess of music presided bright,
Shaming the jasmine, moon, snow and pearl
She revealed her heavenly brilliance;
Then she softly strummed the veena
To the melodious notes of 'Ma', 'Ma' and 'Ma'.

Like the breezes of spring, the divine sounds
Made the mother's heart burgeon into leaf,
And on her lips blossomed at once
The rash hues of coral-red.
And the flowering buds of their teeth
Grew slowly with the moon's radiance.

The flaming mind, like the sun,
Occupies Indra's throne, the East,*
And moving to the North – Kubera's* vault,
Joyfully enhances the glory of its face,
Believing that in its hands (rays) are held the world,
And all happiness and good fortune come.

The princes drawled their childish babble
Resembling lotuses in half bloom;
The manner of their prattle and winsome glances,
Their lovely forms and charming postures
Filled the heart with thrill,
And made the mind's realm throb in ecstasy.

In time the princes learned to sit,
To crawl on all fours on the earth;
The Virtuous One, beckoning fondly from a distance,
Braced up their strength of movement –
And the princes would smile in anticipation
Hurrying towards their mother.

Sometimes with clay in their hands,
They would begrime their tongues;
But if the mother gave them ripe fruits,
They'd shake their heads and throw them away;

---

* Indra and Kubera are presiding deities of the quarters mentioned.

Their pretty, unruly curls would quiver
And appear like flower-tossed bees.

Soon they learnt to stand up with their mother's support,
And fast enough, supported by their own feet,
Began to walk, gripping their mother's hands.
In time they walked on by themselves;
When they stumbled and fell, crying aloud,
The mother would humour them kissing their faces.

Delighted at the gorgeously coloured forest birds,
The princes kept calling out to them;
Longing for the peacock's many-splendoured tail,
They would chase the bird with hopes of catching it;
They would lay hold of the fawn and play with it,
Making a dress for it with wild flowers.

With much delight the hermits, men and women,
Took them round the woods;
They would rock them in swings of flowery vines
And deck their tufts of hair and cheeks with blooms;
Bursting out with buds of glee, the princes would then
Insist for more and more.

Brightly blue, the limbs of the princes
Looked enchanting on the flowered swings:
The goddess of the woods, as if adorned with emeralds,
Like a royal empress coyly moved about;
With the swings shook the branches of the trees,
Taunting, as it were, the beauties around with quavering eyebrows.

Five years slowly rolled by
Moulding the princes with the valour of lions;
With full freedom they roamed
Around lakes, meadows, gardens and woods,
Their fearless hearts weren't bothered the least
With the danger of the beasts of the wild.

The ritual tonsure of the princes over,
Valmiki, the ocean of wisdom, admitted them
Into the woods of learning, of tough access,

Making them five-faced like Siva,*
And the princes, ranging through that world,
Laid low the elephant of ignorance.

Those epic-peaks laden with *rasa*-gems
Were occupied in glory by Rama, the lion,
Where the blood-streams of the elephant Ravana
Flowed down in sounding cascades,
And lionesses kept weeping in the caverns
From the agonies of the tusker's charge.

The towering sage made the princes
Skilfully scale those very summits.
As he taught them how to frisk as fawns there,
They ranged about as tigers;
They felt Rama was indeed a lion,
But did not know, they were the lion-cubs.

They would sing before their mother
The *Ramayana* composed by the great sage;
Playing the *veena* with true tone and rhythm,
Their minds absorbed in the *rasa* of Rama's devotion,
They would move their hands and eyes
Agitated by the waves of love.

As one song after another expressed
Defiance, challenge, lament and laughter,
Their arms and chests would swell
And at times their tear would run;
Sublime poetic feelings would then sink
Deep into their inmost beings.

The new-born Muse upon child-tongues,
Clear and bright and of enchanting form,
Weaving strange and gracefully tender movements,
Dispensed cheer and joy all over,
That rose in the shapes of clouds,
Showering the rain of nectar into every heart.

---

* Siva of five faces symbolises complete vision.

Drinking the pure nectar of the music,
Their hearts melting in joy and grief,
Their eyes streaming with tears,
The women ascetics availed in limitless measure
Torment and peace, sorrow and joy,
Sadness and cheer in the company of Janaki.

And yet, the princes had not an inkling
That Sita, the central gem in the necklace
Upon the heart of Raghava, *Ramayana*'s hero,
Was their own mother, living there
In the forest on the banks of Bhagirathi;
That was kept a secret on the great sage's orders.

In utmost delight they would sing
Of the glories and virtues of Rama and Sita;
Which that jewel among the Pure Ones heard
And bashfully exulted in the recesses of her heart;
And with extreme care kept up her disguise,
Biding her time in the forest as a hermit-woman.

The deer, hearing the exquisite verses,
Their ears erect and eyes absolutely still,
Forgetting their food, drink and frolic
Stood transfixed, as though of wooden forms;
Flocks of birds, fallen silent,
Filled their hearts with the riches of the ears.

The trees, too sang after, filling their deep tresses
With bouquets of flowers as upon flower-pots,
And moving their creeper-arms in graceful drama;
Tamasa flowed by hypnotized,
Helpless under this rare ecstasy.

On the earth's breast ran streams of nectar,
Dancing to the tunes of thanksgiving;
The forest-dwellers gathered from all over
To float dreamily in the rush of nectar;
Having flooded innumerable ear-holes,
The stream deluged the city of gods.

Hearing the chants, Brahma, Indra and Rudra
Joyfully offered their felicitations;
East, West, North and South,
The maids of the cardinal points danced with delight;
Making a proud display of their own musical fare,
The *apsaras* danced with the *gandharvas.*

Narada* travelled from world to world,
Full-throated in voicing his pleasure,
Singing the praises of Valmiki's poetic *rasa*
And the spotless fame of Rama and Janaki;
He sang after the princes,
After their *veena*-like, nectar-raining voices.

He, whose *veena* was renowned in the universe,
Now extolled the boys' *veena* that had enthralled him
Proclaiming its excellence;
Glory to him, divine sage!
For he enhances his own glory
By joyfully singing the praises of others.

Worthy oneself, if one excels
In glorifying the virtues of others,
He only makes his own tree of virtues bear fruit;
The arrow, after all, is pushed forward by the bowstring,
And the breeze that carries the fragrances of flowers
Heightens the delight of the world.

When the princes came into their eleventh year,
Their sacred-thread rites were performed;
Soon they acquired eyes of wisdom
With their studies of the holy Vedas –
And Vaidehi surrendered her sorrows
At the genius of her learned sons.

Their flowering youth made a charming image like the Sun
Casting his rays on the waters of his daughter, Yamuna,
It borrowed the gleams of precious stones
From the treasuries of the sea-god,

---

* Mind-born son of Brahma, the Creator; tours all three worlds singing the praise of Vishnu to the accompaniment of his veena.

And then with superb skill
Decorated slowly the blue limbs of the princes.
Their wisdom-honed words
Purified both ear and heart,
And their ways, imbibing the virtues of the words,
Made their character godly.
Brightened were their minds, speech and limbs,
Creating in their beings waves of grandeur.

The mother's soul filled up with the light of joy
At the reading of the holy verses by her sons,
And her nights of sad memories
Grew more pleasant as time went by;
Only the grieving one knows the value of happiness
Which the joys of the ever-happy can never match.

The fresh, blissful faces of the princes
Were like piles of gems to the mother's eyes;
And to the mother's ears their praises
Became a spring of nectar.
To add to it all, rising steps of her husband's glory,
Became for the Virtuous One a ladder to heaven.

From the day the twins left their mother
To roam the countryside without fear,
Janaki, in ceaseless manner, began
To engage herself in austerities and vows;
She surrendered her mind at her husband's feet
And prepared herself for the end of her life.

Like a river's flow in the scorching summer
The Virtuous One's being grew leaner;
Like the moon in the dark fortnight,
It fixed its gaze upon the dark night of death,
And in the belief her husband was the sun,
Became hopeful for a near union.

She thought: 'If I could only once
Look upon my husband's sacred feet,
I would leave the twins in his hands
And pull down the prison of this body;
The deer of my soul should flee at once
And dwell in that forest of freedom.'

CANTO - XI

Once the Lord of Day, the radiance of his limbs
Dimmed with sweat from the toil of circling the earth,
Went to the Western Sea longing for a bath
And plunged deep into the cerulean waters.
Unable to leave her husband behind, Day
Hurried after him abased, not lingering a moment.
But the innocent lotus-maid wouldn't leave her home,
For she didn't know the torments
Of a wife living away from her husband.
In a trice, looting the pink-apparelled treasury of the lotus
Night spread a carpet of twilight over the sky.
At this humiliation of the tender lotus-girl,
The rain-tree let its leaves droop in shame.

At sunset, the magnanimous sage
Prayed to Fire, and then invoked the blessings of Siva.
In the hermitage he sat, adorning a seat of grass,
Contemplating on Rama's bountiful rule.
He thought too, of the training of the princes,
And of ways to present the father to his sons.
He mused: The princes are now at the threshold
Of knowledge in the science of archery and kingship;
Should they be living on with ascetics in the forest,
Their most precious time would slip past fruitlessly.
As princes, if they aren't skilled in princely duties,
Their virtues would be worthless as a barren tree,
Sons of a hero, if they acquire not heroic virtues
An intolerable stigma would attach to a heroic race.

Who can say that the royal throne of Kosala
Wouldn't need someday the jewel of Rama's son?
If he hasn't then the skill to protect royal honour
A pitiful ignorance would be all-too-manifest
And yet, how could the princes, living in these woods,
Be skilled in these arts without the right models?

Especially known for their charity are Raghu's race of kings,
How can an ascetic's cottage provide for such virtues?
The princes' forms are exactly in Rama's mould,
True mirror images from limb to limb.
Once he sees them, Rama would surely recognise his sons,
And his doubts dispelled by Shatrughna,
He would accept the princes when presented before him
And I would be the object of reproach no more.
But then in fear of public scandal, with a ruthless heart
Under the pretext of fulfilling her desires
When she was heavy with child, he had sent
His pregnant wife away into the forests,
Wholly convinced of her faithfulness to him;
It doesn't seem likely that after twelve long years
His heart would be aroused in filial affection.
To his subjects he has passed on his filial love,
And would certainly seek their consent now;
For one who has no confidence in his beliefs
What good would our thousand pleadings do?
To be sure, it seems proper to consult
Vasistha and Laxmana on this matter.
A royal messenger arrived at that moment
And with folded hands presented a letter to Valmiki.
The great sage read it through, and found
A way open for attaining his wish.

Raja Ramachandra had issued an invitation
For an *aswamedha-yagna** he planned to perform,
And the noble sage thought: Providence is indeed kind,
To point to the shores in this sea of concern.
We shall take the princes with us as our novices,
Attired as sons of ascetics to witness the sacrifice.
Kusa and Lava shall recite the new epic *Ramayana*,
Moving from place to place at the site of the sacrifice.
The story of Rama showering nectar of delight
Will surely hold the minds of people spellbound;
They would observe the princes's likeness to Rama
And certainly conclude they were Rama's sons.
Ramachandra himself would immerse his heart
In a well of nectar-like love in his image's form,

---

* Horse-sacrifice.

And if Rama is hesitant to accept the princes,
Wouldn't Kausalya in anguished protest throw herself on the earth?
All would be happy to hear from the *Ramayana*
That Vaidehi had not been sullied by Ravana's touch.
Whose hairs would not stand taut in wonder
To hear of the Virtuous One's ordeal by fire?
The *Ramayana* would manifest the nimbus of its words,
And all three worlds shake off the murk of scandal.

As he pondered thus, the chief of sages
Felt an exhilaration flow through his inner being.
With sweet words then he asked the messenger to rest
And asked some novices to take good care.
The sage then went joyfully to the mother
And broke to her the news of the impending yagna:
'The messenger of Rama is here with an invitation,
And tomorrow I leave with the disciples.
Kusa and Lava, too, would join in as novices;
They shall meet many sages there and get their blessing.'
The Virtuous One welcomed the great sage's suggestions,
And ardently made over the care of the boys.

The sage then announced to the boarders;
At daybreak we leave for the *aswamedha-yagna*,
All you novices, along with Kusa and Lava,
Keep yourselves ready with your travel requirements.
Dear Kusa and Lava, carry your *veenas* along,
Make your learning fruitful with your song.
That very Rama who is the hero of the *Ramayana*,
And who has been the source of joy to your hearts,
It is he who performs this famed *yagna*.
Nobles from various lands would visit there;
Bibhisana, Lanka's jewel, must have come,
Crossing the seas with his band of *asuras;*
Great bear-and-monkey heroes like Angada and Sugriva
Would also come gaily with scrubbed faces;
The mighty hero Hanuman of immeasurable valour,
To whom mountains appear as but bits of stone,
Would be roaming in the place like a lion
Happily displaying on his chest
The necklace of pearls gifted by Sita;

Numerous *savaras*[1] would have accompanied Guha,
Decking their bodies with colourful garlands of feathers.
And Bharata, who on the strength of his brotherly devotion,
Spurned the rare love-embrace of the royal goddess,
Living on fruits and root for fourteen years,
Paid homage to his elder's sandals upon the throne,
Wore a knot of matted hair, and raised his life so high,
The Himalayan peaks had to gaze up to see;
The same Bharata would be there, following Rama around,
With his splendour of glory like the sun in the sky.
You shall also see Laxmana, the rare-born,
The one who has no equal on this earth,
The one who ground under his feet the arrogance
Of the demon that terrorised the god of thunder;
News of the same Meghanada's death, as a terrible flame,
Which entered Ravana's heart and burned furiously –
Growing more awesome with the sacrifice of the personal guard,
In it the demon-chief heated his bright, mighty missile,
And hurled it in rage at Soumitri,[2]
It is the same Laxmana who justified his name
By bearing upon his chest and back the weapon's scars.
With your eyes you will see what you've seen in words,
And sing of them all in the presence of the people:
For your songs will be heard by hundreds of kings
And by numerous ascetics penance-splendour filled.
When anyone there questions your identity,
Answer simply: "We two brothers are Valmiki's disciples."
If Raja Ramachandra calls you over to him
Sing the *Ramayana* again in his presence;
If then he is curious about your identity,
Tell him, "We brothers are twins, disciples of Valmiki."
If he offers you rich gifts, humbly say without temptation:
"What should we do with riches in the hermitage?" '

And there, hearing of the *yagna* from the sage's lips,
A searing pain suddenly struck Vaidehi's heart,
She pondered: 'It appears certain that the crowning jewel

1. Of the tribe of fowlers; Guha, a friend of Rama, was their chieftain.
2. Son of Sumitra, Laxmana.

Of Raghu's race has held in his lap a second wife.
Praise be to the fortunate woman – the tree of her penances
Has borne as fruit the sea-moon of the Sagara dynasty.
My temptation is great for those penances of her.
Whaterver austerities she performed and how,
Should someone reveal to me those rites or her penance
I would surely perform them with a keener rigour –
But can any one tell of her previous penances?
Yes, mighty sages like Vasistha would know,
Or else how would they nominate her as Queen?
My Lord must have wed on their advice,
And by some means now I must have that mystic mantra.'

With these thoughts the Virtuous One composed an humble letter:
'To the One whose banner assures protection of suppliants,
And who is a prod against elephant-like enemies
Whom the wise see as a thunderbolt against the mount of sorrow,
At the lotus-feet of that king of kings
This poor beggar-woman bows and worships from afar.
In great distress she sends an appeal from the forest
To tear apart the darkness surrounding her sweet hopes.
Oh mighty king, you are initiated for a grand rite,
With your new wife gracing your left lap,
Each virtue of yours must be waxing larger
For the rapt wife to be in raptures a hundredfold.
You shall gift in observance of the great *yagna*,
Silken apparel, gems and riches boundless.
All the needy will feel fulfilled there;
An humble appeal rises in my mind, Lord,
Do not be niggardly at my small request,
For you are an ocean of benevolence, full of the gems of compassion.
It is not necessary to know who I am,
For you are always the dispeller of the worries of ascetics.
There is nothing you' d ever refuse a hermit,
You must not then ignore me, a poor female anchorite.
The entire world must be watching with reverence
The one who is worthy today of your embrace;
What arduous penances had she done in the past,
Where, and how long, and what mantras did she chant –
This alone my Lord, kindly let me know,
For I have no need of any other wealth.
To me that would be far more precious

Than all the riches donated in a billion sacrifices.
There is but one more request:
This unhappy woman's sons are quite innocent,
They haven't had the good fortune
Of sitting in their father's lap, nor of having
A father's love since their birth;
They only know to make the mother's soul run with tears,
Singing the *Ramayana* to the strumming of the *veena*'s strings.
Who, with a human heart, would not weep
At all that makes plants and vines distraught?
Enamoured themselves with the story of your life,
The twins are visiting you with the great sage;
Their own minds entice them onward
For a sight of your lotus-feet.
They shall recite the tale of your past sorrows,
A tale, when heard, that cuts through the heart of this wretched woman.
And if not heard, the mind keeps running to it,
The longing to hear it becoming irrepressible.
Oh Lord of steady reason, if on hearing this tale,
The hapless Vaidehi's memory comes to your mind,
Then think of Vaidehi's love as but a dream,
Cherishing the joyful face of your new beloved.'
The Virtuous One wrote on in her heart's misery
And her tears kept washing the letters she wrote.

As she pondered over what next to write,
Kusa and Lava came in, laughing away in zest.
They said: 'Oh mother! Marvellous indeed is the Lord of Raghus,
And blessed is his beloved, the fortunate Virtuous One.
The son of Kausalya is about to perform an *aswamedha-yagna*,
And a messenger is here with an invitation.
That which we knew from the messenger makes us feel,
The world is blessed because of Ramachandra.
Rama had silenced the public scandal
Banishing Sita, his soul's beloved;
Now he has installed at the site of the *yagna*
A Janaki of gold as his wife by his side;
Mother, was a wife for him so hard to find?
But no, Janaki's consort did not wish for another wife.
Mother, where did Janaki go? May be she isn't alive;

We could glean nothing of that from the *Ramayana*.
We will go there, Mother, and see Rama's lotus-feet,
For the great sage has promised to take us along.'

The words of the princes, like waves of a nectarous sea,
Bathed the whole being of the virtuous Sita.
Her heart that had become a hot bed of sand
Was flooded with the waters of Rama's sea of love.
She said to herself: 'Oh, I am ever the sinner,
Writing words that would have scorched my master's heart!
I am a frail woman, weak within,
But deep and boundless is my lord's compassion.
Forgive my wrongs, my Lord, Ocean of Mercy,
Destiny has made me your heart's poison.'
She hid the letter, and exclaimed with joy:
'Go, my sons, behold the lotuses of royal feet,
Father said you would be singing there,
And that in itself is of the substance of nectar;
It would spread from heart to heart, saturating all,
At the sacred place of sacrifice, like a surge of nectar.
Present yourselves to the scion of Raghus
If you are called, and bow at his feet with devotion.
There, you shall see too, his younger brothers,
Offer your homage humbly at their feet.
Bring fulfillment to your lives, accepting on your heads
The dust of the holy lotus-feet of the queen-mothers.
Janaki's three sisters would be there beside them,
Offer obeisance at their feet as if they were a Janaki each.
And should someone ask you whose children you are,
Say in reply: ' We are the treasure of a woman ascetic.'
The princes were delighted with the mother's words,
And the excitement of new wonders filled their minds.
They had little desire now for food and sleep,
Their hearts kept dancing to vie for Rama's glories.
Thus as both the brothers kept talking of Rama,
They were soon overtaken by sleep.

But Janaki's soul floated on the flood of devotion
To her husband, and spun helplessly around in a whirlpool.
When the goddess of sleep failed to bring her

Into her lap, she sought the help of Jogamaya.[1]
She ventured: 'Oh Goddess, this day the soul of Janaki
Has crossed the limits of the human heart.
For twelve years now, flooding her pillow.
Every night with tears, for a while at least
She would gently slide into my lap.
With whatever honeyed words I invite her tonight
She pays no heed, but retreats towards the world of heaven.
The very pupils of her eyes, her two sons,
Would soon be out of her sight
And all the cardinal points will darken for her.
There is no sunrise for her in this life.
What becomes her fate with such devotion for her husband?
Lighten up her future, that the unhappy woman might see.
The helpless one grew a garden of devotion to the husband,
Pouring the water of her tears in the pits round life's roots,
But it never flowered, nor did it bear fruit;
Think how very tormented would such life be!'
Jogamaya enjoined: 'Let us go then, friend,
The cool night is soon coming to an end.
Let us hurry to the Virtuous One
And reveal to her the mystery of her future.'

Jogamaya left at once, accompanied by Sleep,
And entered Janaki's cottage of leaves.
The forest grew resplendent with celestial light,
And heavenly scents filled the planes of the earth.
Janaki's soul was thrilled with the fragrance
And her eyes closed at the enveloping radiance.
She looked then transfigured with many-splendoured light,
Brightening the entire earth with her brilliance.
There sat Ramachandra, radiant upon a jewelled throne,
She by his side, her countenance aglow;
Kusa in Ramachandra's lap, Lava in Sita's,
And Urmila's consort[2] alongside, royal umbrella in hand,
With Bharata too, at the duties he loved,
Waving an elegant silk-tasselled, moon-white fan.
Shatrughna also was there, fanning

1. Goddess who sustains all life with her yogic power.
2. Laxmana

With one fashioned from peacock feathers.
And the light of all their lives surged to the future
Like the fast-moving currents of a river.
Innumerable men and women bathed in the sacred stream
Deeming it the holiest of holy places.
The stream ran on toward the far shores of Eternity,
Spreading its banks wider and wider with time.
Immortals and celestial musicians kept
Showering exquisite flowers from above;
Gods, demons, serpents, humans and *apsaras*
Filled the earth with cries of 'Victory to Sita-Rama.'
In homes and hearts and cities everywhere,
In rivers-boats, ocean-vessels, over all the hills,
Through the night, at dusk and dawn,
In joys and sorrows, in the beings of the rich and poor,
Shouts of 'Victory to Sita –Rama' went up;
The most virtuous among women all, watched, entranced.

Original translation – **Jayanta Mahapatra & Madhusudan Pati**
Revised by – **Madhusudan Pati**

PRANAYA BALLARI

CANTO - I

Shoot of Love

Praise be to Vedavyasa, and praised be Kalidasa,
    Loved sons of Saraswati, goddess of word and song.
Like marks of sandalwood paste, O teachers wise,
    On the forehead of the company of poets you shine.

To your feet is my heart
    Tethered by fate in unyielding knots,
And following you with humility I adore
    Saraswati's holy feet.

The path you struck and roamed, O masters,
    Through sylvan tracts of poesy in bloom,
I shall walk those selfsame paths, and pluck the flowers
    That chance across my view.

Those that my eyes spot high atop branches,
    Beyond my assiduous hands,
I will quietly desist
    And strive not after them.

But with the flowers I'ld have gathered
    A garland I would string for mother Utkal's bosom,
And immerse myself in joy, offering devout worship
    At the mother's lotus feet.

King Dusmanta once in his chariot,
    Shining with bow and arrow in hand, merry in heart,
Was ranging through the woods,
    Pursuing game in sporting abandon.

As he coursed through the forest
He came upon a deer, right on his path
Which cast at the armed king a swift glance,
And then sped away in quickened terror.

Even as the charioteer, urged by the king,
Hastened in pursuit of the fleeing deer,
Seeing that the path was rugged and rough,
He could not wholly slacken the reins.

The black buck, its feet only now and then
Striking the forest ground,
Leaping with an ingrained force
Almost flew through the air.

Shrinking its back and tightening its tail
Frightful of some striking arrow, off and on
It turned its neck to glance at the chariot,
And in frantic speed ran on.

From its mouth agape with exhaustion
Fell the dribble of half-chewed grass
Here and there
All along the path.

Soon as the charioteer upon level ground
Urged the horses on a longer rein,
They bent their heads, flattened their ears
And raced away with long outstretched legs.

They sped on with their tails raised
Outstripping far the trail of dust their hooves stirred;
Whether their feet touched the ground at all,
Or they only flew, hard it was to know.

All that to the king had seemed
Tiny and small from the distance,
Before his eyes now loomed
All at once, tall and huge.

On either side objects bent and crooked
Caused an illusion, appearing stretched out straight,
And things discrete suddenly seemed as one,
While the uneven looked all plain.

Quickly did the chariot close upon the deer;
And finding it near,
The eager king,
Promptly on the bowstring fixed an arrow.

But at that moment was heard a cry,
'Kill not, kill not, this deer is of the hermitage.'
Hearkened the king, and when he saw there approaching
Two monks, he stood mortified and stunned.

Quickly he regained his composure then,
And ordered the charioteer to stop.
While hurrying up to him, the monks
Offered their blessings with upraised hands.

They said: 'O King, this deer of the hermitage
Isn't game for royal hunt;
On this tender-bodied animal loose not your shaft,
Like a fiery missile upon a heap of cotton wool.

To your arrow of the element of the thunderbolt,
Hardly is a match this frail life of the antelope,
O King, your arrow is not for killing the weak,
But to protect all those in distress.'

The king then withdrew his arrow
And humbly offered his salutations.
Rejoicing, the monks extolled him,
'Bravo, bravo, O lion among kings,

This act indeed, is worthy of your race;
Praise be to you, O scion of the Purus,
May you be blessed with a gem of a son,
A valiant monarch, storehouse of virtues all.

Our hearts at your royal visit,
Abound in jubilation;
Deign to shower more delight on it,
Accepting our hospitality in these woods.

Look, yonder on the Malini's bank,
Stands sage Kanva's ashram clearly visible,
The great ascetic is out on a pilgrimage,
But his daughter is there in the cottage.

Living in your kingdom and engaging in pieties,
Never ever suffering a breach of peace,
The sage keeps showering eulogies
On your royal highness' rule.

His sacrificial rites over, everyday
The sage offers prayers for your prosperity;
Had he been here today, surely
Gratified he'ld have been at your royal visit.

Your royal highness is with us today,
And should you return without being treated here,
When the great sage comes to know,
All of us would suffer his harsh chiding.'

The hermits' cordiality, knew the king, was a blessing;
And so, accepting their invitation with polite words
He moved from there with animated bearing
To go round the hallowed space.

Entering the hermitage, curious and charmed,
He found the ground under the trees
Bestrewn with wild paddy,
That had dropped off the parrots' bills.

To him it seemed the birds there had
Long forgotten the fear of fowlers,
And living in ease had enhanced
The forest's beauty with their emerald presence.

All at once then
The sight of turtle-doves with rubied beaks
Seized the king's mind
And enthralled his heart.

Elsewhere he found some glistening slabs of stone
Made smooth with the oil of *ingudi* fruits,
Stones that carried a clear proof
Of *ingudi*s crushed by the monks.

Herds of deer that habitually ate
Young shoots of grass profferred by sages' sons,
Continued to graze in peace
Unruffled by the sight of the wandering king.

Water from wind-tossed canals
Washed the trees' feet, and yet,
Their foliage looked so dull and pale
Blown by sacrificial smoke day after day.

Shedding his hunting habit some way ahead,
Leaving behind the car with the charioteer,
The king advanced in humble dress,
Following the path to the ashram cottage.

Slowly he walked, relishing
The ashram's honeyed charm;
It wasn't easy, whichever way he turned,
For his enchanted gaze to be withdrawn.

Forced to withdraw from one direction
Forthwith it was captured by another view:
Not simply an enchantment it was,
But the bliss of some nectarous shower.

The king whose handsome form let flow
A cascade of joy in a million hearts
The same exalted one was enthralled today
At the sight of the ashram's charms.

Refreshed by the tender shades of trees
The lord of men thought to himself,
'So insipid the shade of the royal umbrella,
No match indeed to this cool, soothing shade.

And so it was that the kings of Raghu's race
Handing over the kingdom's burden to their sons,
Used to repair onto the hermitage at the end,
To savour unbroken peace in the tranquil range.

The king's vision swam on the splendid scene
And his heart on a new-roused emotion,
And then on his ears fell,
Delightful notes of maidens' voices.

He looked around startled, but found none nearby;
Cautiously then he made for the sound,
And keeping behind the trees, through the cobwebs peered –
He saw, not far from there,

Figures of maidens three,
Ravishingly beautiful, idols verily of joy,
Who with their exquisite feet could trample
All the nymphs of heaven in the war of charms.

Left arms encircling pitchers of water,
Their vine-like bodies bent to the right,
They came at a slow pace,
Swinging their right hands rhythmically.

They ambled along,
In a close, single file,
Engaged in friendly chatter,
Diverting themselves in fun and banter.

From their conversation learnt the king,
One was named Shakuntala;
And Anasuya and Priyambada
Were the other two maids.

Shakuntala was Kanva's daughter
And the other two were her companions;
Like a budded flower between two leaves
Stood out Shakuntala between her friends.

The sweetness of her form at once
Seized the realm of the royal heart,
And memories of the beauties in the harem
With folded hands acknowledged submission.

Shattered the creeper of the wild
The pride of the creeper of the royal gardens –
How should the *basanga* flower ever equal
The rose, even if it be inside a forest of thorns?

Finding the moment propitious
For a sight of the beautiful maid,
The heart embraced on a sudden
Ecstasy and wonder both.

The pitcher in the arm-hold of the delicate one
Ushered into the mind twin images
Of lightning-befriended thunder,
And thorns upon the lotus-stalk.

Beholding her elegant tender limbs
In bark-clothes clad, ruefully mused the king –
'It is like the goddess of a royal house,
Her person clouded over with anxieties of war;

And yet, the splendour of her feminine grace
Manifests clear,
Like the moon upon Shiva's matted hair,
Or an algae-encircled lotus.

Even the dark spot sitting on the moon's lap
Delights the eyes:
Indeed, to a body that is naturally graceful,
What doesn't serve as ornament?

Seeing the oozing beads of sweat
On her gleaming face of youthful sheen,
Reflected the king – 'It's like the fall of snow
Upon a newly bloomed lotus;

Curious it is, with what thoughts has the sage
Enjoined upon this maid such a trying task;
He has used a silken rope, as it were,
To bind an elephant of the wild;

But, of course, by the powers of penance
What is impossible may be made real – is it thus,
That the sage, with the edge of a petal of blue lily
Here tries to saw a tough *shami* tree?'

Her two friends began pouring water
Into trenches encircling young plants;
Then Shakuntala approached near
And stood beneath the mango tree.

Placing the pitcher on the ground
And straightening her well-wrought exquisite body
She stood, bringing into play in the king's heart
The image of a creeper of gold in the royal mansion.

A creeper whose rubied leaves were her palms,
And diamond-buds her shiny nails:
But those were crafted by the goldsmith's hand,
While the architect of the world had designed hers.

Wondered the king, 'Would this creeper ever
Adorn someone's garden of good-fortune,
Or keep to the hermitage for all time
Beautifying its woods?

No mere creeper this damsel, but a crest-flower picturesque
Shining upon Providence's creative vine,
A flower, indeed, to bedeck Goddess Fortune's head –
Priceless, nonpareil.

For whosoever's worship be meant this flower,
Blessed are my bee-eyes
That at a moment propitious
Partook of its honeyed beauty.'

The beautiful one then glanced
At the *niali* creeper, the loved mate of the mango tree,
That only after long three days
She had today been able to see.

Clusters of buds had reared themselves
Upon the nodes of the *niali* branches;
And of them some had meanwhile
Burst through their natal sheathes.

Many of them too were poised to bloom –
All eagerly in wait,
With pollen-covered bodies
For the advent of an auspicious dusk.

A few of them having bloomed
Had fallen and got caught in cobwebs
And a few others lay supine on the ground
Brought down by riotous bees.

When she saw the birth of maiden flowers
Upon the jasmine she had nurtured by hand
Her heart and eyes surged at once
With a vivacious new cheer.

Her blithe face was decked with a smile,
That showed forth not, yet was palpable;
Her feelings she could not now contain
But had to reveal them to her friends.

Beside herself in joy, she called out to them,
'Come, come quickly, my dears,
See how my jasmine today
Is wreathed in virgin bloom.'

The words of the fairest one held
    A sweet laughter innate,
As in the juice of sugar-cane its sugar,
    Not clearly set off, though real.

'Oh where, indeed,' the two friends cried,
    Swiftly coming over at her call,
And went round the vine
    Fondly inspecting its tendrilled limbs.

Said one, 'O friend, certain it is
    This bud here'll bloom out today;'
While the other one happily exclaimed,
    'Here, last night this one blossomed.'

Priyambada cajoled, 'Friend,
    The auspicious hour is come,
Now get the mango tree united in wedlock
    To the vine that delights the forest.'

Shakuntala smiled, and in banter said,
    'I know not the rites of marriage,
If you know, do act as a priest
    And instruct me the proper way.'

Priyambada rejoined in fun –
    'Make this avowal, dear maid,
That at your wedding, my right
    To act as priest would be inviolate.'

Colouring bashfully Shakuntala complained,
    'How shrewd you are –
You play on future suppositions
    Avoiding matters in hand.'

This when he heard, hopes of marriage with the damsel
    Sprouted fast in the heart of the king,
And his right arm then auspiciously throbbing,
    The vine of hope burst into lush foliage.

The king's conscience spoke to his charmed mind
In affectionate, sweet reproach:
'Whence comes this your latitude today,
In desiring another's thing?'

Answered the mind: 'This gem unclaimed
Lies in the womb of a mine;
No reason at all for it to be spurned by the king,
By whom first it has been seen.'

Retorted his conscience: 'She's the daughter of a sage,
Reflection of a star in the water of the well;
If some deluded greedy one leaps in, believing
It is but a mined ruby, he'ld only meet his doom.'

But he heard Priyambada say, 'O beautiful one,
Would your thrilled mind, lured by the love
Of some noble king, look for me then
Ignoring the royal priest?' –

And happily thought, 'That which I took for
A meteor coursing through the sky,
Now appears to be a mass of virtues,
Soothingly bright, that has fallen from heaven.

She is, for sure, as is clear from their talk,
A Laxmi risen from the sea of royalty,*
But it is unclear why this supreme beauty
Keeps sporting here in the wild.

The monks said, in the hermitage would be Shakuntala,
The sage's daughter; but her friends now suggest,
The sweet tender one of lovely tresses,
Is a proper person for a king to woo.'

The king's mind mounted a chariot of curiosity,
To pierce the formation of mystery,
But proceeded not, held back by the appeal of Desire
To stay on and watch the delightful play.

---

* The story of Laxmi, goddess of prosperity, rising from the primal ocean, is under reference.

He mused, 'If I am not fated for the joy
Of this priceless touchstone of beauty,
Then destiny has showed me this splendour today
Only to keep me pining all my life.

Is it all real that I see here now
Or a dream that would suddenly be shattered,
And this blissful sleep would never more conjure
The beautiful form that is rare for the gods?

When she the queen of my heart's kingdom
Departs from the throne of my eyes,
Unruly memory would most easily then
Swamp its subject, my life, in a flood of revolt.'

Anasuya meanwhile continued, 'Friend Priyambada,
Your priesthood wouldn't do here,
For the community of jasmine vines
Boasts its own eminent body of priests.

A splendid canopy studded with stars
Would be elegantly raised above,
All around would the towering mountains stand
Sporting burning torches in hand;

The forests of bamboo would be loud with bursting crackers
And comets would flare the sky ablaze,
And *hulahuli* would be intoned in *malli*-forests
With the sweet drone of honey-bees.

The partridges and tattler-birds rejoicing
Would be raising a chorus of auspicious songs –
And at that hour would the wind-god unite
The hands of jasmine and the mango tree.'

At these words Shakuntala laughed aloud merrily
And commended her, 'You've spoken true, indeed;'
The two friends joined in the laughter
And then left to finish their chores.

Shakuntala began to pour water
At the roots of the *nabamalika* vine, when
A bee which had sat on a jasmine flower
Suddenly flew at her.

It settled on the face of the beautiful one,
Then quickly rose and settled back again,
Thus it went on hovering up and down,
When driven by her time and again.

It circled round her sometimes
With a long unbroken drone,
And the eyes of Shakuntala followed,
Unwinking, whichever way it flew.

Stooping, straightening, flailing her hands, whirling about,
Heaving her bosom, twisting her neck and waist,
She of the fleeting sidelong glance, kept driving the bee
Graphing many a posture of artistic dance.

Alas, that none was around to enjoy
The good fortune of watching this entrancing dance;
If the chief of gods had witnessed this, he'ld have
Decided, the dances in heaven were utterly drab.

Performance by heaven's courtesans
Were bereft of shame, and by self-interest tainted –
How could then the king of gods ever know
Such graceful movements of artless simplicity?

The Sun-god, driven by passion for Aswini,
His forest-hidden wife, could not watch the dance:
His honour was made secure
By curtains of thick foliage on trees.

Only the sovereign king of Hastina saw,
And stood transfixed like a statue:
Marvellous it was that he could harden his heart,
As a thunderbolt, and did not melt away.

Anxiously called out Shakuntala to her friends,
'Come, come quickly here, my dears;'
And the deep accents of her speech
Served to orchestrate the graceful dance.

From the woods rose echoes
To act as chorus to the musical notes –
It seemed the god of love had imbued it with a spell
Drawn from moon-dropped nectar;

Or, it was as if the love-god's wife had kept tuned
Her *veena*, which now she began to strum;
And the king who thought it was a resonance
From cupid's bow of blossoms, lost all his self-command.

She called out again, 'Oh, come my friends,
This wicked bee that from the jasmine took off
Refuses to be restrained,
And makes me all frantic.'

Feigning innocence rejoined Priyambada
In artful words of pun; 'How come,
In the kingdom of Purus, and that too in a hermitage,
Of a drunkard[1] you now complain?

Who is that wicked one, who presumes she is helpless [2]
Even while we are there;
And hasn't he yet heard of
Dusmanta's compelling power?'

Finding the moment opportune, the king
Swiftly moved near Shakuntala,
And asked, 'What's the matter, O gentle one,
Which villain troubles you here?

Fear not, fear not virtuous maid,
When the Puru-king is there;
Who would even a whit tolerate
Atrocious behaviour with a hapless female?'

---

1. The words carries two meanings – 'the bee' and 'the alcoholic'.
2. 'jasmine' and 'friendless'.

Dazed was Shakuntala to behold
A handsome person rare, surpassingly youthful:
Was he of mortal limbs or the ethereal god of love,
Or was he the moon in the guise of a man?

She looked at his lustrous countenance once
And quickly lowered her face –
Was it that some hand had touched,
On a sudden, the sensitive plant?

She was all flustered, and knew not
What to speak nor what to do;
Fast was her heart's space of overcast
With clouds of wonder and amazement.

Bashfulness, her unfailing mate, quickened her
To set in order her loosened cloth of bark,
But both her eyes remained fixed
On the beauty of the royal feet.

Seeing on the ground those coloured feet,
With their shiningly ranged rows of toe-nails
She fancied it was the *kunda*[1]-teethed earth-maiden
Of bright *bandhuli*[2]-lips, smiling out in delight.

Now as she stood there quiet and still
She thought of her friends, and they,
Before she could properly meet their eyes
Had already flanked her close.

Her two companions, when they saw
The youthful form, calm, composed, radiant,
Were struck by wonder, and mused–
Was he indeed Dushmanta the king?

Then sweetly said, 'We have no fear, sir,
In this hermitage: it was only a honey-bee
That turning riotous
Was troubling our friend.'

---

1. A small white flower.
2. A red flower.

Respectfully with polite words
Priyamada led him to the tree-shade,
And extending her hands
Presented a seat on a polished slab of stone.

When he was seated she gestured to her friend
To offer the guest some ceremonial water;
The king read the hint, and in polite dismissal said,
'No need, the guest has been properly welcomed.

With your sweet endearing behaviour
Already pleased and contented am I,
And if you could just sit here awhile
My delight will increase a hundred-fold.'

As if only obliged to please the guest,
But inwardly jubilant, the maids began
Prodding each other, making signs
To sit down there on the ground.

Pressing one another's hands they finally squatted,
As if forced against their will;
And all this playacting went on
Cleverly, as it were, out of the sight of the king.

And the king kept watching on the sly
Sitting there impassive, pretending ignorance,
But engrossed in their maidenly flutter
That was so sweetly hushed.

When he enquired about their well-being
The sages' daughters politely said –
'By virtue of your kindness, noble sir,
All is well with us.'

Said the king, 'Right at the first glance,
When one observes you here,
The cheer on your faces straightaway
Reveals the well-being of the hermitage.

So very closely matched, the three of you –
So young and graceful and amiable –
Make this sanctified forest here
An abode of joy-filled love.'

Like waves upon the sea
Rose and fell the maidens' simple hearts
Throbbing in curiosity to ask
Who that guest of handsome limbs was.

Anasuya and Priyambada exchanged a few times
Coaxing, suggestive glances;
Unable to contain herself any more then
In an eager voice Priyambada asked –

'O gentle and noble sir, forcing which kingdom
And the ornaments of which race, into unloveliness,
You favour us with your visit,
Embellishing these our forests here?'

At the maiden's words said the king,
'I am born in the race of Purus,
Whose customary duty has been
To suppress the unruly and keep the subjects happy.

While pursuing game through the woods
I felt a desire to visit this ashram;
And as I was moving around here I heard
The king's name uttered, and so I have come.

I can easily see, you three
Are the ornaments of the hermitage;
But strange it is, those born as fruits of penance
Should themselves like hermits be.

My mind is seized with wonder, too
And I feel so intrigued:
How had the great sage Kanva, a celibate all his life,
A daughter born of him?'

Hearing these words said Priyambada –
'Once god Indra, the Lord of clouds,
Saw the great ascetic Kaushika*
At rigorous penance, and took fright.

To cunningly rob the sage
Of all the wealth of his pieties,
As enjoined by Indra, the charming Menaka
Descended upon the earth.

The great sage sowed in her field
His unfailing powerful seed,
From which sprang Shakuntala,
A wondrous creeper of gems.

A creeper that nurtured by father Kanva
Has grown here full in the forest;
But when he finds a proper match for her
She'ld be duly made over.'

The king's tree of hope blossomed at once
At the vernal touch of those words;
'That which had seemed a flaming piece,' he happily thought,
'Has turned out to be a gem;

A maiden flower she is upon a celestial vine
Resplendent in heavenly charms;
Heavenly her fragrance and heavenly the tenderness,
That virginal remain, yet to be inhaled and kissed.'

Whenever the king shifted his gaze from her
Sidelong she'ld glance at his face
But would quickly withdraw the moment when
He resumed his sight of her.

If forced by shyness she'ld rise and leave,
An insult it might mean to the guest –
So thinking she kept sitting there,
Seeming preoccupied, and as if on the point of leaving.

* Biswamitra.

She hung her face down, and kept busy
Counting the multi-branched veins on a *saptaparni* leaf,
But every now and then experienced a surge of joy
Stealing quick glances at the king.

Again and again he watched
Her countenance beaming with heavenly sparkle;
Conversation was merely an ancillary matter,
The chief attraction – the sight of her lovely face.

Straight was the parting line of her hair,
And her forehead, entrancing with careless curls;
The cheeks of the maiden were like petals of lotus
Made lovely with strands by the ears, like kissing bees.

Deep blue eyebrows that thickly ran
To the margins of forehead and cheeks,
Flaunted their eminence long and full
With the charmingly lidded eyes.

Exquisitely sculpted nose, rounded chin,
And alluring lips – rivals all
Engaged in a contest of beauty
Keenly struggling for supremacy each.

And the ears, too, ambitious for rule
Over the beauteous realm of the face,
From the borders on either side
Pressed their charge.

The manifold beauties of her person
Drew each towards itself the guest, the royal vision:
Upon the vast waves of the sea of beauty
The king's eyes were but a tiny skiff.

Now and then as their eyes met,
A lightning of love would flash within
And illumine suddenly
The entire field of their hearts.

Little scope had the king
To scan the grace of her limbs,
But the maiden with her head bent down
Could keenly observe his charming feet.

When she saw the dust
Of the ashram's grounds clinging there,
She, the most glorious of maidens, kept wistfully thinking
That she herself might wash and wipe them clean.

She longed too
That her friends should force her
To offer him a respectful welcome,
Putting on his forehead a mark of sandalwood-paste.

But just then rose a commotion in the forest
Caused by the fear of a wild elephant,
And the maidens rose in alarm
Their furtive eyes agitated and anxious.

Someone out there shouted – 'O forest-dwellers,
Be careful, for on a hunting expedition
Has king Dusmanta come,
And is walking the grounds here.

Armies of men with elephants and horses
Have advanced into the ashram,
And the animals here grown restive,
Unmindful of their grazing run hither and thither.

And the forest is covered with dust
Raised by the hooves of horses,
The vast mass of the dust having enveloped the trees
High into the sky soars.'

Just then came a young fawn
Racing fast towards Shakuntala,
And stood there panting,
Under a length of her outstretched bark-cloth.

Now again was heard – 'A gigantic elephant
Is striking terror here;
It has already broken its tusk
Pulling down in mad fury a huge tree-branch.'

With concern stood up the king
And made ready to depart,
Though loath to forswear
The entrancing company of the maidens.

He said – 'Let me go and see for myself
How a tusker, having entered the ashram,
Wreaks havoc here all around;
I must prevent it at once.

I harbour this belief that you won't
Take offence at my abrupt leave;
But, yet, I promise to return here soon
To get myself properly pardoned.'

The maidens replied, 'We, too, feel sad
Not having offered any hospitality;
If you do not come again, O Noble Sir,
In our hearts we'ld deeply be aggrieved.'

In a deprecating voice said the king,
'Utter not such words, please,
Never can I forget through life
These your affable courtesies.

I leave you, sages' daughters,
Owing a debt of friendliness to you;
But how should you trust
If I pledge not something with you?'

Saying so, hastily from his finger
The king pulled out a ring,
And holding Shakuntala by her hand
Adorned her finger lovingly.

He walked away fast, but his mind
Raced constantly back,
As a banner of cloth flies backwards
While the chariot speeds ahead.

His heart was warm with the thrill
That the delight of her hand's touch had yielded,
And the power of that sensation
Subdued all his might.

Her two friends took hold of Shakuntala's hand
And closely examined the ring;
They found, the token of new love bore
The name **'DUSMANTA'** in letters bold.

They were seized with amazement,
Exchanging questioning glances, and Shakuntala then
Was petrified; they couldn't be sure
If hers was a living body or a stiff corpse.

Some irresistible current of a new emotion
Swept her being away; the two friends
Laughed aloud and saying, 'Let's move,'
Headed for their cottage.

Poor Shakuntala was feeling so faint,
Her feet could hardly move;
She dragged herself slowly, but as she went forward
Her eyes towards the king were drawn back again.

Feigning, she then complained to her friends,
'Oh, dear, I am caught by *kuruvaka*[1]-spikes,'
To which Priyambada teasingly rejoined,
'O fish-eyed one, is it the *puruvaka*[2]-beak that has pierced ?'

The king from her sight had disappeared,
But remained firmly anchored in her heart;
In the being of the damsel naturally then
Sprouted fresh a shoot of love.

---

1. Amaranth plant.
2. The Puru-stork, referring to Dusmanta.

CANTO - II

New Leaves of Love

The king rushed to the royal camp
And ordered his men,
'Keep the animals bound or chained,
Don't leave them free in the woods.'

Under the pavilion then he sat
And looking at his ringless finger
Happily thought, 'To that ring I owe,
The exquisite touch of the beauteous hand.'

Of the wild jasmine he had brought from the forest,
A few still lay in hand;
These he inhaled deep with tender feelings,
For they were dear to the noble dame.

With their scent enchanted, the king mused happily:
'At the time I touched her lotus-hand,
I obtained in exchange of the ring,
The fragrance of her balmy palms.'

Smelling at it again and again, and recalling
The sweetness of the charming one's leaf-like hand,
He filled his heart with a rare rapture,
Savouring the flower's delectable scent.

On the lake of that rapture rose waves of joy,
And as it received in showers
The memory of the new love-token of the maid,
Overflowing, streamed out of the heart.

The maiden was a storehouse of gems, the sea,
    And her simplicity a clear blue sky,
Which with a cloud of bashfulness was overcast
    On the advent of the king as on new monsoon.

Her sidelong glances were like lightning flashes
    That had danced out again and again
To dispel all the murk
    Of despair in the inner kingdom.

As his heart now streamed out,
    It rushed towards that sea, searching for passage
Through the deeply forested ground
    Of rules and customs of royal marriage;

It saw, the two companion-maids close by,
    Propitious and helpful both,
Had formed themselves into banks, as it were,
    To carve for union an easy path.

With the smiling acceptance of the ring had flowed
    A high tide through the path,
And so the king's heart-stream rushed on
    And comfortably spread out on the sea's bosom.

Now that the heart had advanced, his conscience
    Sought sanction for an intimate contact;
The mind then reared up and affirmed –
    ' O conscience, what you are looking for is already achieved;

For you have yourself witnessed,
    The close union of palms,
And you must have realised, the maiden hadn't been
    Loath to offer her hands.

If you still desire some proof
    Of her heart's consent – didn't she get herself
Caught in the amaranth – thorns just to look at you?
    What more could she have done?

You might say, the mind of a girl
Is under her father's rule;
But no child she, a full-grown maid,
And no more is her heart at her father's keep.

A free maid she, with a free mind of her own
Has offered you her hand,
With her friends, her heart and the trees,
All bearing witness around.'

Questioned his conscience – 'Should the sage grow angry,
To hear of her self-willed act, what then?'
But reassured the mind – 'Isn't the conscience of a sage
Of lifelong austerities, more mature than yours?'

But his conscience demurred – 'When was that union of hands,
Consecrated by oblatory water, when was auspicious *hulahuli* intoned?'
Thereupon the mind argued – 'The nature-queen had
Raised *hulahuli* in the voice of the mynah.

And though you could not understand,
The lotus-hand of the maiden was wet,
And what you thought perspiration was, in fact,
Sacred water poured by the god of marriage.'

But Conscience raised a doubt – 'There was no priest,
Who then chanted the vedic mantras?'
And Mind replied – 'The spring-cuckoo had loudly chanted,
The holy words, "As Rama's with Sita."

Argued Conscience – 'Wasn't it coercion,
To make free with the hand of a weak female?'
And Mind retorted – 'A maid, though deep in love
Is not allowed by her shyness to offer her hand;

In the kingdom of love, it is ever the case
The beloved expects to be forced by the lover;
For without friction by the cloud-mass
Lightning in its lap plays not.'

Conscience said, 'Compelled by the cloud, if lightning is pleased,
Why then is the roar so fierce?'
Corrected his mind, 'Hardly a roar it is; rather the roll
Of the couple's love-drum resonating through the world.'

Now the heart intervened: 'If the body does not follow
Where I have sojourned,
All life's joy would be vitiated
By the fatal poison of separation.

The world in the absence of her company
Would utterly insipid be;
Dull will be the bejewelled throne
And dull the gem-studded palace.

She is verily the goddess of royal prosperity,
Incarnated with all her charms;
The ruby-studded royal umbrella*
Would be lustreless without her light.

Helped by the radiance of her lotus-hand
And her immaculate pair of lips,
The bodies of topazes and rubies there
Would spring into lumious splendour.

When the blue tresses and eyebrows
And gleaming pupils of her eyes
Approach close, the bodies of sapphires would
Streams of refulgence let flow.

If strings of pearls have the good fortune
To serve as figures for her nails and teeth,
In the eyes of men would they suffuse
A new glamour rare and sweet.

As the moonstone at the sight of the moon
And the 'sunstone'-ruby the sun,
So would all gems swell in joy
When they watch this glorious maiden.

---

* Kept raised above the king while he presides in the court.

Wide open is the path of prosperity –
Move forward and delay not,
For if one sleeps beneath a tree open-mouthed
No fruit would enter on its own.'

Sonorous beat the drums in the camp then
Announcing the hour of midday rites;
The king at once rose from the platform
And repaired into his royal tent.

Out there Shakuntala entered her cottage
Restive and unquiet in mind;
Again and again she stole a sight of the ring,
Unnoticed by her friends.

On some plea every now and then
She escaped from their midst,
And secretly reading the letters upon the ring,
Into raptures threw her heart.

The king's love-image
Newly installed in the temple of her heart,
Kept her being filled
With a heavenly sweetness rare.

The splendour of that idol of love
Brightening quick the shrine of her heart
Lighted up the courtyard of her face
Silhouetted in the gloam of her contracted eyes.

Thrilled was the damsel recalling
The royal hand's blessed touch,
Like a bud of *malli*
Unfurling in joy as the night spreads.

She mused – 'The one whom I adore in my heart,
Can I also offer him adoration with my hands?
He has incited a hope of another meeting,
But would he, at least for once, really come?

Oh, how sweet his form,
And how full of honey his speech –
No words those but sprinklings of nectar
On this new shoot of life.

No wonder it is, the entire being
Should burst into foliage with that nectar;
Even an inert form would assume life with its touch
Like Ahalya rising with the dust of Rama's feet.

Yes, doubtlessly he'ld come; but then
If he accepts me not as a maid at his feet
I'ld bide here, a hermit by name only,
Pining for him in my heart's agony'.

Her mind lay absorbed in thoughts of the king
While her hand performed the chores;
And she kept herself busy with other work when
The assigned duties were over.

She began weaving for him a garland
With flowers that were collected for the deity's worship;
And then, instead of fig-wood for sacrificial rites
She focussed her eyes on sandal-wood.

Her companions at the sight of her ways
Easily fathomed her mind,
And silently drew each other's attention,
Exchanging signs with their eyes.

For inside the cottage there sat,
Gautami, an old and revered female ascetic;
So the two friends were perforce mute,
Unable to tease the girl.

They mentioned in brief then,
Soliciting Gautami's view –
'The virtuous king of Hastina
Is camping here in the woods;

Quite likely it is, he would
Come over to visit this ashram;
Who, then, should extend him hospitalities
Since our father, the chief of sages, is absent?'

Calmly Gautami replied, 'Don't we have with us,
Flowers, fruits and water?
Easily with these can Shakuntala
Treat in due form the king.

She, you know, is the child
Of an illustrious one from the pure warrior-class;
And she would please the eminent warrior-king,
Ritually washing his feet.'

Priyambada cast a look at Shakuntala
And with mischief in her eyes said, 'Do you hear, friend?
Remember this counsel
To properly treat the royal guest.'

When she heard these words,
Bending her love-drenched bashful face
Shakuntala to herself intoned: 'This indeed is,
A most welcome coercion by friends.'

The sun then set, and with it ended
Shakuntala's innocence of earlier days;
A new evening now came for her
Grafting a new nature in her being.

It was a new life that transformed in her eyes
The sky, the wind, and the woods;
And in the heart of the new damsel grew
With the evening's deepening hue, a tender desire new.

New to her freshly-lit eyes appeared
The gleaming galaxies of stars;
And the flowers diffused a new fragrance
Displaying a splendour new.

As thus to her the world became
Sweet and enchanting, her heart longed
To enjoy the love of all dear ones
Condensed in a single being.

The friends with whom she had passed her days
Merrily roaming and playing around,
All the frolic and fun, and their company, too,
Seemed today dull and drab.

If one is used to saltless curry,
Quite pleased is the palate with that;
But once the tongue has tasted of salt
Does the heart any more cherish the earlier stuff?

The maiden now wistfully nursed a thought,
In moonshine she with her lover would stroll,
And hanging on his chest an exquisite garland,
Gratify her heart to the full.

The fragrant breeze of the garden then
Should be caressing his person,
And she should be joyously displaying to him
Creepers and plants she had herself grown.

Moonbeam-adorned leaves,
Tremulous in the soft breeze,
Should then make her feel fulfilled, as they
Steal away the loved one's heart with their silver sheen.

Clusters of flowers, blooming atop branches
Rubbing themselves against the loved one
Should consummate all her long effort,
In watering and tenderly rearing the plants.

As they would walk upon Malini's sands
The soft ripples, sparkling in moonshine,
Should delight the loved one,
Sprinkling diamond-like particles of spray.

Time and again she then should watch
    The dear face in contentment suffused,
Filling her being in bliss,
    While by a fountain of love would the eyes be flooded.

The young maid of new hopes
    Harbouring many such fond thoughts
Spent her new night,
    Full of new excitements and longings new.

The shoot sprung from the dear one's sight
    Watered by hope-clouds of future meetings
Caused in her heart to glisten forth
    Freshly reddened leaves of love.

CANTO - III

Flower of Love

The king passed the night in
Honeyed thoughts;
In the morning came nature
Baring a rare sweetened form.

He finished his morning ablutions,
And as though to take a turn thro' the woods,
Set out alone, grooming in his lotus-heart
The sweetness and grace of the maiden.

Things lovely as seen the day before
Today seemed lovelier far,
As if all those had been
Freshly washed in Shakuntala's sheen.

On whatever his eyes lighted, it seemed to say,
'Here in the woods is she, the beautiful one.'
And his mind wherever it journeyed,
Her charming image was upon memory's mirror flashed.

All that had yesterday appeared to his mind
Full of a soothing peace,
The same very things looked changed today,
Brimming with sweetness and splendour.

That which the king had earlier thought
Was covered with ash from sacred smoke,
Today he believed, it wore a coat
Of shining diamond-powder.

Flowers that with their lustre and fragrance
Had released a fount of devotion,
Their same very smell and colour today
Ignited flames of love.

That branch from which the parrot had seemed to preach
Glories of ascetics in the woods,
Seated on the same branch lauded the dove today
The good fortune of happy couples.

The deer and the doe that made one believe,
Had the nature of hermits imbibed
Appeared today changed, blissfully attached,
In ties of connubial love.

From the freshly-bloomed *bahada* tree
Wafted out fragrance sweet
While on every one of its branches were at play
Flocks of birds newly seen.

The gigantic Sal had decked its head
With a huge bouquet of flowers;
And the pink pollen of *kamalagundi* served
As coloured powder to beautify the woodland goddess.

Numerous creepers and trees unknown
With blossoms in myriad colours
Unceasingly adorned one another
In an urgent passion of love.

Bees stretching out all their six legs
Clasped the flowers time and again;
And humming sweet tunes of love kept
Smothering their faces with unending kisses.

Elsewhere the butterfly justified its other name,*
Fulfilling that which the god had ordained,
As a young groom visiting the city of blossoms
Its body in exquisite colours painted.

* Prajapati means (i) 'butterfly' (ii) 'God Brahma, ordainer of marriages'.

In leisurely steps as thus sauntered the king
Upon the banks of the river Malini,
And witnessed those scenes, his mind
Took fire at once and grew restive.

The universe so contrives
That men reap fruits after their natures alone;
The noble mind in elevation has nectar
While the debased has only venom.

And the mind of the lord of men,
Scintillating, exalted and virtuous,
Naturally impelled him towards
A gem dug out of the celestial mine.

He descended from the bank
And walked on the sands by the stream;
Soon he observed a forest of rushes,
Exquisite and dense.

A sandy path that led up there
Bore marks of advancing feet,
But none of retreat;
And so wondered the king –

'Who are the ones to have got in there,
And what are they engaged in;
With what intent do they tarry so long
When the sun is already strong?

The sands with the passage of time
Would grow hotter and hotter;
If they do not get back soon
How can they walk back later?

Or, maybe, the daughters of sages
Have chosen this entrancing spot
The scorching midday hours to spend
Inside the arbour of rushes.

With the transparent Malini nearby
Flowing on a gurgling note,
Whose heart wouldn't a captive be,
Of these lovely sandy bowers?

The couple of ruddy sheldrakes
Sitting on a branch, shaded deep
Keep ruminating there all by themselves,
Utterly quiet and still.'

Choosing a cool, smooth slab of stone
As a proper seat, the king
Settled down in a sequestered nook
In that enchanting forest of rushes.

Soon was heard nearby
A song in a dulcet voice,
And the king, first startled,
Sank into absorption rapt.

Sang she – 'Inside the woods behind a hill
Bloomed a lotus in a pond;
From its birth it had never known
The resplendent rays of the sun.

But now came the sun into her view
After finishing his southern tour;
It'ld have been well if he had granted only
His sight; but he also extended his rays (hands).

He had imparted hopes of coming up
In the morning once again,
And so the lotus had been alert and keen
Ever since dawn, waiting for his advent.

Doesn't he, the day's lord, the one
who illumines the world, know
The poor lotus, in all three worlds
Has no resort other than him?'

With the melody of the song was hushed
The liquid warble of the stream,
And stifling the crickets' chirp, the silent woods
Joined in imitation sweet.

Not high and treble was the song,
But sweet and gentle and deep,
It had not the strength nor pitch
To corss the banks or the hills.

The sheldrake on hearing the song
Tenderly gazed on his mate;
The *nadikulabandhu** too excitedly
Called out to his beloved to hearken.

Surprised, the dove fell silent first
And then poured out unbroken notes;
And the master-singer cuckoo cooed after,
To endorse the melodic tune.

The king's love-pool overflowed
With the continuous stream of songs,
And the river of his being swelled up, flooding
The scorched sands inside his heart.

Tossed here and there by the sweeping flow,
Leaping up, as it were, in frenzy,
Upstream sped the trout of his mind
Charged with a new energy.

As the peal follows the lightning
So the king catching up with his mind
Moved up the slippery path
And hurried near the arbour.

Keeping himself concealed he peered
Through a chink into the womb of the creepers
And saw Anasuya carefully weaving
A garland of forest flowers.

---

* A bird which prefers to live near river-banks.

Shakuntala sat there, her mind elsewhere,
But her eyes upon the garland,
And it seemed as though Priyambada it was
Who had just finished her song.

Now she smiled and to Anasuya said–
'Put away your garland for a while;
I sang as I could, and now,
Why don't you, too, sing?'

Anasuya rejoined merrily– 'My song
Is not something ordinary like yours;
Once I sing, the lord of her heart,
At once would come rushing in.

And then if the garland is not ready,
With what would Shakuntala worship her lord of life?'
But Shakuntala's mind was elsewhere intent –
She heeded not what they said.

Well knew Priyambada Shakuntala's state;
Artfully doing her friend's coiffure
Her ears and tresses she decked
With a dainty arrangement of flowers.

Meanwhile Anasuya had leisure enough
To finish making the garland,
And Priyambada coaxed again, 'Friend,
Do now sing a song.'

Play-acting, and laughing aloud, Anasuya
Cautioned her friend –
'Watch out, for the lord of her heart would come,'
And then began her song:

'The cuckoo arrives when the mango is ripe
And coos her bewitching words;
And so the lord of one's heart comes,
To fulfill one's desire when pieties are matured.

The moon, only when it sails upon a clear sky,
Can be drawn down on a mirror in hand,
And so would the lover come
Only when love is pure and strong.

Never has it been heard before
That a virtuous nature goes crooked;
But is it, god forbid, my friend's destiny
To suffer an exception here?

A connoisseur of jewels, can he ever,
Having seen a true one, turn his back?
Whoever under his feet tramples down
A flower in full bloom that has come to hand?

To whom, unless his tongue has gone sick,
Would nectar taste bitter –
Of which a small droplet even
Revives into lush foliage a dried creeper?

O my friend's lord of life,
Why do you only hide inside her heart?
Appear before her once in person
That joyously she might offer you adoration.'

In merry banter Priyambada chimed –
'Leave aside your song, my dear;
Compelled by your noble frog's croak
The king with lightning speed has come.'

Startled with the words, 'The king has come,'
Shakuntala turned her gaze, and saw,
The king, dear as her very life,
Standing at the mouth of the arbour.

The two friends jumped up,
And Shakuntala too at once sprang to her feet;
In a tide of embarrassment her companions
From tip to toe were sunk.

Shakuntala's heart swung to and fro
Floating upon waves of love;
All three stood, their heads hung down,
Not able to utter a word.

Priyambada then made signs with her eyes
For Shakuntala to hasten,
And wash the king's feet
With water stored in the gourd.

Shakuntala passed on the burden
To Anasuya, indicating with her eyes,
While in her heart of hearts she wished,
Her friend should decline the duty.

Anasuya meaningfully smiled and said,
'Bear your own burden, friend;
Fate hasn't granted me, nor have I earned
The right to such good fortune.'

Shakuntala performed then the customary washing
With love-tremulous hands,
While Priyambada prepared a downy seat
Spreading out fresh new leaves.

The hand of the maid and the young king's feet
So thrilled at the mutual touch,
That the wealth of the Lord of heaven, as it were,
Couldn't surpass their glorious luck.

On Priyambada's request then the king,
Squatted on the soft seat of leaves;
And felt a rare comfort and joy,
Transcending the feel of his jewelled throne.

At her friends' bidding did Shakuntala,
Hang the garland on the neck of the lord of men,
To her the lord of her being, offering withal
The dower of all her love.

With a smile said Priyambada, 'O king
With what gift can our friend,
A hermit-girl in a hermit's bower,
Please so noble a guest?'

'From your acceptance of water (hand) yesterday
We know, you are gracious by nature; and so,
It's only redundant for us, sages' daughters,
To speak thus, O generous one
(May the daughter of the sage be your wife).*

The only precious thing we have in this ashram
Is the wealth of flowers in the virgin's care
(Is the wealth of the flower-like virgin);
Make our hermit-world feel fulfilled
Receiving this gift with pleasure.'

The king lauded his own fortune, and happily mused:
'Whatever the sick man was longing for,
The doctor has prescribed, quoting authorities,
As the medicine proper for a cure;'

Then spoke aloud, 'The fruits of penance, too,
Are part of the royal revenue,
But you have made it, O hermit-maids,
(Only you have made the hand of the hermit-maid),
A deeply cherished necklace on my bosom.'

In the same vein rejoined Priyambada,
'Will the forest-flower be cherished
In the royal garden (harem),
Where there is a concourse of exquisite blooms?'

Replied the king, 'When from the heavenly garden
The flower-divine *Parijata* drops to hand
Naturally ignored and left unattended are
All other earthly blossoms.

---

* From this stanza onwards the puns are inscribed in brackets.

One of Shakuntala's friends then quizzed–
'O friend, how would the heaven's garden gain
(What would our friend's offspring gain?
After all, rivers, sharp-clawed animals, and kings,
Are not to be trusted in this world.'

And the other one replied, 'What would it avail,
For us to enquire of the heavenly garden,
(For us to enquire about the future son?'
At which the king exclaimed, 'True it is, all true,
She has the right to my answer
(He would be my heir).'

With the *rasa* of idyllic purity was mixed
Rasa of urbane grace; when the *rasa* of love too commingled,
As at conjoint Saturn, star Swati, and new-moon night,
They raised a squall of wild ecstasy.

As the sun in the darkening squall,
So was the king's royal pride,
Forced by the gale of love,
Sunk into oblivion in the arbour-sky.

Even the dry upland of the hermit-maids' beings
Was submerged in the flood;
The wisdom-ways were all lost to view
And their hearts went berserk along unknown paths.

Even though she understood all,
Shakuntala sat feigning ignorance,
With her head bent in bashfulness
And her heart aflutter and thrilled.

Her friends then noticed a fawn
At the mouth of the bower,
As if looking for its mother
In the throes of hunger and thirst.

Priyambada at once stood up exclaiming,
'Ah, how distressed is the poor fawn in hunger!'
Declaring then, 'Let me carry it to its mother,'
Quickly she left the arbour.

Anasuya stood up too, and playacting anxiety
Said, 'You take care of the fawn,
Giving it first a drink of water;
I will fetch its mother at once,' and forthwith left.

Shakuntala rose then exclaiming,
'Oh, I am left alone,' upon which shot back the king –
'Who then has kept me in this arbour
Having bought me with her love?'

'I know not'[1] she intoned quick and made haste to leave;
But the king played cleverly on her words, saying,
'Skilled if you are in the art of writing,
Compose here golden words, undisturbed.'

Replied Shakuntala, 'A forest-dweller am I,
I do not even know what is composition;'
And the king rejoined playfully, 'True, as you say,
O you of ambrosial speech, composition is a globule of nectar.'[2]

'From where can I have a nectar-globule,' exclaimed she,
'They say, it is only there in a full-moon.'
'That is speckled,' said the king,
'But your immaculate lips are nectar-full.'

Thus the hours slid by
In fun, frolic and banter,
Observing their ways through pores in the bower,
The sun felt impassioned and charmed.

Ever it is true, on watching another's love
One's own passion waxes large,
And so the sun extended his hands (rays),
Longing for his beloved Shade,[3] to the roots of the trees.

---

1. The letters differently spaced, the words would mean, 'I am familiar with the point of a pen.'
2. Pun on the Oriya equivalents of 'even' and 'what' to suggest 'nectar' and 'globule' respectively.
3. The Sun's wife.

And, she, too, with the sun's embrace
Swelling in joy, left the shelter of the trees,
And hurried out in eager passion
To sport in the arbours of the eastern hills.

Before she left she stretched herself long,
On the ground, clasping the mighty tree's feet,
And saying, 'I shall surely come, if
My companion of the moon-beam comes.'

From the nearby forest called out Priyambada
With suggestive words clever–
'O couple of sheldrakes, take heed,
The sun has already departed from the lotus.'

The king then left for his camp
And to the cottage was conveyed the lass;
In the heart of the beautiful one
Bloosomed out the flower of love.

Recalling to her mind again and again
The king's image as he took leave with a longing look,
And enraptured in thoughts of the sport of love,
The beautiful one passed her night.

The king spent a few days in the woods
Blissfully in love's abandon,
And then left for the city with a promise
Shortly to fetch her thence.

CANTO - IV

Fragrance of Love

To his capital returned the king,
                And in the forest bided Shakuntala;
In the damsel's heart kept frolicking
                His varied sport and fun.

Things that had always engaged her
                Now her heart grew weary of those,
And memories of new-found joys instead
                Crowded in to fill the space.

The forest-girl's world of fancy
                Was bustling with novel forms:
Palace, city, royal pelf, horses,
                Elephants and attendants - male and female.

Often was she in a flutter within
                Planning to leave for her husband's place;
But felt aggrieved, too,
                Thinking of parting from her childhood friends.

Soon she'ld depart from the deer and the birds
                Whom with such fondness she had reared;
So time and again her loving gaze
                Caressed their tender forms.

Sometimes she would keep standing near
                Trees and creepers she had grown,
And with pangs of envisioned separation
                Keep brooding over their future.

The affection showered in the ashram
Joined to the love-gale blowing from Hastina
Raised in her heart a squall,
Sending shivers of thrill, ever and anon.

For her in the beginning
In wild torrents rushed past time,
But as the days rolled by
It slowed to a languid pace.

For a sight of her beloved husband
The girl's yearning by degrees peaked,
Slackening time's pace to a point of stillness,
Evermore blocking off its course.

And then with her heart joined time
Ebbing away backwards,
While her imagination ushered in the ashram's guest,
The Lord of Hastina's land.

Engrossed it was in him wholly,
As she conversed in bowers or roamed through the woods;
Finding Time and Heart in delight thus,
Conscience as servitor followed.

Such the state that her body only remained
Seated before the cottage,
With no one nearby –
Neither her friends nor the hermits –

When arrived as guest the great ascetic Durbasa,
And stood there waiting in the courtyard;
He saw the young girl sitting in front
But speaking no words of welcome.

'Here am I, a guest,' announced the sage,
But Shakuntala heard it not,
For how could she, with her own heart
So far away, a guest to someone else!

Amazed stood the great sage;
Smarting under neglect and piqued,
He then upbraided aloud – 'You proud girl,
Where has your mind strayed?

Living in a sage's ashram, yet
You are so negligent of ashram-ways,
Forgetting the assigned duty, your mind
Keeps sporting far away!

Reap then the fruits of errancy
In refusing to honour a revered one;
He, in whom your heart lies rapt, would know you not,
Even when you reveal yourself in person.'

With these words the sage was walking away
When her two friends overheard,
For they were collecting flowers in the adjacent forest,
And now were greatly distraught.

Anxiously they rushed and prostrated before the sage,
And pleaded with prayerful words:
'O father, be gracious upon this poor girl,
And mercifully forgive her fault.'

The wrath of the sage cooled down
With the flood of the hermit-maids' tears,
Like a fire-singed mountain
Receiving showers from a pregnant cloud-mass.

Said the great sage relenting, 'If she has a memento
From the one she was recalling,
When she presents him that token
He would recognise her at once.'

Reassured returned the hermit-maids, and together conferred –
'The shores of the sea of peril are found,
But all these matters must not be
Revealed to the innocent girl.

The king has earlier gifted her
An exquisite ring of gold,
The same ring would now serve
To rouse him from the curse of oblivion.

Specially since on the ring is carved
The name 'Dusmanta' so deep and clear,
All the knots of suspicion would it
Sever away like sharp scissors.'

But one of them raised a doubt – 'Friend,' she said,
'There is one thing that makes me feel unsure,
In our conversation with the king
We had slyly parried with double-meanings;

And if perchance now he
Explains the words to her disadvantage,
Ah, then, the life of the young one would go waste,
Floating on a sea of infamy.'

At which the other one argued – 'Virtuous people
Ever read wholesome meanings,
And men of sound character always preserve
Harmony of thought, speech and deed.

Having acted then lovingly how should he
Now unfavourably interpret the words?
The essence of his speech and heart
In action were clearly manifest.

The countenance wreathed with feelings,
Is a content-page for the book of the human heart,
And the printed matter which follows
Brings out the sensations in elaborate form.

To me it seems the heart of the king
Is large and clear and pure;
It cannot ever generate
Dissimulation and guile low.

Remember, a king he is, and must be busy
Discharging the duties of royalty,
And, moreover, the sage's curse would block off
The path to his remembrance of love.

The promise he made to visit the place
Won't now possible be;
What is needed now is some occasion
To ensure a meeting with him.

As father says, "The richer the source of joy
The greater are the convergence of impediments;
You shall never have happiness if
Afraid of sorrow, you begin to fret." '

Both the hermit-maids then
Went near Shakuntala
And saw her still absorbed in thought,
With her left palm against her cheek.

She sat there like an idol;
And on the floor before her was written,
'Dusmanta,' which she kept tracing
With her writing-chalk again and again.

When her friends read aloud the name 'Dusmanta,'
Shakuntala looked up in excitement;
But there was no Dusmanta, only her friends
Standing there by her side.

At first she knew not what she had written,
Seeing which her friends so laughed,
Then read it herself and in love-stirred bashfulness
Hastily wiped it off.

Ignoring the friends' teasing she quickly then
Ran over her head her dusty palm,
One of the maids at which exclaimed, 'May all sorrow be dispelled,
By the power of the holy ash smeared on her forehead.'

With Gautami thereafter joining in,
The flowers that her friends had collected,
They offered in worship to the deity in the temple
With hearts all pure and clear.

Some days later sage Kanva of high wisdom
Returned to his ashram;
Shakuntala offered her obeisance at his feet,
And then quickly withdrew from his presence.

The other hermits, male and female
Greeted him with reverence, touching his feet,
And on the sage's kind enquiry
They were all very well, they said.

Then with the sage's permission they left
Each to his appointed task:
Some engaged in studies and some others in rites,
In their habitual manners each.

Shakuntala constantly kept to her friends,
And whenever she saw the sage,
With some excuse or the other betook herself away,
Always lowering her face.

Her virgin-like simplicity
Forswearing its natural ways,
Screened itself behind shyness –
With limbs drawn in, fearing discovery.

As he sat at the foot of a tree one day,
The great sage thought to himself,
'How is it that in Shakuntala's behaviour
Appears so much change?

Why doesn't she as before
Come to my presence and freely talk:
Whenever now she chances upon me,
With lowered head why does she slink away?

Not for once is she now to be seen
Careless, as before, in covering her body,
And the shine on her face looks different –
What, in fine, has become of her?'

A crow that sat atop the tree
Then cawed the message;
And listening intently the sage,
The secret history learnt.

Thoroughly then he knew
The love of Dusmanta and Shakuntala,
And felt happy that the mango-tree
Had courted the proper vine.

Happier still was he to know
The vine had already borne a tiny green fruit;
Content to know that his wish had fructified,
He lauded his daughter's good-fortune.

It was not proper, he reasoned,
That the daughter should now be in her father's house,
And so decided to send her with an escort
Soon to her husband's place.

He summoned Gautami and declared,
'My wish is now fulfilled.
I had gone out to perform some rites
So that Shakuntala might have a worthy husband;

And returning now I know, the King of Hastina,
Himself visiting the hermitage,
Has joyously accepted
The hand of Shakuntala in marriage.

Let her then leave for Hastina
To serve at her husband's feet,
No more is it proper for her to engage in
Austerities in this forest.

Rising very early in the morning tomorrow,
Accompanied by two other ascetics,
Convey my darling Shakuntala
To the palace of the king of Hastina'.

The words of Kanva like a joyous stream
Coursed through Gautami's ears,
And causing a tumult across the field of her heart
It swept on strong and fast.

Whose ears indeed wouldn't feel fulfilled
To hear the honeyed words,
That the girl one had nursed in one's lap since birth,
That image of affection, will be a kingdom's queen?

And, yet, naturally does the heart crack
As one begins to reflect,
That the very pupil of one's eye
Soon will be lost to it for ever.

The news spread quickly
From cottage to cottage,
Like the shadow of a thing that stands
Close to a lamp, lengthening itself out.

Laughing aloud, declared some female hermit,
'Well I knew it long before,
That the capital city of Dusmanta
Would be enriched with Shakuntala's presence.'

Another one put in, 'When dear Shakuntala
Attains her royal status,
The fortune of our ashram shall surely
Climb to its very zenith.'

Some one then snidingly said, 'Ah, such a lot has happened,
And I hadn't the slightest wind;
But who would know, if one on fast
Should gulp down water while taking a dip?'

And another chimed in, 'Oh, this lass Shakuntala,
How simple and innocent she looks;
But see how cleverly she has
Erected her fortune's mansion!'

Another one explained, 'You see, good luck favours
Those who come of a noble stock;
The mighty king has accepted her hand,
For she is a girl of royal blood.

It is, moreover, their innate qualities
That make individuals excel:
The point of the thorn of the wild
No one assists to sharpen.

Hearts of a common breed
Throb with concordant feelings;
Thus the cuckoo-chick, though nursed by the crow,
Is able to join its flock.'

Greatly pleased, addressing Anasuya then,
With a smile Priyambada said, 'O dear,
At last the canoe of uncertainty
Has touched a land of gold.'

Anasuya's face, too, was swathed in joy,
And happily declared she –
'True enough, friend, in all good things
The Omnipresent One is the unfailing support.'

When Shakuntala came to know
She feelingly reflected –
'No one in the world would equal a father
In forgiving the daughter's lapse.

Father has nurtured me in the ashram
With love of both the parents in one,
And yet I made over my life in a hurry
Without speaking to him a word;

Praised be father, the magnanimous one,
So indulgent with his dear daughter,
Even after he had noted her aberration,
His affection abated not, but his gladness grew.

My puny heart had restive grown
Without plumbing his depths –
For how should the coral creeper know
How deep the ocean is?

My husband had promised to return soon,
But has not come; and how should I
Fathom his love too,
For that also is like the ocean!

If my husband's love be like the sea,
My love would at least be a stream;
And a stream never demurs
Flowing into the ocean's bosom.

High hopes nursed of a noble person
Do not ever go in vain,
When the column of water-vapour upward climbs
The rain-cloud welcomes it in.

But will the bevy of his queens in the palace
Snigger at this my hope?
No matter; the river that plunges into the sea
Cares not for raised eyebrows of sneering waves.'

Fancies and conjectures of various kinds
Animated thus the ashram world,
And all felt excited to know that the day after
Shakuntala would leave for her husband's place.

Only for a day now would she be an ashram-girl,
And then move away to live as queen –
Knowing this the daughters of the ascetics
Flooded her with their ardour.

Unwilling were they to leave her presence
Even for moments few,
And kept by her side, looking at her
Time and again, in fond cherishment.

Shakuntala had no leisure at all
For any of her private thoughts,
Extending whoever came to her
Her affection and cordiality in double measure.

Observing such fervour and fondness in an ashram
The sun grew disgruntled and livid,
And angrily hastened to set
With a face all swollen and flushed.

Gods find it hard to brook
If the humans ever transgress proprieties;
For they always keep themselves restrained
Within their sacred, sanctioned bounds.

The evening in the forest of the sages
Resonated with vedic chants;
And for Shakuntala in the grip of impatience
It sped away fast.

Duties and rites of the evening over,
She retired for the night with her friends;
But they only lay on the beds with bodies stretched,
Keeping themselves busy in animated talk.

All three friends were keen
To convey their feelings in full;
So no sooner did one end her speech
Than another one began.

Sleep could not succeed that night
In advancing near the cottage;
She made for it time and again, but returned
When she saw the open door from a distance.

At long last did the sleep-goddess, followed by the goddess of dreams,
Push her way into the cottage,
And skilfully patted the maidens' ears
With tender, delicate hands.

But the girls kept waking up again and again
Resuming their pleasant talk till,
In the fond embrace of dream,
Their consciousness surrendered in defeat.

On dream's conveyance journeyed Shakuntala
And at the city of Hastina arrived;
To her the city seemed full of cottage-ranges
Large as hills.

In the king's palace hung diamonds and sapphires
Like clusters of *amla* and *harida* fruits,
And the women of the city were brisk,
Like ascetics' wives, in animated chores.

The bedsteads had feet of unblemished ivory
And their bars were made of gold,
Of a width that would equal, she thought,
The village carpenter's plane.

Strings of silk had been drawn across the bars,
On the bed were spread puffed cotton quilts;
Nearby were jewelled lamps on gold-stands set
With their wicks perennially lighted.

The queens were dressed in gold leaves fine
As bark clothes worn in the ashram;
They cast at her sidelong glances
As a does at a mare in contempt.

Before the crow had cawed came Gautami
And called out Shakuntala's name;
But the calls to rouse her
Uncannily slipped away into her dream.

Still wandering in her dream-world
It appeared to her as if,
Someone from inside the royal palace
Had called her by her name.

But Priyambada woke up quickly
And as she shook her friend who lay lost in dream,
Shakuntala felt it was some royal lady
Affectionately petting.

Her dream broke when she was harder shaken,
And the delicate one, with a start, opened her eyes
To realise she was still in a forest-cottage
Far from the forest of affluence.

Gautami called out again and said,
'Shakuntala, leave your bed;
Come, Priyambada; Anasuya, come,
Only a small bit of night is left.

A long time since have the drongoes called
Again and again in the woods;
The darkness at the night's end
Would in no time be all lifted.

The smaller stars are dissolved from view,
And the bigger ones are growing paler,
It seems the sun's path of ascendance,
Is already being swept clear'.

With a start then, as it were, the crows
Began loudly cawing on a sudden,
As if, they being asleep, some others were
Stealing away their treasure.

With Gautami the three girls then
Went to take their bath,
By which time a number of young ascetics,
With their bath over, had finished their vedic chants.

Her friends rubbed soap-clay
And washed Shakuntala clean,
And smeared on her body an *angaraga* then
Of powdered *gorochana,*[1] *nageswar,*[2] and *kumkum.*

Bath over, with her hair still wet and loose,
She put on some charming clothes,
And offered her salutations
Seeking the blessings of elders.

Blessing her Gautami said, 'O my daughter,
May you earn glory as the chief queen;
While another wished, 'May you be like Sita,
A mother of heroes.'

Someone there hearing the words,
Uneasily reflected within:
'Did not Sita give birth to heroes,
While in banishment in the woods?'

At this moment the moon with his silvery beloved[3]
Covered his face in pallor
And approached his western mansion,
Filling with discontent the eyes of men.

In the other direction the sun, keeping in front
Aruna, the blazing charioteer,
Was hastening to touch
The top of eastern hills.

Both these stellar beings showed to the world
Reversals they are to suffer:
For even as one is rising high,
The other one declines lower.

---

1. Dried yellow substance extracted from the brains of a dead cow.
2. A white flower of four petals, with yellow stamens and pollen.
3. Moonshine pictured as the moon's beloved.

The beauty of the lily now departed from view
And took residence in the city of memories;
No wonder that, for when the lover is abroad
Who can nurse any cheer in her being?

And so the bee forswearing the lily's quarters
Came to the doors of the lotus,
And chanting aloud like a morning-mendicant,
Annihilated her sleep.

The dew-drop upon the ripe blue water-lily,
As it swayed in the morning breeze,
Exultant with the embrace of the rays,
Trounced the pride of the ruby.

Giving up their sleep, the peacocks
Came down from cottage roofs,
And on the whetstone of sunbeams
Rubbed into radiance their jewelled feathers.

Near platforms their hooves had made uneven,
Stood the deer and does,
They straightened their necks, and back and forth
Stretched their bodies spruce.

Then, as ordered by Kanva,
A sage's son, Harita by name,
Brought there for Shakuntala's wearing
A tray-ful of ornaments.

Flocked a company of female hermits
And seeing the jewellery exclaimed:
'Oh, wherever lay hidden
Such splendid treasure!'

One said, 'These marvellous jewellery
Can't be of this earth:
It must be the celestial woman, Menaka,
Who brought them in the night.

It is said, all the earth's joys and sorrows,
Are clearly visible to heaven,
And the earth isn't so far away that
When spurred by a daughter's love, she cannot traverse.

Woman alone understands the feelings of her kind,
How by nature to ornaments they are drawn;
And even if she be inhabiting heaven,
Can a mother ever give up her filial love?'

Another suggested, 'The great sage himself
Had stored these precious things
So that his dear daughter wouldn't lack
Any ornament cherished by her.'

Harita clarified: 'The power of the sage is such,
This is hardly a marvel
That each tree in his hermitage
Boasts a treasure-trove.

Numerous kings, too, serve the lord of sages,
Each a huge tree of that kind;
Is it any wonder to acquire then
These few gifts from them?

You should know, accomplished sages never desire
Money or gems or ornaments;
All such riches crowd at their doorsteps
To be made sacred by their touch.

I went round the garden, you see,
At the sage's behest, carrying an empty vessel;
And no sooner with my hands did I hold it out
Than poured in ornaments from various quarters.'

A ticklish problem then arose
With the hermit-women at a loss,
For they could not guess, which of the ornaments
Should be worn on which limb, and how.

An itinerant female-hermit there
Explained it all to them;
Happily then Priyambada decked
Shakuntala's person with those jewels.

Finding a place on her body,
So innately charming and pure,
The ornaments shone out with a new animation
Like the lotus in the sunrays' bosom.

The rays of the morning sun, too,
Falling on Shakuntala's ornamented limbs
Felt blessed and danced in excitement
Spreading themselves out in exultation.

After being readied thus the new bride
Took from her friend a saree of red silk
And elegantly draped round her slim waist
And her body so graceful and fair.

Only that day did she know why it was
That in childhood her ear-lobes had been pierced,
And that day only she could feel
How silk differed from a barkcloth.

The great sage came then,
And with his loving eyes fixed on Shakuntala
Thought with a pang – 'Presently,
This my forest would be bereft of her.'

The heart of the noble sage
Was churned and convulsed with thought,
Like a pond in turbulence, as when
An elephant rushes in longing for lotus-stalks.

With agitation his eyes
Began filling with tears
As water-drops gather on lotus leaves
On their own in a disturbed pond.

If he had spoken then
The tears would have rolled down, for sure,
For if the body of the 'travellers'-tree' is pierced
Can its water be held back anymore?

Sentiments in a man's life
Would break forth clear at given moments;
And who in the world has sentiments none –
Whether house-holder or forest-dweller?

When she saw the sage there, Shakuntala,
Upon Gautami's advice, bashfully
Prostrated at his feet,
While her eyes were flooded with tears.

Thrilled with joy, in a choking voice
The sage pronounced his blessing:
'May you, my daughter, in all felicity,
Be a Ganga to the ocean, your husband.

And may you be blessed with a son
Graced with birth-marks of a supreme monarch.'
Delighted was Gautami as she commented,
'This is boon in the guise of blessing.'

The sage in a moment composed himself
And making Shakuntala sit by his side,
Lovingly counselled: 'My daughter,
Today you would leave for your husband's house;

Diverting yourself merrily with friends
You lived in a hermitage, an abode of peace,
But presently into affluence you would enter
Upon the wave-tossed waters of the worldly sea.

One who enters the sea without a boat
Courts terrible perils; and you must know,
For the worldly ocean the only ship
Is the husband's revered feet.

For a woman her husband is verily the Lord,
And heaven is at his feet; to the loyal wife
The goddess of wealth is a never-failing mate
And in the love for the husband her salvation lies.

The husband is a teacher, the most precious friend,
And service of husband a religious duty,
So you should perform all your actions there
With a mind in adoration tethered to his feet.

Even if it be some arduous task, delay not
In acting upon his words;
And never again take to a path for which
He has expressed his disfavour once.

The moment you see him coming,
Forget whatever grief you may have within,
And if he engages in banter, do not you
Retort, for he is not the one you should tease.

You must eat and sleep
Only after him;
And get up early in the morning
Before he leaves his bed.

Allow not your eyes the licence
To gaze at some other man,
And even if someone is a brother to you
Allow him not your company, when alone.

Should your husband get angry,
Or even talk chidingly to you,
Do not take it to heart, but serve him well
Bearing it all with a bowed head.

Cook his food and serve him
The dishes you yourself have made,
And while he is eating
Be by his side fanning him.

Engage not in your husband's service
Another female in your place,
As for maids who are not on the payroll,
Banish them at once from the palace.

Your husband has shouldered the world's burden,
And his feet now rest on your head;
Hence you should always keep in mind
The vast forbearance you need.

On jewellery and fineries be not vain,
And do not ever persist in pleading for them;
Whatever he offers, contentedly accept,
Trusting that as proper for you.

Regularly serve the mother-in-law's feet,
Taking her verily as a deity of the house;
She is the worship-altar of your husband,
She, too, the mine of all his affluence.

Do not feel put off by the sister-in-law's nagging,
Rather lavish on her yet more love;
If you find her in some sour mood,
Draw her to your lap and cuddle.

Look upon the other palace-women
Verily as your sisters,
And never do anything
Which they might view as an insult.

Rise from your seat at once
When elderly persons come near you;
Show your regard humbly, then offer a high seat
And speak in a voice gentle.

Do not laugh loudly,
And never ever in derision;
And by way of even a joke or in fun,
Treat not slightingly your maids-in-waiting.

Be always clean, and keep your chamber
All neat and tidy;
Pay heed to the woes of servants
And help them out of their grief.

If someone comes to you uninvited
And heaps on you gratuitous praise,
Know for sure, the visit is made
To deceive you with some guile.

A woman who narrates your husband's faults
And tries to rouse your pique,
Know for certain, she is an enemy to you
And treat her words as deadly venom.

Till today you thought this ashram alone
Was all your cherished wealth,
But now you must consider
The whole earth as your prized treasure.

The affection you profferred the ashram-trees
You must now offer the world,
And the love you had reserved for the deer and the does,
Now must embrace the humanity at large.

Like a sage your husband, too,
Adorns an ashram – the one of kingly rule,
You must then make yourself capable
To uphold its norms.

And, now, my daughter, come, proceed at the auspicious hour
With your mind focused on the lotus-feet of your husband;
Gautami, accompanied by two other disciples
Would escort you safely there.

O Saradvata, begin your journey,
Lead your sister along the path,
And Gautami, accompany your daughter,
While Sarngarava follows in the rear.'

And so walked Gautami, heading for Hastina
With Shakuntala's hand in hers;
Walked, too, the chief sage with all the ascetics
And all the ashram maids.

Shakuntala walked watching longingly
All her creepers and trees,
And painting them all in the canvas of her heart,
She treasured them coloured with love.

Now and then she did extend her hands
And caressed those vines and trees,
While in the guise of opening themselves out
They revealed their thrill, as if with hair on end.

A few of them when touched by her fingers,
At once shed their tears –
Some in the form of dew-drops,
And others of cascading flowers.

Those of the plants the gentle one
Released from her tender grasp,
They looked as though, with the pang of separation,
Deeply winced in heart.

The doleful plaint of the dove was heard
Pulsating through the woods,
And all the vegetation appeared to be
Spurting tears in recurrent grief.

But the forest's mate, the cuckoo,
Sweetly exclaimed with cooing notes;
And it seemed as if the woodland goddess
For the auspicious departure had a *hulahuli* raised.

Deer and does, peacocks and peahens
Stood along the path in rows,
Giving up their food and frolic
And looking on with sorrowful eyes.

Stealthily moving away from the flock,
A young fawn, hiding itself
Behind the end of Shakuntala's saree,
Kept trotting along close to her feet.

Some distance away when Shakuntala saw,
She tenderly stroked its body and face,
And expressing her sorrow before her father-sage,
Eyes filling with tears, said:

'O father, you know it how,
As you nurtured me lovingly in the ashram,
I, too, have fostered this fawn,
Orphaned since its birth;

I feel so anguished within
To sever its string of love and depart;
If I leave it behind, for some days now
It'ld be in agony, desperately looking for me all over.

And so, if you permit,
I would take it along with me;
If not, wrench away this child from me,
As I am being wrenched off you.'

The great sage shed tears when he heard,
And held the fawn close; then said,
'O my daughter, I know now,
How well you have known my pain.

The sun of love that manifests itself
Looming over this fawn as on the eastern hills,
Its rays would range through the city of Hastina,
The kingdom entire, its mountains and forests all;

Let this small fawn be here in the forest,
A crimson sky at dawn;
Now you move on, my dear, may all misfortune
Lie shattered into dust at your coloured feet.'

Then he turned towards the forest and said,
'O you creepers and trees,
Your friend from childhood leaves now,
On way to her husband's place.

That one who never took a drink of water
Without first watering your roots,
Who when she saw new flowers on you,
Used to be in ecstasy,

And used to celebrate the occasion
So excitedly with her friends;
Who used to preserve your heavenly beauty
With such tender care;

Who though craving for ornaments,
For fear you might be disfigured
Never stretched out her hand
To pluck even your leaves;

The same Shakuntala now departs:
All of you cheerfully then
Grant her leave,
May her parting be auspicious and sweet.

May her path be entrancing
With lotus-decked ponds by the side;
And bearing the fragrance of lotus,
May the breeze be pleasant and reviving;

May charming new sights occur to view,
Imparting joy to her eyes;
And may shady trees relieve the heat of the sun,
Refreshing her fatigued limbs.'

Pleadingly then Shakuntala enquired, 'Father,
Wouldn't my two friends accompany me?'
The great sage declined, saying, 'They, too,
Have attained the age of marriage;

It is not proper that they should now
Visit the city and the royal palace.
Gautami will travel with you,
But your friends will stay back here.'

Anxiously she asked, 'O how shall I,
Deprived of father's secure lap,
And away from both my friends,
Be able to survive among unknown women?

My sorry state would be like
A sandalwood creeper's –
Uprooted from its own *Malaya*-mountains,
And transferred to someone's garden.'

The great sage consoled her – 'When you are with them,
The ladies of the palace will
Keep your heart pleased
With honeyed words and sweet regard.

Happily would your mind enter
Your husband's forest of affluence,
And wouldn't allow a moment's leisure
To nurse for this ashram any wistfulness.

And a son would adorn your lap
Like the sun in the lap of East;
He would light up the whole palace
And be for you a source of ever-growing joy.'

Her friends then said, 'O dear one,
To whose care do you consign us?
Remember us, friend,
While sauntering thro' the royal gardens.'

The gentle one replied, 'I leave in your hands
The care of my trees and vines;
Immersed in the pool of your love, too,
The fawn wouldn't pine for me.

I know, even though I depart from you
I shall never be exiled from your hearts.
And, my dears, for my sake regularly water
The *niali*-vine's roots.'

She prostrated at the sage's feet
And then held her friends in an embrace,
Clasping them against her bosom,
Wetting their barkclothes with her tears.

Then said Priyambada, 'Friend,
You have forgotten the ring;
Take it here, keep it with utmost care,
This first token of your love.

Your husband, if he finds it missing,
Might suspect your affection has waned;
As a symbol of his love then, preserve this ring
With his name etched, as your most cherished treasure.'

Priyambada and Anasuya in a fast knot tied the ring
In Shakuntala's saree,
And mumbling, 'You'ld now be gone,'
Burst into tears before their childhood friend.

The sage had composed and sealed a letter
Which he now placed in Saradvata's hand,
And asked him to hand it over
While presenting Shakuntala before the king.

But again enquired Shakuntala – 'O father,
When may I next
Visit this hermitage,
And see your lotus-feet?'

Tender and solemn, the great sage said, 'When
The royal umbrella shines above your son's head,
And all the ocean-girdled earth is animated
In the shade of that protective cover;

And your husband, seeking liberation
    Comes to live as a forest-dweller,
And you, too, for salvtation desire to settle here
    Serving his feet – then, my dear, you come.'

Shakuntala then greeted in parting
    The holy folk assembled there –
Touching someone's feet, kissing another, and
    Embracing some other, as was her wont.

Then moved Gautami with Shakuntala,
    Saradvata leading the way,
And Sarngarava following behind,
    As a guard for the rear.

Slowly the fragrance of love
    Spread through Shakuntala's heart,
To dispel as she walked
    The overpowering strain of travel.

The large-minded sage returned to the ashram,
    Holding as equal both joy and sorrow,
With him went back the other inmates
    And repaired to their respective tasks.

CANTO – V

Worm Inside the Flower

Seated on a jewelled throne
The king of Hastina shone:
Verily, incarnate righteousness imaged on
The bright mirror of wisdom.

Exquisitely were ranged on either side
Ministers and courtiers –
Justice, Conscience and other virtues, as it were
Carrying the human form.

The king's countenance and his courtiers' faces,
Cheerful, glowing, clear and serene,
Looked like the consort of the autumnal night
Shining among a starry constellation.

The footstool near the throne
Was decked with gleaming jewels
To hold in embrace the gems
Upon the crowns of a throng of vassal-kings.

Clear Yamuna-water in a gem-studded pitcher
Was kept stored by its side,
To ritually fructify the tree of wish
That the earthly-gods planted, pressing their suits.

The royal sceptre in the king's right hand
Blazed with awesome splendour;
At its mere sight from a distance, too,
The pride of enemy hordes lay shattered.

Elephants' pearls that the mountains
Used to offer the king,
And the carefully chosen jewels
Which the ocean used to give,

Hanging with bowed heads
From the roof of the court-pandal,
Were dazzling gaily to receive
The fiery rays of the royal rod.

As serpents slither away to hide
When Garuda gives out a deafening screech,
So did the demon-hordes at the twang of his bow
Abjure the kingdom and their pride.

Compassion within the king's bosom,
And the silk raiment without,
Shone as his apparel, outer and inner,
Sovereign in the world of grace.

Irresistible on his heart was the hold
Of the virtues of the wise;
To him a blade of grass was the human body
On which jewels were but drops of dew.

Truth and fame in his own life
Were ever in contest,
With transparency and nobility
Vying with one another.

The king who was adept
In trying his subjects' cases,
Made over the right to the people at large
To judge that struggle between truth and fame.

Whenever he heard another praised
In delight his heart grew warm,
And then he applied himself all the more,
To surpass the good deeds of the praised one.

As the sun courses unresting,
As blows the wind night and day,
So was the revenue-earning king
Always at work for the weal of his subjects.

Ever was he keen, courting hardships himself,
To dispel his people's pains,
As does the tree which yields shade,
Bearing the glowing sun's scorching rays.

His rule was luminous
But its fury, too, was colossal –
No one could tread the evil path
Breaking through the fierce bulwark.

Into the court advanced a chamberlaine,
And with folded hands submitted –
'O Lord, some ascetics have come
From the ashram of sage Kanva;

There are two women,
Accompanied by young neophytes two;
With the noble master they desire an audience
But with what intent, it's unknown.

Of the two women one is old,
And the other is young;
I believe, a sage's daughter she is not,
But some divine damsel from heaven.

In the company of the ascetics, the maiden's beauty
Shines out with enthralling grace
Like an exquisite new one
Among pale, wizened leaves.

It appears the great sage has deputed them
With a letter in their hands,
If the noble master so instructs
They'ld be conducted to the royal presence.'

The king felt surprised
To hear the words of the chamberlaine,
But calmly ordered, 'Lead them directly
To the sacrificial fire-chamber, where I now proceed.'

At the lion-gate out there stood Shakuntala,
Thinking within herself:
'Oh, now would my husband hasten here
After he knows I am come.

Maybe he would himself lead me in
Holding me by the hand,
Or, perhaps send some female attendant
To cordially welcome me home.

Whatever be it, it is certain,
I shall soon my husdband meet;
But I wonder, where would he convey me,
Which mansion furnish for me!

Oh, how large are the buildings, how lovely,
Tall beyond the Sal trees;
How glistening white – the sheen of royal swans
Would look so poor by their side!

How should I know the revered mother-in-law,
And my sister-in-law, too, among all?
Whom should I embrace in affection,
And whose feet should I honour?'

Why these idle thoughts, O you anxious one!
For your future is all so different;
Ah, that human intellect were granted
Entry into the city of the things to come!

At this time approached the chamberlaine,
And conveying royal consent
Escorted all four visitors
To the king's presence in the fire-chamber.

Saw the king – among the ascetics
A lovely girl, tender-limbed,
So easy to distinguish, like a piece of diamond
Among pebbles of rock.

With cheerful demeanour the king
Cordially greeted the hermits
And made kind enquiries of their well-being,
As also of the sage and the hermitage.

Saradvata responded politely, saying
All were in excellent state,
And the king then wished him to make plain
The purpose for which they had come.

And Saradvata made over to the king
The epistle sent by Kanva;
Breaking the seal as he cheerfully began to read,
The king's heart was filled with wonder.

The lotus-heart of Shakuntaka meanwhile
Had not the slightest inkling
That soon in the fire-chamber's flames
All her hopes would be singed.

The king read through the letter, looked upwards,
Then read the piece again,
Turning the matter in his heart,
In disbelief, over and over again.

Again and again he looked at Shakuntala,
His eyes in apathy shrunk;
And his heart growing sorrowful, thought –
'Most astounding this, indeed!

It is nothing strange at all
If a knave commits hundreds of frauds;
But most strange it is if
A hundredth of a perjury in a saint is noticed.

Chicanery which fills the sage's letter
Exceeds a hundred frauds; it'ld make even a sage
Tear in exasperation his matted hair, and die;
Should such a thing ever be read or heard?

I fail to know if magic or truth it be;
What answer can I possibly give!
Or is it that I misread?' Thinking so
The king read through the letter again.

No doubts now lingered about its import,
Yet he cogitated in silence –
'Oh, this must be some delusion
The gods wish to beguile me with.

Else how is it possible to find such beauty
Down below here on the earth?
And how incredible that Kanva the old ascetic
Should have such a daughter with him!

The limbs of the hermit's daughter, again,
Are decked with heavenly jewellery;
Am I such a fool, then, not to understand,
And take this letter on credulous trust?

Oh, come my wits, my conscience come,
Preside over my heart and strengthen me;
So that, whether this be truth or guile,
I respond wisely.'

Thinking thus he said aloud, 'O young ascetic,
I have read the missive, and its sense I gather,
But what the sage has written is not
An act, or a duty that my position behoves.

I never entered into wedlock
With this girl here; and so,
Before a scion of the Purus today
Has been enacted an absurd play.

If the girl were not already married
And if she weren't quick with child,
I would not worry the least
In carrying out the sage's wish.

I wonder how, being himself of the Puru-stock
The sage had this urge,
To paint in dark the glorious moon
Of his own ancient race.'

At this was Saradvata inflamed and asked,
'Is everything false here, then?'
And the king retorted with a smile,
'O ascetic, this indeed is magic plain!'

Saradvata turned to Shakuntala and said, 'Look, dear,
Remove the dark film from the eyes of the king,
And prove how you became
His lawful wife.'

And Shakuntala murmured, 'I understand not,
Whether all this is real or a joke;
But I tend to feel certain
He is only probing my heart.

Only the clever ones know
How wittily talks the king,
And frames his utterances in jest,
Endowed with multiple meanings.'

Dusmanta queried then, 'Is it true, O beautiful one,
You know me well, and I have courted and held your hand?
Have you, indeed, looked upon Dusmanta's face
As that of your husband?'

And Shakuntala answered, 'I hear right now
The voice that won my life;
Has the lotus ever blossomed,
Without herself gazing at the sun?'

Dusmanta asked her again, 'Look at me closely,
And judge if, indeed, I had courted you;
Do you firmly believe
That I was the one you really married?'

Saradvata joined in, 'Sure, observe the king's face
And prove the truth of your marriage.'
Shakuntala demurred, 'How should I look at his face,
When he doesn't admit he is my spouse?'

But then continued, 'However, I have his love-present,
A ring with his name inscribed;
That is the testimony of our love,
Please place it in his lotus-hand.'

And the king said, 'If that is in your keeping,
Why all this needless talk?'
Quickly then she lifted the end of her saree,
But, alas, there was no knot, nor ring!

This end and that she desperately twisted
But no sign was there of the ring;
A long time before had ill-luck
Cleared its passage clean.

At her discomfiture then laughed out the king,
And said, 'Look close and search,
And let it be proved that king Dusmanta
Blatant falsehood speaks.

Find out, O ascetic, and delay not,
Present the ring before me,
And right now will your hermit-girl
Be anointed Hastina's chief queen.'

The heart of Shakuntala winced and shook
Shamed by the sharp insult,
And quick out of her eyes flowed
Two long streams of tear.

She recalled in pain, her friend had said,
It was the key to her heart's love-temple;
But she had been remiss, and after the loss
To go on living, she felt, was impossible.

The world grew dark,
She went dumb,
And all her Himalayan hopes
Were turned into dust and blown away.

She wasn't sure
If her body still pulsed,
And couldn't know
Where she might go, how stay.

As she fainted and sank down
Gautami held her close, sat on the floor
And looking at her face agonised,
Uncertain whether she lived or had died.

'Alas, alas!' cried the two young ascetics,
As they sprinkled some water on her face:
They found her breathing faintly yet,
Though the pupils of her eyes were set.

But the king was sore, and mocked,
'Why do you put up this terrible show;
Why don't you speak out quick and free
What design you have in view?'

Touched to the quick retorted Sarngarava,
'Little do we care for wealth and status,
But the leading character of this drama
Will certainly meet his doom.

Alas, O Destiny, alas the god of justice,
That we have to listen to this charge –
That one nurtured from infancy in the ashram
That innocent girl, is an impostor!

Now kingly duty is reduced to
Deceit and torment of women;
O goddess of wealth, with what temptaion do you still
Refuse to spurn this palace?'

The king rejoined, 'O young ascetic,
Blending anger and pity, but without
A grasp of things, why do you
Exhibit such puerile temper?

When one sees this young maid's misery
Sharp does one's hair stand on end;
I believe, someone in my guise
Has deceived her cruelly.

By this lovely maid, a fountain of beauty,
Even gods would captivated be;
Some lecherous one, adopting guile
Must have stolen there a dip.'

Sarngarava argued, 'If gods felt tempted
Why should they adopt your name?
Couldn't they have succeeded in their amour
Keeping to their divine forms?'

And Dusmanta said, 'Women by nature fight shy of the gods,
And seek rather the web of human love.
Hence it was that gods took Nala's form,
Hoping to gain Damayanti's favour.'*

Said then Sarngarava, 'In all our thoughts and deeds,
Such our training, such initiation,
We never wish to be falsified,
Nor anguish to enter the pious life;

But every living being must partake of action's fruit,
And none can subvert the rule;
Crossing over hundreds of hurdles it pierces –
So inexorable the fruit of action.

---

* Story in the *Mahabharata*.

And so Shakuntala, stay on, your duty follow
And bear your fruits of action.
No more must we persist here in vain
With non-holy petitions.

Brother Saradvata, lead on please,
We shouldn't here tarry a moment longer;
Let us go, Gautami – else we might fall
A prey to terrible sin.'

And so began Gautami walking away with the hermits,
Leaving the hapless girl near her husband:
When the sorrowing one returned to a shadowy sense
She thought she had been left to her consort's care.

Observing the ascetics' conduct
The king in derision said,
'How marvellous, O hermits, you leave behind
The "fruit of action" with me;

The dynasty of Purus would be widely famed
With this glory of a bastard child!'
Hearing which in Shakuntala's credulous heart
The creeper of hope brought forth fresh foliage:

For the poor simple girl had mistaken a letter,
And understood 'whose' for 'a bastard';
Like the *chataka*-bird that drinks the new rain
But regards not the fearsome roll of thunder.

How should the *chakora*, that sustains itself
Sucking nectar from the beams of the moon,
Ever a suspicion admit
That from the very same orb would drip poison?

How could she believe
That the waters of the king's love,
So ardently wherein she had immersed herself,
Had into a rock of ice now turned?

'So be it', loudly pronounced the hermits,
And hastened away from the palace:
Thus it was that in the womb of Kunti
Their words on the Purus took effect.

No one can get away with
Sneers at pious folk;
And, yet, even the taunt that hits the pious
Comes to serve some human good.

Nor did the word-sense Shakuntala held
Finally come to be wrong,
For her son in time was able to achieve
All that his mother had cherished.

Those naturally virtuous in their hearts' innocence,
If perchance from their path they stray,
Destiny forgives them the lapse
And fructifies all their auspicious desires.

Soon then the dazed girl
Regained her sense,
Nursing within herself a belief fond
That all that drama of rejection had been merely for fun.

Since the sorrowing one knew
The great king excelled in humour
She drank up all that poison
Thinking it was but nectar.

So the native lustre returned to her face,
A new splendour swathed her being;
And the astonished king then wondered,
Was she the goddess of royalty incarnate?

Always had the care of that goddess
Cheered and animated his life,
But the care of the present goddess, he was afraid,
Would insufferable and crushing be.

The great king was in distress,
Dazed and bewildered, unsure of his duty,
Ruing his ill-luck that so unforeseeably
A mole had entered the cobra's throat.

When the royal priest saw the king's state
He reassuringly said, 'O great king, do not grieve;
Your son will be born
With the signs of a monarch on his limbs.

So many sages, and astrologers many
Have affirmed this time and again;
That alone would the right test be
Of the truth of Kanva's missive.

Let this youthful dame till the birth of her child
Be housed here with care;
And then the royal master may decide,
Whether to accept, or repudiate her.'

The king consenting, in gestures asked
The priest to take her home;
As she stood there with her head meekly bent,
The innocent poor thing noticed it not.

The priest then kindly bade her, 'Come, child, come
Let us now leave for the quarters;
Have faith in *dharma*,
By the power of that shall you prosper.'

And so walked the priest with Shakuntala behind,
Her eyes unwaveringly on his heels,
And the unlucky creature thought she was
Being led to the apartment of her heart's master.

Had she known she was not being escorted
To the hallowed mansion of her lord,
Her very life would have been in jeopardy,
And how could her feet have moved at all?

As they walked there appeared on the way
    A woman of rare splendour,
She drew the girl by her hand and said,
    'Come, my daughter, let's go to my place.'

Confounded as the priest stood there, and mumbled,
    'Oh, what is this; Oh, what is this,'
He could know nothing of the uncanny woman,
    From where she came, and where took the girl away.

The king came to know from the priest
    How the girl had been spirited away;
But could not know how a canker-worm
    Had forced itself into love's blossom.

One whose mind is pious, ever upon her life's path
    Is auspiciousness crafted by *dharma*;
Thus the world which Shakuntala came to inhabit
    Against shafts of grief was armoured.

CANTO - VI

Fruit of Love

In the home of Winter was born a son,
A cherub bewitching,
Seeing which He, in unrestrained joy
Went reckless and wild.

He gifted away baskets numerous
Of thickly woven cobweb-apparels,
And purificatory feasts spread out,
Offering countless ripened grains of wheat.

He flung into the wombs of fields
Sugarcane sticks in pieces
And to the gallants doled out
Multi-coloured fineries patterned with blossoms.

Turmeric-hued letters, sweet and auspicious
Were flown in all directions;
And for the heat-oppressed people
Numberless umbrellas were unfurled.

To deliver the message to skiey tribes
The whirlwind carried the cards,
Raising for itself a stair of dust
In spiralled columns tall.

With his heart by pity moved
He brought back the lotus from exile,
And freed Morning that was shivering in cold
From the prison-house of mists.

Night was suffering a long sentence
Bearing fiery braziers;
He granted her pardon and handed a reward
Of ambrosial moon-beam candies.

Persistent and nagging, the damsels of the quarters
Took all the fine, crimson silk,
And ever greedy for radiance, the constellations,
Looted the fair of splendour.

The yellow-flowered *sunari* and date-palm,
Kept busy crafting necklaces of gold,
And the silk-cotton plants their needles plied
Weaving away canopies day and night.

The missives received, all trees and creepers
From the woods, cities, gardens and villages,
Assembled in the hall of Winter
Their hearts with cheer filled.

Dwarf plants like the *palasa*
In the company of lofty Mangoes and Sals
Displayed their hauteur,
Drawing strength from their wooded fraternity.

And behind them stood ranged
The *mahua*, *sirish* and *kanchan* trees
Decked in fineries and jewellery,
Each to the measure of its wealth.

Dazzling the sky with a white coat
In great arrogance the towering Neem,
Pierced the formation of plants
And occupied the pavilion in the assembly of trees.

Dressing them as heavenly men and maidens,
In divine ornaments arrayed,
Into the inner courtyard had *champak* conveyed,
Jasmines various – *madhavi, niali, malli*;

And by them stood for service
manjuati, kuruvaka, karnikara,
Baula and *bakama*, carrying on their heads and ears,
Clusters of colourful flowers.

Came there blossoms in groups,
Came, too, the concourse of birds,
And embellished the meeting place
With exquisite charms, exotic and native.

The south-breeze came there to convey
Gracious blessings from sage Agastya,
Pausing midway upon the Malaya mountains,
Lured by its sandal-wood fragrance

At the auspicious naming ceremony,
Sweetly the honey-bee blew a conch,
And all there assembled concurred,
The young child's name would be Spring.

A feast of honey was laid out,
With groups of flowers merrily serving,
Where the conch-player bee swallowed more and more
With many a wile and guile.

After they had lapped up the honey,
The priests (birds) kept eating up the containers,
Watching which startling scene, the trees around
Stood there dazed in wonder.

The cuckoo which had come from afar
Sweetly intoned a benediction,
And all the priests endorsed the wish,
Shouting in chorus, their assent.

The body of Winter aged soon
And became weak and wan,
But Spring waxed larger like the moon-digit
And grew accomplished in his tasks.

Winter then made over the kingdom to his son
And settled down by the hills,
There shed his body in rigorous penance
Lighting up a fire around.

Having been born he had to die,
So would he be born again,
And all that he had gifted away
Would be stored for his incoming reign.

King Dusmanta upon a day then,
Desiring a view of spring's enchantments
Was loitering by himself
Inside the woods upon the river-bank.

And there into his ears flew
Tuneful melody of a female voice,
And his being was seized with a thrill,
As the mushroom's upon the cloud's rumble.

He followed the song in bated stealth
And arrived near the source;
There stood with his ears pricked
And the sweet song joyfully savoured.

But the more he heard the song,
The more restive he felt within,
As if he was desperate for the shore,
Lost in a sea of oblivion.

Saw then the king a woman there,
In her lap she held a child,
And a young girl by their side stood
Thrilling the woods with her pulsating tune.

Sang she, 'With what hopes of bliss
Does the bee a fresh-blown lotus spurn,
And in futile exercise
Keeps hovering near the bamboo-pores?'

Approached them then a man,
Carrying varied flowers in hand;
And the moment the child saw him
It sprang out in joy from its mother's lap.

'Father, my father,' it called aloud
And clambered up his breast,
When the man joyously held it close
Extending his eager arms.

All four were alike endowed
With beauty's affluence,
And when they grew jubilant together
Four-fold grew their splendour.

As the *chataka* when in the sky it sees
All four clouds* gathered on a sudden
So in the king's heart they roused
A longing sharp and intense.

But like a herd of deer
At the scent of a tiger,
They glanced around furtively
With their hearts going aflutter;

And in a moment vanished into the forest
Far out of the king's sight,
While his heart kept throbbing
With their loveliness dancing within.

To his eyes then seemed all dry and joyless
The forest range and the plains,
And he slowly returned, pausing ever and anon,
With his heart pining for that bliss.

All royal pomp and pelf
Lost their allure,
And the sweet vernal days and nights
Felt drab and dreary.

---

* *Drona, Puskara, Sambartaka and Abartaka*, as mentioned in the Puranas.

His mind failed to grasp
What joys his heart now sought;
And whatever pleasures the mind prompted
The heart, revolted, at once spurned.

Rising love for Shakuntala in the king's heart,
Compelled by Durbasa's curse,
Like a hungry tiger inside a cage,
Had grown fretful and unquiet.

One day thus as the king in the pavilion sat
The police chief approached;
He bowed to the king, and
Handing over a ring, humbly said –

'O Lord, in course of the patrols today
A fisherman has been caught;
He had with him this royal ring
Which had been missing earlier.

The fisherman claims he caught a fish
In the waters of the holy spot of Sachi,
And as he cut the fish,
He found this lodged in its bowels.

Supporting his claim
The ring does carry the smell of fish;
The royal master's name, too,
Is clearly engraved on its face.'

'Oh, is that so?' exclaimed the king,
And as he began to examine the ring,
All at once flew open memory's doors
To light up the event of his wedlock.

Knew then he, what sage Kanva had written
Was true to every letter;
And the king fell speechless awhile
Stuck in amazement, anguish and remorse.

Seized with wonder he then mused,
Marvelling in astonishment,
But succeeded not in piercing
The forest of mystery, dark and deep.

On the king's orders then,
Brought into his presence, the fisherman
Spoke in deep humility
Shaking the while, and his voice all tremulous –

'O great king, Justice-incarnate,
I am a fisherman, and no thief.'
Said the king, 'I don't wish to know
What caste you are.'

O lord of virtues, I only caught the fish,
Punish me if I have erred.'
'Ah, trite it is
To narrate the story of the catch.'

'O great king, I am the lone earner
Feeding a family large.'
'Fisherman, needless it is
For you to be so garrulous.'

'Save me,' cried the fisherman
And fell at the royal feet,
Wetting the ground with the sweat of his body,
Tears streaming down his eyes.

The king turned to the cashier, saying,
'Bring a hundred coins of gold,'
Hearing which the fisherman,
His wits all gone, went limp in his heart.

For he had lain prostrate there
With his forehead upon the floor,
And thought he had been fined
A hundred coins of gold.

A terrified being always mistakes
Every wholesome thing for evil,
Even the note of the cuckoo startles him
As the voice of some malevolent spirit.

So wailed aloud the fisherman,
'O great king,save me, O save,' he begged,
'Not in seventeen generations have my forefathers
Ever seen a hundred gold.

And if your highness, unconvinced,
Decides to punish this poor thing,
Do the favour with a kindly heart
To order me into the prison.'

The treasurer then returned
Carrying in his hand a hundred coins,
And the king spoke to the fisherman,
'Here, take these as your reward.'

All were uncertain whether it was
Remuneration or a piece of sarcasm;
The fisherman stood up, and seeing the coins
Closed his eyes and hung his head low.

Then slowly spoke, 'O Sir, I couldn't know,
It was the royal master's ring;
How could I, an illiterate, lowly thing?
Had I known, I'ld have brought it directly here.

Let the royal master keep his ring,
And allow me to return home,
And if such be the master's kindly wish,
Only some copper coins let me have.'

At the king's bidding the police-chief
Took the sovereigns himself
And forcing apart the fisherman's joined palms,
Filled his cupped hands with gold.

'Go, go now,' said the king,
And the fisherman slunk away,
Pausing on the way off and on
And looking back with incredulous eyes.

The king had the ring,
And his life was anguish-filled;
Not for a moment then he had the wish
To engage in diversions or royal duties.

Wherever he was he thought he heard
All the world iterating a complaint –
'King Dusmanta upon his spouse inflicted
Humiliation unspeakable, unmerited.'

When he sat upon the royal throne,
It questioned him, as it were,
'You repudiated your innocent wife,
How are you then worthy of me?'

When inside the palace, it seemed
The royal mansion chided –'You have spurned your own';
And if he went into the garden he felt
The trees were shaking in terrible ire.

When he went round the city he thought he heard
His subjects saying to one another,
'Ah, what a pity, the king allowed not
His charming wife, wholly guiltless, into his quarters!'

The shelduck lamented through the night,
Wailing till she was spent out, questioning,
'Would my husband, too, spurn me,
On the precedent of king Dusmanta's justice?'

At night's end heard Dusmanta
The drongo voicing his faults,
And in the morning he noticed the bee
Whispering to the flower – 'Dusmanta is a traitor.'

Flocks of birds sailing across the sky twittered,
 'Though born in the race of Purus,
King Dusmanta in rejecting his lawful wife
 Performed a heinous act.'

Eating lotus-stalks in a pond
 Noisily squawked the swans:
Believing it was a piece of lotus-stem,
 The king has swallowed venom.'

Imagining nature thus full of scorn,
 Brooded the king –
'I have sinned greatly
 Spurning my beloved dear.

Like one gone insane I thought
 The great sage's honeyed words were bitter;
I renounced wisdom, grew dead in reason
 What escape can there be now?

What might the great sage be speaking of me
 And what my beloved's feelings be:
What strength of righteousness do I have now
 To punish lecherous hypocrites?

The king who is himself by a sin tainted
 And punishes another for a similar fault,
The God of Justice in severe wrath
 Scourges him a hundred-fold.

For which of my virtues would now
 The goddess of royalty be fond of me,
When rule of law is debased into
 Falsehood, betrayal and innocent-shaming?

What fiend was it that seized my mind
 And caused such awful delusion!
I took the encircling arms for a serpent's coil
 And the goddess of grace for a demoness.

Will I ever find my darling again?
I made her suffer, and am in torment now,
I might search and spot her in some ashram or woods,
But with what face can I then approach her?

After they have known of their friend's sorrow
What must Anasuya and Priyambada be saying?
Ah, that I sought my might to display
Hitting a tender *sirisa*-flower with a lethal mace!

Striking the flint of trickery,
Their cordial garden-hearts I set aflame,
And now having singed them, I burn myself
Consumed by terrible agony.

What can I do with a mind caged in this body
Like a nested bird in a fire-gutted wood?
To prescribe atonement for my sin,
Even the scriptures would be beggared.

I have decorated my chamber-walls
Painting her figure with these my hands;
But how should I see her in person now,
For she might take fright at my tigerish face!

Bashfully when the beautiful one
Used to detach herself from me,
I used to protest, "O my dear, you can't ever thus
Run away from my heart:

For when at the end of the day
The shadow recedes further and further,
The tree keeps her tightly close
To its root in a clasp of love.

But ah, tender one, delicate are your limbs
Like the *sirisa*-blossom,
And I harden your heart
Like its tough green stem."

Alas, that I distanced her,
Making of myself a stone –
Harder has my heart now grown
Than the ruthless thunderbolt.

And so the divine family in these woods
Inhaling my nauseous reek,
Couldn't tarry here a moment even
Fearing the contagion of sin.

Oh, how sweet and moving
That divine one's filial affection:
Even before he had extended his hands
The love-glowing child had raced to his laps.

Merrily laughing and forcing his way
The young one climbed his father's lap,
And at his feet placed, as it were,
All the three world's joy and grace.

She upon whose laps the child played,
Must have been his mother, I guess,
How blithely did he rush from there,
And adorned his father's lap!

Such was my nature, every mite of virtue I saw in another
I'ld imbibe and enlarge – making a palm-fruit of a sesame-seed.
Oh, the pity that with my own hands today
I have emptied my dower of filial love.

Fascinated by the delights of
Roaming thro' the woodlands here,
The divine family had come from heaven,
To savour the sweet ambrosia of spring.

Ah, damned be my wit,
That I viewed my beloved, the ornament of the woods,
The very image of spring-time grace,
Only as a sufferance!

Matched with my beloved's charms, sugar-sweet,
Mere molasses are spring's beauties;
Could there be a greater dunce than me
Who thought the sugar was sand!

It was my beloved's company
That enhanced the world's beauty,
Which in the grief of her separation now,
Lies pitifully crushed and bruised.

The flowers and creepers and trees
That in the ashram I had seen,
Used to appear to my eyes
As if freshly come from heaven;

But the full-blown flowers, creepers and trees,
By men even more adored,
To my eyes appear today
Harsh and pale and rugged.

My beloved's company had attuned the ears
Keen to the sweetness of sound;
And the call of forest-birds because of her
Lent a warm ardour to the heart.

Parrots, mynahs and cuckoos with their notes
Should natutrally delight the ears;
But all their mellifluous tunes today,
Jar when my beloved is away.

The very same flower in my beloved's hand
That gladdened me with fragrance sweet,
With its scent wafting into my nose now
Rends my heart with a searing conflict.

While eating fruits from her hands
I had counted even ambrosia as nought;
Without her by my side, to my nostalgic palate
Even more luscious fruits taste bitter.

When I sat beside her, I learnt
The surpassing worth of a seat of leaves.
But now in her absence the silk-cotton downs
Prick as a bed of its thorns.

All the world's joys are of a union born,
As warmth and coolness in summer and winter;
When either is absent the other becomes
The dwelling of terrible pain.

My beloved as winter, away from me,
Must be shivering in pitiless cold;
While I a summer, without her,
A burning frame here inhere.

Will ever into this scorched life come
The season of fragrant union,
And all at once dispel my day of heat
And the accursed dark night of her pain?

Like the wintry night my beloved
Must be dropping unending dewy tears,
As my eyes like rain-clouds
Send down unremitting showers.

Will the severity of my misfortune
And the dense mist of her grief, ever dissolve,
And the sky of my fortune clear up,
Bright with the happy moon of autumnal union?'

He then looked at the ring with tearful eyes,
And said in sweet chiding,
'Alas, you luckless ring,
Incomplete must have been your penance;

The merit of pieties that placed you
On the exquisite finger of the beautiful one,
When those pieties got exhausted
You couldn't stick a moment more.'

Moving into the inner apartment
Where the portrait of Shakuntala hung,
He held it in hand, drew close to his bosom,
And kissed the face time and again.

Upon the forehead of the painted beauty
Glistened drops of sweat;
And strands of short, curly tresses
Sodden, stuck upon it as if glued.

The starry pupils lowered in bashful glance,
She had cast an oblique look,
The gaze that had caused to sprout in her heart
A fresh young shoot of love.

Closely as he peered once and again
The vision of the king grew blurred,
But the image of his beloved and the ashram
Rose clear in his heart.

His mind was sucked into the image,
The sense of the outer world was gone,
And like an inert figure of wood
The king dropped to the ground.

A long while later he regained his sense;
And gazing on the image again and again,
The rare and sacred glory of love
Enhanced a hundred-fold.

In sorrowing nostalgia thus spent his days the king
Recalling the joys of his beloved's company,
And his conscience with his heart and mind
Rested in the shade of a creeper of hope.

Earth has no perennial joy nor grief;
All things suffer here decline -
The face that with cheer is lit up today
Tomorrow is shadowed by grief.

In the same measure as someone enlivens the heart,
So, too, the same one causes anguish;
For the more a thing can absorb heat,
The more, too, it gathers cold.

The earth gets immersed in murk
For the same length as it brightens in light;
So the fruit of true love is
Bitter as much as sweet.

CANTO - VII

The Shade of Love

By the seashore below the blue hills
Strolled along one day the divine daughters –
Peace, Geniality, Compassion,
Mercy, Fortitude and Devotion.

They culled from wooded creepers
Malli, madhabi, niali and other jasmines various,
While the bees kept flitting about
Between their baskets and the blooming vines.

A joy natural to their hearts,
To which was joined the bliss
Of a sweet melody one of them poured forth,
Thrilled their inner beings.

Upon their backs swayed
Thick plaits that tapered down,
With their ends grown bulkier,
Decked with wreaths of stringed pearls.

The damsels' limbs shone clear
Through diaphanous clothes;
And all four quarters were nectared
With the splendour of their faces.

The forest ground grew beauteous
With their feet that gleamed as water-lilies,
Feet that lured the hearts of ascetics
Craving for godliness.

The young leaves were elated
To kiss the sheen of those lovely hands,
And swelling in joy the blossoms, their trees and vines left
Hoping to be cuddled by those divine palms.

Birds and deer crowded near them
To play and frolic like children;
Some opened their bills, some longingly watched,
Conveying their hunger and thirst.

There then arrived Violence,
Daughter of the king of demons,
Her nails were like the kites' talons,
And her teeth as those of tigers.

Bear-eyed and owl-voiced,
Of speech loud and harsh,
She insolently claimed her supremacy
And towards Compassion charged.

Seeing the demoness the deer and the birds
Took to flight uncontrolled,
And the forest-ground with its trees and creepers
Shook in startled fear.

Irate, the demon-princess picked a quarrel,
Seeking to drive away the divine daughters;
With her tongue single in a slanging match
Trounced she the entire host.

The damsels from heaven using strong words many
Chided her long and loud;
One of them taunted – 'Your tongue lolls and drools,
At the sight of birds and deer.'

Another spurned her – 'Go, touch not, touch us not,
For you daily eat horse-flesh and beef.'
Yet another jeered – 'Your limbs are bloated
For you gorge on pork and lard.'

In anger shook the demoness,
She charged with her teeth and nails,
And bruised deep the limbs
Of all the divine daughters.

Their bodies were bathed
In streaming blood,
But restrained by the words of Mercy
They withdrew from fight, and for heaven left.

Demoness Violence went to her father
And against the heavenly maids complained,
Bitterly narrating how they had
Rebuked and treated her with contempt.

The demon-king waxed wrathful
To hear of the insult to their race;
His eye-balls rolled furious
And his body uncontrollably shook.

Indignant, roared the royal minister,
'These selfish gods, they guzzled all the nectar,
And still in unappeased hunger,
Our food they thieve and plunder.

Using guile, and on plea of sacrifices
They eat up horses, oxen, sheep and goats,
Never have they refrained from the evil deed
Of looting our share of food.

That exquisite forest
By the sea-shore below the blue-hills
Where fowlers weave their nets
Has always been our domain.

Those daughters of gods our realm trespassed
And fearlessly roamed around,
And, on top of it, scolded our princess, too,
Mouthing harsh words long.

Should we ignore this now,
Where a finger has entered the whole arm would soon follow,
For an entire vessel is drowned
By water pushing in through a small orifice.

Often have they taken us for a ride
With various deceits and tricks,
But can they really resist
If now we exert our might?'

The courtiers stood up one by one –
Avarice, Arrogance, Hostility, Guile –
And with loud voices endorsed the words,
Shouting, 'True,entirely true it is.

Promptly then the demon-chief
Advanced with all his army,
And with shouts of furious challenge
They shook the gates of heaven.

When the king of gods saw the demons
Mounting an assault at the city's gate,
He despatched an army
Backed by warriors experienced and skilled.

The chief among them were,
Zeal, Daring, Intelligence, Patience and Might.
They engaged with the demons in pitched battle,
Displaying fierce valour.

But the demon-hosts
Of Passion, Greed, Arrogance, Indolence, Luxury,
Charging from the evil camp
Swallowed up the strength of heaven's army.

Some hid under damsels' aprons,
Some ran to their kinsmen's shelter,
While some others torrents of perspiration shed
Inside mansions treasure-filled.

In that fierce demonic war were heaven's soldiers
Hit by swarms of arrows, poison-tipped –
Some on the head, some on their chests,
And some others all over their bodies.

Steadily rose their pain,
And agonised they lay,
Not having any ready relief
Even in Aswinikumaras'* hands.

Rushing to the king of gods, ruefully the general said,
'The demons' skill is invincible;'
And these words pierced through the ears
Indra's heart. He quailed in fear of the demons,

And turning to heaven's preceptor beseeched:
'Revered teacher, kindly advise a remedy,
Else all this realm of the gods
Would be vandalised by the demons.

Lord Hari had instructed
That we should protect the blue-bills,
But the demons who have directly pushed into heaven –
How can they be curbed on the earth?'

To read with his wisdom-eyes, Brihaspati,
Drew the lines that reveal truth,
And reciting from scriptures before the king of gods
Explained the effects of action.

'O Celestial Monarch,' said he, 'A great sin it is,
To beguile saints with deceitful temptation;
The tree you planted wrecking Biswamitra's penance
Has borne its fruit today.

Also Durbasa, considering not
That for a woman her husband is foremost
Among those worthy of reverence,
Wrathfully upon Shakuntala pronounced a curse;

---

* Divine physicians.

Under whose influence a blameless Dusmanta
Suffers now deep torment.
And because of the grief of a pious being
This world of the gods has its glory lost.

King Dusmanta is righteous and just;
If you can properly honour and please him,
The demon-menace will soon be dispelled
By the power of his virtues and pieties.

That king bears in his noble person
Essences of various gods,
And he is eminently skilled
In extirpating demon-hosts with his divine shaft.'

The king of gods when he heard,
Ordered his charioteer Matali –
'Go soon, make ready the carriage with care
And quickly journey to the earth.

There you offer king Dusmanta
Our invitation as cherished friend,
And cordially seating him in the divine chariot,
With due regard conduct him into heaven.'

Bowing to his master in obeisance,
And having decked his carriage
With flowers from the Nandan garden and jewels many,
The divine charioteer left.

Soon he presented himself before the king
And conveyed the invitation of the chief of gods;
With various delightful words then pleasing the king,
Persuaded him to ascend the chariot.

Ritually purified, respectfully the king
Went round the divine car and ascended it.
Driven by Matali, the horses then
Pulled the chariot upon the path of the gods.

Fast it moved and reached
The eastern portals of the celestial city
Where lofty bejewelled gates
In splendour shone;

Where spread across the quarters, like clouds,
Troves of gems brought from the ocean's depths;
Densely strung together,
They filled the sky with a starry radiance.

Man's instinct of greed in abasement recoils
When the gem-studded skies he beholds;
For, dismayed he reflects, 'How can a well,
Hold in its womb all the rains?'

But only one greed had filled the king's heart –
To savour the excellences in others,
Which the art of heaven's architects appeased,
And in pure joy his inner being revelled.

Through the spacious gateway the king
Entered the city of gods,
Where he saw the lovely forms
And exquisite attires of heavenly folk.

Goddesses with their bodies pure and fair
Dressed in shining raiment,
With loving eyes and cheerful mien,
Intently gazed at the king.

A woman he saw stood watering there
The root of a plant in the garden,
She looked at the king with a saddened face
And then quickly lowered her eyes;

Again and again watched the king
The face of that beautiful dame,
And mused – wasn't it she who had once
Beautified the woods upon the river-bank?

Again he watched and saw
Her companion-maid walking through the garden,
Carrying upon her hip
The child he had seen in the forest;

The youth who had collected flowers there
He saw there wandering,
Paying no heed at all
To the advent of the king or the chariot's sound.

Curious, the king asked Matali –
'Do these four in the garden
Ever remain confined to heaven
Or, on occasions, roam the earth?

May I know, O divine charioteer,
What their names are?'
'Hear, O King of the Hastina region,
Their names,' said Matali,

'Love is the youth's name, Affection the dame's,
And Felicity the name of their son:
Sometimes they visit the earth,
When some place fascinates them.

The one to whose bosom the child clings merrily
Harmony is her name.
The community of gods is nurtured well
On fruits in their orchard grown.'

At once then the king understood
Why they had vanished from the woods,
And sadly bowed his head to know
Even while in heaven, of heavenly joy he was shorn.

Meanwhile the chief of gods, when he heard
The king from earth had arrived,
He came and escorted the guest by his hand,
And seating him on a throne offered a divine welcome.

Then he narrated at large the story
Of vandalism by the demons,
Hearing which at once the king
Set out to destroy the evil host.

Demon-messengers rushed to their king
To convey him all the news.
'O Demon-chief,' they said, 'King Dusmanta
In high spirits advances to do battle with us.'

The demon-king turned to his preceptor,
Soliciting his opinion; whereupon the latter
Pondered a while and enlightened him
With a wise reading of the past:

'O demon-chief, when the gods are
In fear of the demon-hordes,
They fall back upon the prowess of humans
Which they strengthen with divine powers.

The great warrior Ravana of ten heads
Had vanquished the heavenly beings;
But with all his clan Time's subjection he bore
Afflicted by fiery shafts from human hands.

The root of contention was then
Ravana's sister, Surpanakha by name;
And now it is because of your daughter
That our demon-race is grown belligerent.'

Hearing the words of his preceptor
The demon-chief understood;
But putting on a brave front declared,
'In fighting an ordinary human, what glory is there?

If in fear of us the gods have now
Turned to the humans for help,
Clearly exposing their pitiable strength,
Doesn't it prove we have won?

Let us then unfurl our banner of glory
And march back to the beat of victory-drums,
Leaving the craven hearts of the gods here
Quailing in fear of demons for ever.'

Thus with all his army and attendants
The demon-chief withdrew to his realm,
And heaven's herald declared the happy news
In the presence of the king of gods.

And so Dusmanta's expedition turned into
An ocasion festive and grand,
And all the damsels of heaven
Showered flowers upon his head.

The world of the gods with sweetness overflowed,
With *apsaras* dancing and nymphs singing;
And loud did the divine chamberlaines shout,
'Praise be to the scion of the Purus.'

In his immortal form came Yayati,
And joyously blessed the king;
So too in his heavenly shape came Puru
And gifted a celestial garland.

Fondly then Indra placed Dusmanta by his side
Where his son Jayanta rightfully sat;
Melted in deep joy then,
On the neck of the king he hung his divine necklace.

Then approached both Harmony and Love
And embracing the king
Happily said, 'Go, O lord of men,
On the earth you shall now have joy.'

And so the king bowed at Indra's feet
Humbly seeking His leave,
And Matali was instructed by the chief of gods
In comfort to conduct him home.

Indra himself gave a hand,
Helping the king ascend the divine chariot,
And cheerfully wished, 'Go son,
On the way may your desires be fulfilled.'

The king on his way back
Visited the *Nandan*-garden,
Where along the path strewn with flowers of gold
Tree-trunks bore some inscription.

Approaching, he read the divine letters,
And knew they were verses metred –
'With the fragrance of King Dusmanta's pieties
Delighted is the realm of the gods.

In the guise of the flowers of Nandan
Have bloomed the petals of his fame,
And amid the petals the image of his inner being
Shines as lustrous gold.

Only pure and sacred love resides
As honey in the womb of those blossoms,
And the Great Friend of the universe,
As tender dew there His blessings drops.'

Perusing no further his own eulogies,
The king wished the chariot to go faster,
But when he alighted on the sands of the heavenly river,
Saw he again hundreds of elegant scripts.

With strings of shells had been written out –
'Bravo, bravo, the race of the Purus,'
Which the royal swans of heaven read
And recited upon the river.

The king took a turn while listening to them,
And then climbing the chariot again,
As he proceeded, thanked his good fortune
In the hearing of the divine charioteer.

Crossing the sphere of clear winds
　　Soon did the carriage reach a realm
Where cloud-masses kissed
　　The heads of lofty mountains.

Droplets of clear water that the chariot wheels
　　Sprayed out in friction with the dense clouds
Happily did *chataka* birds drink
　　Issuing from rocky caverns.

Often did the bodies of the horses
　　Blaze forth in lightning-flashes;
And soon thereafter came into view
　　The earth's green surface.

Peaks of mountains appeared as if
　　Climbing upon skiey steps,
And the earth seemed holding aloft
　　The hills in its giant hands.

Was it that suspecting the king
　　Of celestial amours, and piqued,
The earth-dame was receding farther and farther,
　　As the chariot neared more and more?

But soon it seemed as though her companion,
　　Sweetly reassuring the earth-dame,
Was escorting her near the noble king,
　　Returning in glory from heaven.

Trees that had seemed supine on the earth
　　Now appeared to be raising their heads;
Like sleeping birds as they woke up,
　　Flapping their wings and popping their crests.

On the way was a mountain, Hemakuta,
　　Where lived the semi-divine *kimpurusas*.*
The mountain glowed like a cloud-mass,
　　Glazed in twilight by the sun's rays;

---

* Mythical beings – half human, half divine.

Whose feet were washed with sea-waves
By the chief of gods and the god of the sea,
Who offered *arati* with the sun every morn and eve,
And chanted aloud prayerful verses;

Attaining the bliss of tender friction
Upon whose colossal form,
Clouds remained glued like fragrant smear,
Forgetful of the task of showering rain;

Where all twelve months
Revelled spring, sporting every kind of flower,
And in great jubilation wandered the bees
While the community of cuckoos kept cooing;

Where pool after pool did lotuses of gold
Spread out their beauteous fare
And where in the houses of the *kimpurusas*
Resplendent gems dispelled murk;

And so in stealth did the rays (hands) of the Sun,
Full of trepidation,
Advance upon the deserted noon-hours,
To touch once the golden lotus-dame.

Melodious bird-calls there
Were the only rivals of *Kinnaris'** songs,
And the only kind of rain they knew
Was the everyday shower of flowers.

Dew-drops fell in proper measure
To nurture the blossoms and fruits;
And roots and fruits in abundance lay littered
After all had had their fill.

A community of ascetics on the mountain lived
Secure in their performance of austerities;
And the god of success, too, offered daily worship,
Finding it hard to leave the place.

---

* Semi-divine women.

There lived Kashyapa with his divine consort,
Progenitor of gods and demons:
The devotion of both the races
Lighted up the mountain exalting.

Animals that lived upon the mount
Had no enmities ever;
They were always at pains rather
To serve their mutual good.

With keen affection did the tiger there
Carry fresh shoots of grass to feed the fawn,
And the baby elephant was delighted
Eating wood-apples from the paws of the lion.

Eagerly did the king solicit Matali
To expound the mountain's glory,
And the latter in effusive terms
Dwelt on the joys of the place.

The king wished the chariot should touch down,
And he should at Kashyapa's feet pay obeisance –
He marvelled to see it gliding at once
Upon the ground as in the sky.

Its wheels did not sink in dust and sand,
And bumped not on uneven ground;
Sailing along, as it were, like a swan
Upon wind-free, still waters of a deep pond.

And so the king turned his gaze on Matali,
Full of incredulous wonder,
And came to understand how the cars differed –
Those of the king of men and of the king of gods.

Not far from there he saw a sage
Standing still like a rock,
His body from toe to waist
By an ant-hill covered.

Along with the sacred thread was slung
A band of scales a snake had shed,
And a tangle of withered creepers encircling
Afflicted his neck.

Immobile stood the sage
With his face towards the sun;
In the matted hair flowing down his shoulder,
Some birds had made their nests.

The king stepped out of the carriage
And respectfully greeted the sage with palms joined,
Then filled his heart and being
With heavenly bliss at the ashram's view.

He saw the shaded ground
Under the ashram's wish-fulfilling tree,
Cooled by irrigating water
And heavy with fragrance of golden lotuses.

Ruby-stones like slabs of rock
Lay scattered here and there,
And celestial women moved about
Dispensing affection all over.

Watching the ways of those heavenly dames
In the king's heart rose a desire
To adore their feet and please their ears
Fondly calling them 'mothers'.

Wondrous it was that such penance went on
In a world to be attained as fruits of penance;
And so the king reasoned –
Those sages kept austerities only for others' good.

The place was far more enticing he felt,
And more delightful, too, than heaven;
That, he felt sure, was the place,
Where mankind should enjoy all their fruits of penance.

Mused the king – 'Men with selfish ends engage in austerities
And go on courting hardships,
But deep joy is made manifest
Only in penance one performs for others' happiness.

One who has risen from a lowly state
Well knows the things that at the base prevail,
And so he strives from his eminent position
To dispel the miseries below.

Even I experience an impulse here
To gift away all my felicities to the world;
How then should those habitual renunciates
Selfishly savour their bliss?'

Indra's charioteer meanwhile left
To convey the tidings to Kashyapa,
And the king waited beneath an *Asoka* tree
Watching the nearby woods.

Into his ears then entered the words:
'Release it, release it, you naughty one,'
And turning, he saw a young child
Holding a lion-cub by its mane.

At the prowess of the boy
Marvelled Hastina's king,
And slowly approached close
Curious to watch the play.

A female hermit admonished the boy again,
'O you naughty child, let off the cub,
Should the lioness grow angry,
All your childish pranks would end.

How reckless you are, you pull away
A lion-cub while it is being suckled,
And then begin to count its teeth –
Do you think it is just a fawn?'

But the boy was unmoved and pushing out his lips
Taunted her – 'So easily frightened,'
And then all the more forcibly
Pulled the cub by its mane.

Another female-hermit said, 'O friend,
Is he afraid of anyone ever –
Else how could he elicit from the sage,
The name of Sarvadaman*?

And then hinted with gestures –
'Tempt him with playthings and toys,
Else he would continue to detain
And pester the lion-cub.'

The first one sweetly pleaded, 'Free, my dear,
Free this young cub here,
Its mother must be anguished in heart,
To see the distress of her child;

Now take from me a toy
And amuse yourself.'
At once the boy stretched out his hand,
Demanding urgently, 'Give me, give me that.'

In a flash saw the king the child's palm
Lovely as a fresh-blown lotus,
Where all the signs of a future monarch
Were gloriously housed together.

'Wait, we'll get it for you,' said the hermit- woman
And hastened away from the place,
While forcibly holding the cub, the boy declared,
'I shall let it go only when you fetch me the toy.'

One of them returned then
And looking at the king complained,
'O Sir, see how this wicked boy
Doesn't release the lion-cub.'

---

* The All – subjugating One

Observing the boy the heart of the king
Melted in fond emotion,
And he intoned within himself, 'Praised be the man,
Whose offspring is this valiant lad.

A strong desire stirs my heart
To hold him in my lap and kiss his face;
But how would the little boy accept my affection,
For I am an utter stranger?

How sweet must be his touch
Whose sight is so heartening!
The temptation to feel his touch
Seeks to override the joy of sight.'

Thus did two emotions furiously contend –
Enticement of touch and delight of sight;
And the king's heart, like a field of battle,
Into turbulence plunged for a while.

Then said the king, 'O hermit-child,
Why so unquiet? Give up this warrior-mood,
And conduct yourself with the lion-cub
As befits the nature of a young ascetic.'

But the hermit-woman corrected him –
'No, sir, this child is no hermit's son.'
And the king mumbled, 'Oh, I mistook him,
For he lives in an abode of hermits.'

Fondly then the king
Held the boy by his hand,
And, as he gently freed the lion-cub,
Removed, too, his own heart's pain.

As when melted together,
Two pieces of gold become one,
So did the endeared child grow one with the king
With the solvent of sweet affection.

The hermit-woman saw,
The king bore the child Sarbadaman,
An exact likeness of form,
And her heart began to dance in marvel and elation.

The king kept holding the child's hand,
Delighting in the joyous touch,
And addressed the woman, 'O gentle lady,
In which race is this noble child born?'

'He is of the race of the Purus,' he heard her say,
And reflected within,
'Aged Purus during their declining years
Into the forest usually retired.'

He asked her again, 'Is it possible
That humans may scale this height?'
And she said, 'Well, that constraint
Applies not to the mother of this boy.

She was born of a mother
In the line of the preceptor of gods,
It was through her ill-luck that
She had to deliver this child in the woods here.'

'The mirage of hope,' thought the ardent king,
'Is slowly shaping into a lake,
Soon would it be known whether or not,
I enjoy a right of entry into that.'

Then wonderingly asked, 'Do you know perchance,
The name of the boy's father?'
At which she sharply spoke, 'It's prohibited here,
The name of the impious to utter.'

The king was waxing keen to know
The name of the boy's mother,
But restrained himself thinking,
'Most unseemly would be the query.'

Meanwhile came the other hermit-woman
With a clay-peacock in hand,
And coaxed the child, 'See, my dear, for once,
See for yourself this bird's loveliness.'

Mistaking *Shakunta*, the bird, for 'Shakuntala',
The child demanded, 'Where's my mother, where?'
And the woman explained, 'No, not your mother,
I wanted you to see this charming peacock here.'

Cogitated the king,
'Yes, Shakuntala is the name of his mother,
But so many fortunate women bear that name –
This doesn't yet remove all doubts.'

Ran the boy to the hermit-woman,
And took from her the peacock of clay,
His lips wreathed in smiles
Radiating pleasure deep.

The woman saw missing on the child's wrist
His protective talisman,
And so began looking for it,
Anxiously scouring the place.

The king saw it lying nearby,
And even as the hermit-woman in great agitation
Cautioned him not to touch,
Picked up the talisman from the ground.

Seeing which both the hermit-women
Upon their bosoms placed their hands,
And seized with awe and astonishment,
Exclaimed aloud in ruffled voices.

Surprised, asked the king, 'Why, what's the matter,
Why are you so frantic?
Do you apprehend, because of my touch,
Some danger to the well-being of this precious kid?'

'No', she denied, 'No harm at all
To this wonderful child;
But, touched by a man other than his father
The talisman would turn into a venomous snake.

The boy himself and his mother, too,
May safely hold it in hand;
Should someone else attempt to do so,
It is certain to cause his death.

Indra's father had gifted it to the child
When its birth-rites were being performed;
It contains a divine herb that destroys all evil,
And is called *Aparajita*, the invincible.'

Questioned the king then, 'Has it ever
Handled by another, caused his death?
'Not just once, but many a time
Have occurred such mishaps,' she said.

Reassured, reasoned the king, 'What doubts more
After all this evidence?
Certain it is this child here,
Is my beloved Shakuntala's offspring.'

Exclaiming, 'My son, my son', in a surge of passion,
The king clapsed the boy in a deep embrace,
And his tears of joy streaming out
Wetted both their frames.

Protested the child, 'Leave me alone,
Why do you handle me thus,
You are not my father,
He is Dusmanta, Hastina's ruler.'

Refusing to heed the child's protests
The king showered kisses on him,
At which the child and the hermit-woman
Stared wide in utter amazement.

Bliss crowding in on bliss
Waltzed round the king's heart,
And his mind and being in exaltation
Felt completely fulfilled.

One of the hermit-women hastened away then
And to Shakuntala conveyed it all;
Hope in her burgeoned quick, but with it
Faith didn't commingle.

So she went up and herself saw
The child in his father's lap ensconsed;
Her feet were mired in perilous grief
But the surface a throng of gay lotuses adorned.

The boy gazed at his mother's face,
And in wonder and surprise said,
'O mother, why does this person here
Hold me, and keeps calling me his son?

My protest he refuses to heed
And draws me to his bosom time and again,
Just look at him mother, why does he
Feel in his heart so happy?'

Saying this the child stretched his hand
And clutched his mother's,
While his other hand remained captive
In the king's loving grip.

He did not draw away his hand from the king's
Nor did he release his mother's hand;
Pulling them together he dispelled their griefs
And their mutual joy enhanced.

Neither had the scope or leisure
To pour forth the feelings of the heart,
For like Bhagiratha did the child unite
The gem-filled ocean with the celestial Ganga.

When she heard the words of her son,
The being of Shakuntala was in nectar drenched,
And the hair that stood on end at her husband's sight,
Was, verily, a shoot of love sprouted fresh.

Her smile didn't play on her lips,
But suffused her face and eyes,
Like water inside a new pitcher of clay
Seeping out through the pores all over.

Separation from her husband, the beautiful one had believed,
Had been contrived by her own mother,
And so had she lived there, continually
Recalling his love and longing for his sight.

Always had she thought she had herself failed
In requiting her husband's love,
And desired, if she could meet him,
Humbly to beg pardon at his feet.

The king, too, believed he had greatly sinned
In not having adored his idol of love
On the altar of his fervent heart,
Transgressing thereby a religious duty.

How should he now expiate his sin, he pondered,
Offering what excuse –
Would it in any way satisfy his beloved
If he explained the way the ring was regained?

The agony of six years' separation
Was suddenly blown away;
And fondly watching each other's faces
The couple were immersed in a sea of nectarous joy.

Exalting like the moon, the child there
Had stretched out his hand (rays),
So the ocean of conjugal bliss swelled
Breaking loose waves upon mounting waves.

The holy mount itself was thrilled
To watch the joy of pure connubial love,
And all the buds then blossomed out,
And those already in bloom tumbled down.

Seized with a new joy flocks of birds
Chirped out sweet notes,
And the fawns began to frolic and caper
Drawing away from their suckling mothers.

The preceptor of demons and gods
Arrived there at this juncture,
And with their palms joined together
Prostrated at his feet all three.

The great sage smiled and blessed,
'May all your sorrows abate,
And may this gem of a prince in your race
Wax in resplendent glory.

Rising from the bosom of the eastern horizon
The Jewel of the Day adorns his mountain-pad;
Ended is now your night of sorrow
That the darkness of despair had shrouded.'

Loving and genial, the great sage
Led them to Aditi, his divine consort,
And to her introduced Shakuntala
Together with her royal husband.

Humbly did the king with his wife and son
Offer worship at Aditi's feet,
And the divine mother sweetly, joyously,
Pronounced her benediction holy.

In groups came hermits
To see the king,
Some averred he was a man, some god,
And thus went on the debate.

Kashyapa addressed the king and consoled –
    'Entertain not any remorse,
It was a curse by sage Durbasa that had
    Wiped off your memory of love.

The ring whose influence would have
    That memory revived,
Shakuntala lost it while bathing
    In the holy waters of Sachi.

Her heart was rivetted on you,
    All her mind at your feet,
And so she remained unaware when
    The ring through her *anchal*-knot slipped.

A fish which then was sporting in the water
    Swallowed it as some food;
That ring finally reached you
    Through the fisherman who cut the fish.

Shakuntala's mother, when she knew
    A period of tribulation had ensued,
She conveyed her up here
    To be looked after in this ashram.

You see for yourself the potency of this place
    Where pains and sorrows can't enter;
Also you must understand, in your own conduct too,
    No trace of deceit was there.

Rather your glory is enhanced
    By the self-denial you courted in deep remorse,
And under its influence has
    The earth's seed of sin dried up and perished.

Go now with your wife and son
    And happily rule the earth,
Which, in the absence of a lord like you,
    In anguish lies overwhelmed.'

The king offered his parting salutations
At the feet of the sage-couple,
And walked some distance with his wife and son
Upon the holy ashram-grounds.

Then he ascended the chariot
And held the little prince in his lap,
Also made his noble beloved sit by him
Joining his hands to her lotus-hand.

The chariot of Indra by Matali driven
Covering the distance in a trice
Blazed forth its divine splendour
Upon Hastina's royal road.

Seing which the city's inhabitants
Shook the sky with victory-shouts,
And bidding Matali adieu, the king,
Entered his inner palace.

Shakuntala was made chief queen,
And her son the crown-prince;
In all directions echoed the roll of drums,
Spreading the fame of the king and his queen.

The royal couple grew as of one soul,
With only their bodies held separate;
Evermore did their life become pleasant and sweet
In the shade of sacred love.

Madhusudan Pati

KICHAKA BADHA

CANTO – I

Grand upon the earth stands the city of Virata
Pleasure-house of Laxmi,[1] charmer of all worlds;
The market like a wreathe of tall white buildings
Sits enticing as silver hills in array;
Pearly mansions topped with domes of gold
Appear majestic as ash-smeared Shiva,[2] with crescent moon on head.
Ranged are the shops like harlots deck'd,
Shrewdly luring in men, mind, money.
The royal street stretches, charming as Mandakini [3]
With frolicking children as gold lotuses shining.
And women in flower-bedecked plaits,
Glow as creepers of *Parijata* [4] in bloom.
With tender-limbed damsels, lotus-faced and sweet,
The royal house charms as a lotus garden fresh.
Conch-white the king's palace in lofty majesty,
The carved gates arching as resplendent rainbows.
The million-rayed sun showers sparkles
Upon studded arches and edifices of burnished gold.
The inner palace-walls with pictures bright
Dispel all gloom by their jewelled sheen.
Trees and leaves of gold adorn the walls
With flowers of ruby and sapphire honey-bee.
On some gold creeper blooms a nine-gemmed flower
Elsewhere dazzle many a diamond bud.
Gem-studded peacocks and *khanjanas*[5] swift,
Gold parrots and silver doves with ruby eyes;
Quartz ponds with over-arched golden bridge,
Lovely with lilies of silver-white and sapphire-blue.
Gold seeded lotuses with rubied glint,

---

1. Goddess of Prosperity.
2. The Ascetic Lord; the Lord of Time and Dissolution.
3. Mythical river Ganga in the heavens.
4. Celebrated flower in the heavenly garden.
5. A bird that keeps quickly changing its sides.

Balance on emerald stems amid emerald leaves.
Silver royal swans with beaks and feet of gold,
And bent silver cranes eyeing the silver fish.
When the lamps are lighted inside the palace
Dances out the lake in glittering waves.
Rooted solid on marble stones
Tall pillars hold the golden canopy.
The queen's nurslings, lovely young fawns,
Enliven the inner courtyard with frolicsome joy.
Rows of wild-elephants with tusks long and full
Adron the stables, obedient to royal wish.
All wistfulness forgetting, in terror of the goad,
Which they fear is sharper than lion's nails,
They banish from their minds all past revels:
Their gladsome stroll across half-hidden caves,
Moistened by the spray of mountain-streams,
Delighted swim in the waters of deep forest lakes,
Joys of the herd, the beloved's love-embrace,
Unfettered movement, and repast of new leaves.
And horses, too, quick as arrow-shot, glossy and sleek,
Adept at piercing battle formations,
Whose neighing causes shudder in the enemy hearts,
Adorn the stables of the king in royal order.
Blue, red, white, in myriad hues
Were milching cows in millions, the king's great wealth;
Large-horned mighty bulls fearlessly, roam,
Bellowing defiance all over,
While the calves after sucking to their full,
Frisk around in wild playfulness.
Around the city are large mango groves
Lovely with green leaves on robust trees;
With branches intertwined in green embrace
The trees endow themselves with dense foliage.
Piercing the pores of thick leaves, the bright sun-rays
Lie patterned on shaded earth in moving beauty.
And the entranced mind wonders if it is,
The bright gem upon the hood of *Ananta**
Or a white lotus upon the breast of Yamuna,
Or a blooming jasmine upon the icon of the night,

---

* The mythical serpent upon which Vishnu rests; also named Shesa.

Or the glow of past merits in a sinner's life,
Or ascetic trees, standing with upraised hands.
Seeing the crystal city amid dark mango forests
Sky-farers, in wonder, search for metaphors:
Is it a jasmine-bunch worn by the earth in its bun,
Or a cluster of swans on the dark Kalindi?
Flocks of diverse birds in the forests
Animate the place with warblings sweet.
The bright-limbed birds in a riot of colours
Shower love-flowers in the eye's path.
Like a shooting star some lone bird
Sweeps down a tree, and perches atop again;
Other birds dive from the sky to the earth,
Like pearls falling from a *Yaksha** – woman's breast.
Flapping once the wings in still poise, floats a bird
Upon love-streams, and then swims in the ethereal sea.
Now flying high it spins back again
Sending waves of melody in sublime strain.
Sometimes flying in a wavy motion,
Now it soars high, now comes down.
Young boys and virgins downing tree-branches
Swing upon them singing in sweet low tones.
Pleased with their song the goddess of the woods,
Joins in chorus and resonates the final notes.
Resting in shades the black bucks, here and there,
Ruminate with eyes closed, without fear.
The transparent waters of the woodland lake
Shine like a locket upon the forest-Laxmi's heart.
Smiles the lake at night with a host of lilies,
And in the day with a lotus forest.
At night she wears a necklace of starry gold
And at dawn a garland of river-bank flowers.
She delights in the company of playful lasses
And raises her waves in a love embrace.
By the joyous trumpets of bathing elephants
The solemn forest reverberates;
And the hum of honey-bees lotus-juice drunk,
Quavers like the veena of Cupid's consort;
The warblings of aquatic birds rise,

---

* A celestial being.

Surpassing the sweet soft words of a new bride;
Raining nectar in the ears in all these forms
Revels the lake in perpetual music.
The drop on the lotus-leaf is but another guise
For love's tear to trickle from her large wide eyes.
Here roams the royal tusker with vermilioned forehead,
His tusk like the shadowed two-day moon,
Seeing which the *koko*[1] fears it's nightfall,
And gazes upon his lover with a sad, wan face,
But seeing the sun again, up in the sky, the illusion gone,
Revels with his beloved in redoubled passion.
Enjoying such blessedness and beauty
The genteel folk there live amid unending gaiety.
Swinging on the lap of wealth and power
The Virata king happily rules and reigns.
The crest-jewels of a hundred thousand kings
Brighten his feet like lamps of worship.
The hero of truth, Yudhistira, in the guise of Kanka
Lives as a happy courtier in the royal court.
The royal cook there is Bhima, the one
Whose baby-kick had shocked Satasrunga,[2]
In whose hands the mighty were but
Sacrifices at the rites of war, whose
Terrifying mace made the earth shudder.
And Dhananjaya, pleased with whose heroism
Shiva had granted a boon,
The soul-mate of Krishna, the Lord of Yadavas,
The greatest archer ever, worthy of the homage of gods and heroes,
He, too, lives there, a serving eunuch in the Queen's quarters.
The twins of Madri, verily Aswinikumaras [3]
Tend the cows and horses of the king, for a living.
The one who luxuriated in the lotus garden
Of the Pandava heart, where she was
A sporting lotus in the hands of Laxmi, the cosmic goddess,
Now she lives, the same Draupadi,[4] as Sairindhri,
A lady's maid, embellishing the inner palace.

---

1. Koko is the *Chakravaka* bird which is fated not to meet his beloved at night.
2. The *Mahabharata* describes how Bhima, while a babe, had shocked the 'mountain with a hundred peaks' with his kick.
3. The Aswinikumars are horse-tamers and physicians of heaven, handsome and heroic.
4. Also named *Panchali, Krushna* and *Jagnaseni.*

CANTO - II

Message of Spring's triumphal march
was broadcast through the world
When from tree-brought new leaves
the herald cuckoo read.
Heard the planet-king, sun,
the season-emperor's words,
And forsaking the hope for gifts [1]
straightened his course.
Winter dew kills his beloved lotus
in Rain the clouds swallow him whole,
Hence, at the name of the 'lord of seasons'
the sun kept a profile low.
Lucent was the planet kingdom,
the planets revelled in joy,
With exquisite riches of splendour
on their bodies in display.
Pining at her Lord's wintry fall
the day had languished thin
Delighted now she swelled
beaming a face divine.
The *chakravaka* couple regaled,
sensing longer stretch of the day –
Who wouldn't indeed rejoice
sighting a cherished wealth?
Seeing the sun go south,
to the quarter of death
The devoted lotus had drowned herself
in the streaming dew from Vishnu's foot; [2]

---

1. The word 'dakshina' in the original has a pun, meaning 'south'and'gifts to a priest' An altrenative rendering would be:
   'Leaving the southern skies, in fear
   he straightened his course.'
2. In Indian mythology, the sky is viewed as a foot of Vishnu.

By the warmth of the summer-penance again
she revived her beauteous life,
And to her Pole-star-facing husband became
a darling wife.
With the advent of her dear guest, spring,
the lovely earth-queen
Stocked she in her store
all riches green:
Mango, jack-fruit, watermelon
and such other repasts juicy
And for gifts, the *Ijjal*[1]-blossoms,
like a necklace of rubies.
For festive meets the forest was
decorated with care
In clusters of pearly *mahua* and
sapphire-like fruits of *chara.*
Playfully slipping off
the wavy swing of the gem-filled sea,
As fair Spring's mate then,
the Southern Breeze arrived.
He advanced thro' floral routes,
immaculate, exquisite,
And in loving joy revelled
in arbours flower-filled.
Holding as her welcome offering
the *navamalika*[2] in bloom,
The comely Moonshine greeted him
with the *chakora*'s[3] soulful tune.
In shining fineries and ornaments,
of enticing form,
Sukanti, of the charming face,
joined her soon.
Then came the god of love,
world-enthraller,
Peerless tender-limbed youth,
in flowery attire.

---

1. A red flower resembling the ear of corn.
2. One of the five mythical arrows of Kandarpa, the god of love.
3. A bird, famed to drink nectar from moonshine.

Together the five in gay abandon
contrived the *tandava* of Shiva,
No, not that dance,
but a fruity lush *Khandava.*[1]
To eat of the Khandava fruits
the world was maddened in greed,
He who got some danced in joy,
and the one who was deprived grieved.
Tormented was the noon
and evening was mirthful and gay,
The trees into foliage burst
but dry was the river-bed.
Scarlet turned the flame-flower,
the forest rose in splendour,
Delivering the baby moon
pallid went the night-mother.
Couples, in the sea of love
released their passion-boats,
But restive were the ascetics
singed in Cupid's flames.
Meanwhile at the end of spring
came a Tuesday,[2]
Auspicious for Virata women
to worship the Mother Goddess.
Encircled by mango groves
on the shores of the lake
Stood the shrine of Banadurga[3]
bright with domes of gold.
Sanctifying the forest-lake
by her benign grace
Reigned over the region
the supreme Goddess.
The mango groves throbbed
with cymbals, drums and pipes
The bees' antennae vibrated
as did the faces of lotus-fields.

1. A forest in the *Mahabharata*, famous for its rich vegetation.
2. Tuesday at the conclusion of *Chaitra* in March-April.
3. A forest-deity, a form of the Mother Goddess.

Streams of people filled
and flooded the forest
And a din-tide arose
like the roar in the seas.
Dressed in their fineries
the best that each had
From the city hurried the ladies
for the goddess' worship.
One champak-skinned beauty
wearing a silk of charming red,
Shone like a lovely star
cresting the ruddy twilight.
Another gem of a beauty
draped in a green saree
Displayed the beauty of Ganga
on the grassy bosom of the earth.
Emulated another,
the star-filled, deep night blue,
Draped in a blue apparel
with embroidered flowers of gold.
Like a mountain-peak woven
with rays of the rising sun
Gorgeous looked in her yellow
a big-bosomed dame.
Like the *Purbabhadraba* duo
in the *Satavisa* [1] cluster
Glamorous rose one's breasts
wreathed in a string of pearls.
The face of another charmer
wearing a necklace of pearls,
Reminded one of Jupiter
as guest in *Rebati*'s [2] starry space.
A woman's gold nose-ring
undernearth a studded *natha,* [3]

1. A star-cluster with two bright stars called Purbabhadraba.
2. A fish-like constellation of 27 stars. Brihaspati (Jupiter) in Rebati (Pisces in the zodiac) shines the brightest.
3. A crescent shaped nose-ring on the nostrils,

Caused an illusion of the four-digit moon
alongside *Bisakha.*[1]
Offering-plates in hand
the ladies looked enticing,
Like sun-flowers in a garden
in pristine bloom smiling.
Striking in priceless apparel and jewels
stepped forth Sudeshna the queen,
Also Princess Uttara, her daughter,
a beauty non-pareil.
With them came lovely Draupadi,
the earth's adornment,
Laxmi of the clan of beauties
peerless, resplendent.
For the queen and the princess
to offer at the goddess' worship
Carefully carried the maids
gold plates lavishly heaped.
Other women of the inner palace
followed the royal train
All dressed for the occasion
in diverse taste and strain.
Out of the palace, the bevy of women
decked the royal street –
Was it Cupid from his quiver
had released a thousand dart?
Like a locket of diamond
in a gem-studded chain
Fair Sairindhri shone
among the palace women.
Seeing the host of beauties
the fond heart reflects:
Had one's eyes entered
Varuna's [2] secret vault of gems?
Or, perhaps, the soul had,
wandering in its dreams,
Strayed into the exquisite world
of heavenly nymphs.

1. Five stars in a semi-circle.
2. Varuna is the Lord of the oceans.

But no, it wasn't a vault of gems
nor dream-nymphs any,
Verily, a cluster of meteors it was,
foreboding Kichaka's doom.
Beautifying the grounds in
an unbroken rainbow line
The gem-bright, fine-eyed women
moved in ceremony.
In the holy waters of that sweetness
immersing their eyes,
The onlookers purged away
all sins of their sight.
Sitting relaxed, mighty Kichaka
in the balcony of his mansion
Studied the face-flowers
in that large female-garden.
His juice-greedy eye-bee
roving from face to face,
Lighted finally on Panchali's face –
the new floral wealth.
Awestruck it paused
for a stunned moment,
Then slowly indulged in sipping
the nectar of beauty.
"Kissed have I," it thought,
"lily, lotus and *malli*
But none, I'm sure,
was ever sweet as this;
Enjoyed have I jasmines varied –
malati, juthika, navamalika,
But the heart does not fancy
any comparison here.
Varieties of roses have I entered,
and chrysanthemums,
But the mind does not bend
to liken them to this one.
I have roamed through forests
of wood-*champak* and *bakul*
But how would I admit them
as a match to this pearless belle?

The celestial pleasure garden
    of the cosmic couple
Where the star-flowers
    entertain the soul,
Which as they know
    upon new-moon night
Their monthly period is done,
    and so bloom in countless swell –
Even the love of that garden
    is now declined and cloyed,
After seeing this flower
    fallen from Indra's head.
In the moonshine-flowered garden
    on full-moon nights,
I have sucked there often
    love, soft and sweet.
But this flower from the wish-fulfilling
    Eros-tree, granter of boons,
From today has ended my fascination
    for all those delights.'
Seeing her lustre and glow
    it reflected within –
'Was the fair-eyed one made of
    the element of sun-beams?
The light that brightens
    Saturn, Mars, and Jupiter,
The self-same radiance
    is woven in her form.
Black in her bewitching hair
    yellow in her person,
And crimson in her feet and palm
    are all brightly manifest.
On the lips of the lovely one
    the rising sun, as it were, glows
And her lotus-face blooms
    in the pure waters of love.'
Like an impatient *matsya-ranka**
    diving for prey with expanded feathers
Immersed Kichaka's excited mind
    in the flowing beauty of the fish-eyed lass.

---

* Literally, 'fish-crazy' ; the kingfisher.

With his mind and eyes thus enraptured,
the other senses,
Craving for pleasure
took refuge in their habitual modes.
In no time as Kichaka watched,
darkening his vision
Went past that flower-garden
like a luminous procession.
Making the earth music-loud
with their anklet-chime
Vying to vanquish cupid's flag
with their flowing *anchals*,
Brightening the path
with its splendour of gems,
The beauty-stream coursed forward
to the shrine of the goddess.
Like Bhagirath at the head
of the divine stream
The escort of guards ahead
made a passage through human waves.
The afternoon sunlight
like liquid gold
Burnished the bodies,
of the female folk.
Dazzled their foreheads and cheeks,
the faces grew resplendent,
And on their soft glossy hair
gleamed varied oranments.
Jewels on their persons
radiated a brighter sheen
And gold-wombed borders of sarees too,
imbided the lesson.
The gold temple-dome that gifts
radiance into people's eyes,
Excelled, making its glow
scorchingly bright.
Sighting from afar the women-folk –
figures of its own kind –

Did it beckon, to gift yet more splendour
raising the trident high[1]?
Stealing the frolic and pride
of sunlit ocean-waves
That climb the sands
in ray-suffused glory,
The flow of women-folk
adorned in varied gems,
Climbed the whitened temple-steps
in surging waves.
Their hearts filled with love
and true devotion
In half-circle stood the women,
before the goddess' icon.
Was it a garland of diverse flowers
full of beauty and art
Lying as a chain upon
the temple's heart?
Offering flowers, fruits, incense,
devoutly lighting a gold lamp,
Sudeshna worshipped first
approaching close the altar.
Promptly the other ladies
raising their lamps
Followed the rites of the queen
in jubilant concourse.
The lovely women there standing
with lamps raised high in hands
Before the *palasa*-bedeck'd Devi,
contrived an unrivalled grace.
Sighting the welcome entry of *Prava* [2]
the sun's companion,
Did the lotus-forest offer
seeds of golden lamps?
Or did the bosom of the scarlet evening
The Dame Night dress
With a diamond necklace
of dazzling stars?

---

1. Trident on top of the temple, symbol of the goddess' power.
2. Prava is 'glow', presented as a companion to the sun.

Or before the evening surge
had ranged the western hills,
With domes of fire splendid,
as on summer eve?
Ornaments on the women-folk
in the lamp-light gleamed
At the touch of sun-rays, as it were,
water vapour glistening.
Perfuming the temple with incense
the bevy of women,
With flowers of wishes
in their garden-hearts in bloom,
Carrying the holy *prasad*,
they left the deity's place,
And wound their way
slowly to their homes.
Giving their children
sacred *prasad* and flowers,
In joy they invoked the Devi
to keep them in bliss.

CANTO - III

The day's theatre over,
        evening's curtain fell,
Changing the costumes of day
        appeared night sable.
Cutting to pieces, in nature's machine,
        the great gem of the sun,
Made she moon and stars
        to adorn her own person.
Upon the moon-shone starry blue sky
        appeared a nectarous moon
Like Vishnu's *Kaustubha* amid Shesha's gems
        lovely in the milk-ocean.
Melting the sunbeams she poured
        thick into flower-lamp moulds,
And plotting to enrich the *chakora* she stole,
        the gem that warmed the *koko*'s heart.
Shifting Laxmi's camp from lotus-fields
        she pitched it in jasmine forests;
And the sunflower's glow she lifted to grace
        the *navamalika*'s mien.
With pollen plundered from caressing flowers,
        the breeze that had grown dusty
Now danced in soft pleasing capers
        from house to house in glee.
Restive were trees and tendrils
        and fragrant were all quarters,
The erotic sea in men and women
        swelled with rising waves.
The moon-beam-caress-elated sea,
        husband of all the streams,
Had no feeling for his river wives
        and pushed them all behind.
The rivers sulked with swollen faces
        and folks, horrified with the sea's manner,

In mock-reverence did '*juhara*' which,
grown demotic thro' time, became '*juara*',*
The love-inspiring, lush moon painted
women in moony layers,
And applied in all men's eyes soon
the collyrium of passion.
Men of pleasure in elegant attires
wearing garlands of *champak* and sandal paste
Revelled in the company of *champak*-bright dames
and retired upon luxurious beds.
One after another all houses in the city
had their entrances shut,
And the doors of men's eyes belike
were soon by sleep made fast.
On the dream-waves of the ocean of sleep
floated all living beings,
Strange reflections saw they many
of events, subjects, and things.
Only Kichaka was kept out,
anguished in sensual thirst,
His chase was on for vain mirages
that held him tense and taut;
Where Draupadi's luminous image,
a creeper wreathed with floral laughter,
Reflected in his lidless eyes
brought him some cool succour;
But the same coolness soon increased
the heat in his burning heart,
As cool water raises fumes
when sprinkled on a heated oil-pot.
Having enquired of a serving maid
the mighty one had known,
That gem of a woman, Sairindhri by name,
lived in the palace quarters;
Who her father was, what husband she had,
where she hailed from,
And what had brought her there,
nothing was clearly known;

---

* A fanciful etymological connection between '*Juhara*' (putting the palms together in salutation) and '*Juara*' (tide).

From her habits and dress it appeared
a married woman she was,
Her manner and words conveyed clear
she belonged to the genteel stock;
Although a lady's maid, in the palace
when one saw her demeanour
One felt, even the queen of heaven
would be a trite thing beside her.
In discernment she could overtake as it were
the mind of the god of justice,
And had won the hearts of the palace-women
by her love and geniality.
The Virata Queen, too, was in her sway,
of her character and grace, enamoured,
As though she had found the world-coveted
pure touchstone for gold.
All these reports on the elegant dame
were writ on the scroll of his heart
Reading which he was ready to enter
the order of that love's faith.
To possess that gem of youth became
the prime mantra of his life,
And his mind's kingdom soon came under
lust's rule and polity.
All systems of justice and order
summarily were abandoned,
And endless conference went on
with ministers of pride and passion.
Resolved he in various ways
to subject the woman to his will;
Thought he – 'My heroic fame and great wealth
would surely draw the belle.
If she wishes, I shall instal her
as the presiding deity of my home,
Or else shall I, the whole of my life
enjoy her secret love.
Sometimes I would visit her inside
charming creeper-bowers
And cool the heat of my heart's hill
by her massed-cloud close embrace.
She would pour out, the gracious one,
her fount of love-nectar

Drinking which to my heart's content
I would spurn the seat of Indra.
Observing me from her balcony
when she would softly smile
All the joys of heaven would then
fall into my hands sweetly.
Or meeting her, in a lonely chamber
I shall kiss her chin and lips,
And be watching again and again,
her love-swelled lotus-face.
The wishes of the priceless dame
unceasingly I shall serve,
To gladden the tender love-crepeer
would be my life's task.
Let alone other things, to please her,
should the need arise,
I shall not hesitate the least
to offer my life in sacrifice.
Thus in his reveries built Kichaka
a splendid Elysium of hope
Not thinking at all that the insect's race
was only to the burning fire.
Restive he grew, anxious to perform
the much-wished-for act,
And disgusting was the night to him
for it seemed so tiringly endless.
Again and again he climbed up the parapet
of his palace that kissed the lightning's cheek,
And kept watching the base of the eastern skies
for the morning star to rise.
The deluded crow's untimely caws
hearing now and again,
Mistaking it for dawn he sprang up everytime,
eager to despatch his messenger-woman.
Painfully late the ambrosial moon
fell into the jaws of time
And like the *kapittha* [1] swallowed by an elephant
sank into *Baruni*'s [2] deadly grip.

---

1. A round, white, sour fruit.
2. West, also mythical 'elephant of the quarters' in the west.

Losing her lover-moon the grieving night-dame
tore off her garland of flowers
Oh, how long and deep she then wailed,
Mourning in the drongo's voice!
And, last, with the hesper-diadem upon her hair
she entered the pyre of the glowing dawn
Whose smoke rose as the morning haze
upon the heaving waters of the ocean.
Flock upon flock the birds lamented
the death of the pious moon,
The brahmins brushed their teeth, took bath,
and for the dead offered their oblation.*
On the high throne of rising peaks
laying a carpet of gold
Crowned by rays, the Lord of the day
then made his benign ascent.
The lotus raised a royal umbrella
above the sun's image,
And fish and fowl, like priests, coronated him
with crystal water spray.
White swans in melodious voice
chanted Vedic hymns
And the *chakrabaka* came holding a sceptre
of a lotus-stem in his beaks.
The menace of nocturnal creatures
was gone from the solar kingdom,
Thieves quailed, and murky hosts for hide-outs
rushed in all directions.
Upon the sea of the world all living beings
released their vessels of duty,
And through forest and air ranged the birds
searching victims for a hunger-sacrifice.

Meantime a maid brought scented water
in a piped mug of gold
And stood near Kichaka, waiting
for him to wash his face.

---

* In this stanza Gangadhar has poetically exploited three different meanings of the word 'dwija' – 'bird', 'tooth', and 'brahmin'.

She, he thought, would be the emissary right,
  and said, 'Dear Chapala,
Could you, on my burning body,
  smear some soothing sandal-paste?'
Chapala answered, 'No big task, lord,
  if you command, in a trice shall I,
Anoint and deck your royal body
  with sandal paste, camphor, and lotus.'
Kichaka said, 'If truly you can procure
  the sandal-paste I desire
I shall not ever fail
  in gifting the wealth you wish for.
Whatever raiments, ornaments,
  all you'ld covet,
Quite willing would I always be
    to offer as reward.'
The maid said, 'Lord! on which sandal wood is
  your royal heart so set?
Command, my liege, with utmost care
    this slave shall bring it fast.'
Confided then Kichaka – 'O clever one,
    you must have seen
That youthful dame, fair as a goddess,
  who lives in the king's palace;
Has been there for some time,
  known to the women as Sairindhri;
Her company alone I crave –
  she be my life-soothing sandal-paste.'
Chapala replied, 'I know Sairindhri –
  Beauty's soul indeed,
No wonder that a man's heart
  should so by her allured be.
She is lonely like a female dove
  separated from her mate,
Easily can I her heart entice,
  speaking of your heroic fame.
Who would, when it comes to hand,
  spurn in contempt Indra's seat?
Impossible it is for the flower in bloom
  to drive away the bee.

I go now, gallant lord –
by hook or crook or wile,
I shall tie the Beauty in love's noose
and lay her at your feet.
But about this affair, master,
the queen must not have wind,
For if this ever falls in her ear
it's certain I will lose my living.
I will not take ornaments, my lord,
nor shall I wear any silk,
If perchance my mistress notices it
on my head will fall the stick.'
So saying and bowing at his feet
promptly out she went,
Planting in his heart a firm faith
she'd fetch the flower from the garden.

She went then to Sairindhri and sat near her
wearing a sly smile;
And Sairindhri exclaimed, 'Why, what's the matter, Chapala,
today you are so merry!'
Answered Chapala, 'Once one sees your face,
all sorrows vanish,
Your sweetness verily is a thunder here
for all the mountains of grief.
Leave aside me, across whoever's view
your grace flits past a moment,
In that heart do you for all time
preside as an icon of joy.
For many a day not seeing your face
restless was my mind,
And so just to soothe my anxious heart
here have I today hurried.'
Sairindhri rejoined, 'Never do you, Chapala,
speak to me so; why then,
Do you thus engage today
in eulogy needless and vain?
Ignoring them where praise is due
what good extolling me,
Neglecting a garden's flower-plants, what'ld you gain,
watering the forest trees?'

Saucily said Chapala, 'Yes, O beauteous one,
what you speak is indeed true,
Unenjoyed your beauty lies in vain
like the forest-flower dropped to the ground.
If someone then lovingly takes and offers
that flower on the deity's head
Would it not enhance the flower's charm,
as also the pleasure of the god?'
Sairindhri countered, 'Right you are,
I am indeed a forest-flower
But there are, to enjoy my company,
five bright gandharvas ever!
Not to speak of plucking the flower,
should the gandharvas merely hear
That tempted by it someone had entered the woods,
his life would at once be in danger.'
'I think, O charming one,' persisted Chapala,
'With such a lame excuse,
To ignore your joy, fortune, and happiness
is not at all proper for you.
So proud of your merits, if you so wish,
you'ld have a gallant worthy of you –
There is Sudeshna's brother, Kichaka,
verily, a second king in Virata now.
It is mighty Kichaka who holds by the horns
the milch cow of royal wealth,
And the Virata king only lives merrily,
relishing his drink of milk.
Hence, in this kingdom, blazes forth
Kichaka's mighty power
Subjects and feudal vassals all
regard him as royal master.
Moreover he is the queen's brother,
much esteemed by the king –
It's like borax joined to gold
or sweet cheese added to milk.
Whatever commands like petals drop
from Kichaka's lotus-face,
People honour as flowers fallen
from Lord Shiva's sacred image.
Whichever way does Kichaka's mind
swell in a stream to flow,

Hurriedly digs royal power there
a canal for its smooth course.
All minds does wealth delude –
famous is this maxim in the world;
For riches men give away lives
engaging in bitter wars.
Wealth makes one proud and noble,
makes one wise and charitable,
Wealth enhances hauteur and grace,
and only wealth it is that the people serve.
Authority is ever in wealth's company,
only the poor keep straining as slaves;
If you were affluent would you have here
in another man's house stayed?
From cradle to grave, in sun and shower
life does lean on wealth,
So has Lord Vishnu, in his own beloved's hands
vested the boon of riches.
Lovely women of youth and charm
to the rich are naturally lured.
Forced by the impulse that
makes the lightning sport upon water-rich clouds.
One more thing: Charming women ever
look for powerful men,
Thus by a test Sita chose her Rama
as Draupadi did her Arjuna.
Kichaka's palace has grown today
a second Indra's home
And the king of Virata leans upon
the might of his valiant arms.
It is fortunate for a woman to be
love-mate of a mighty man –
The thrill of the sun's love-warm rays
the lotus knows alone.'
Sairindhri retorted, 'I'm no lotus,
and I don't need the sun,
A wild flower am I, lying here
the forest-deity to gladden.'
Chapala warned, 'If you heed me not
and keep to your conceit vain,
In pain you'd have what in joy should have been,
with insult being the only gain.

A ripe mango that adorns the tree-top
and wouldn't come easy to hand,
When children notice, they carry it away
bringing it down with a stone.
Since your sojourn here, O tender-limbed one,
your pride as devoted wife
Has been swaying upon the dancing waves
of Kichaka's passion-sea.
You see, lovely one, in the house the sun
in the sky-kingdom lives,
Other dwellers there, the stars and planets,
do they retain their sheen?'
Retorted Sairindhri, 'For aeons if you
cajole in this vein
Sairindhri's mind will unshaken be
and only heartache you'll gain.
To dwell in different skiey spaces
brighter planets desire
But the tiny pole-star seeks her shelter,
in the northern sky forever.'
Still coaxed Chapala, 'Wherever they be,
your husbands wouldn't just know –
So go on enjoying rare luxuries
savouring secret love.
The lily that beams with moonshine-caress,
the love-joy of the moon,
Does it not mate with darkness
and before the moon-rise, bloom?'
Sairindhri snapped, 'Now I know
your intention is vile,
Never again dare come to me –
and now be gone forthwith.
Know for certain if anyone ever
tries my honour to force,
My husbands will surely despatch his life
to the death-god's abode.
I won't blame the noble king,
for I live on the food he gives,
But if he indulges in unjust ways
wouldn't then Dharma punish?
The king who by passion blinded
abuses royal power,

Gets destroyed soon like fuel
caught in a blistering fire.'
When she heard from Sairindri's lips,
a reply so damp and stern,
Chapala fled like a corn-eating deer
hit by the farmer's stone.
How could Draupadi's mind be trapped
in the ignoble Chapala's net of words?
Of a lioness caught in a rabbit-trap –
has anyone ever heard?

CANTO - IV

Driving her naughtiness all within
Sadly returned Chapala with her hopes dead,
Like Ravana's messenger from Janaki
Returning pale-faced, as a flower stale.
With bowed head near Kichaka, the woman said;
'O crest-jewel of royal gallants,
However engagingly I tempted her
The saucy coquette didn't yield;
Like Vishnu's disc against Rahu,*
She has five *gandharvas* who protect her
From assaults of lustful men.
Strange, I thought, with five husbands already
She should now object to a sixth!
But I have thought out another device;
If it appeals to your fancy,
I shall be the goad of the device
To bring here the lass, the she-elephant wild.'
Kichaka cut in, 'Why discuss at all,
Why do you linger here without acting upon it?
To one who is dying of hunger
You ask if he would relish some nectar!'
The maid said – 'My master,
I will speak to the queen, your sister,
Craftily thus, in confidence: "Last night
Your brother saw in his dream
A woman flash and vanish in a trice.
Since then your brother, all distraught,
Sits like a hermit in her vision lost.
Till he meets her, he has vowed,
He would not touch any water or food".

---

* Rahu was just having a sip of nectar when Vishnu decapitated him.

If your sister enquires about the woman then,
I'll secretly whisper Sairindhri's name.
Sister, no doubt, wouldn't refuse your appeal,
She would certainly try her utmost for you.
And who dares flout her orders here?
Sarindhri, perforce, would her bidding do.
And once the dame then sees your face,
Will cupid ever let her escape?
Without mutual sight does ever love blossom?
Don't you see daily the ways of the lotus and the sun?
She'ld deceive her husbands and set her heart on you.
For know, the loves of women and creepers are mysterious;
Supported by a tree a creeper lives,
But if it finds another nearby
Eagerly it advances for its embrace
And in new tender love clasps in deep caress.'
Kichaka said, 'Your reassuring words, verily,
For my *chataka*-soul bring the rumble of clouds,
In your hand now rests my hope's thunder-showers.
Go; till you return, eagerly 'll I keep watching here.'
Comforting Kichaka's love-lorn heart
Chapala hurried to Sudeshna at once.
Bowing humbly to the ground she touched her feet,
And said, 'Divine Queen, I have an entreaty:
Last night your brother had a dream,
In which a woman showed up and vanished soon.
Ever since your brother with a restless soul,
Sits meditating upon her form and beauty.
Till he meets the woman in person
Food or drink he would have none.
This thing, in confidence, into my ears
He whispered, and said, "Do your best."
The mother knows the mind of her son,
So does a sister know her brother's heart.
In his joys and sorrows she enjoys or suffers,
A sharing that belongs to none others.
When streams dry up as the mountain burns
The river, at that time, in anguish lives;
And when the streams flow and the mountain is calmed,
The river's heart swells in joy.
But the trees standing on the river-bank
Care little about her slow decline:

Motionless they all watch in silence,
And laugh out rather with their flowers and leaves.
To share Kichaka's joy and sorrow,
Other than the noble queen who is here?
Unable to bear the master's anxiety
This slave petitions, for you are the sole refuge.'
At Chapala's words the queen grew concerned,
And asked, 'For whom does my brother so yearn?
Where on earth is such a great princess
Who, gaining my brother's hand, wouldn't feel blessed?
Speak, whose fortune's stores are bared –
Her path of sorrow will in no time be lifted.
Promptly sending a royal messenger today
I shall arrange to conduct her here.'
The maid then prompted, 'O Mistress, she is not far,
Lives on royal bounty in the palace here;
She, who is called Sairindhri, she it is,
Whom your brother has seen in dream.'
Hearing Sairindhri's name the Virata queen
In shock bit her tongue and touched her ears;
Said she, 'This is a tough task,
Drop this idea; suggest some other means.'
The maid pressed on –'He has only seen her in dream,
And wishes to see her face just once;
He would only appease his thirsty eyes,
And wouldn't at all touch her body.'

The queen warned, 'If it's otherwise,
Look you, Chapala, you'll lose your life.
Great is the potency of a virtuous wife,
Little does she brook any authority.'
But Chapala thought – 'She who has husbands five,
How come she is a woman chaste?
She is no Jagnaseni, the soul of the Pandavas
For whose rescue they would all rush.
Even if she has her husbands, how do I care?
Kichaka the great hero is the queen's brother,
I shall please him and carry off rich booties,
Shall earn much goodwill, and live in comfort for ever.
The evening uniting the moon and the night,
Gains coloured apparel and gems bright;
When the dragon comes and swallows the moon

Has the evening ever been blamed?'
Now the queen to Chapala said,
'Is there some guile that keeps you mum?
If there be deceit, go convince him,
Such sin hastens one's death.
When the night-loving moon tries to solicit the dawn
He shrinks as a mouse before the cobra-sun.
The mediating morning star's radiant glamour.
Flashes for a moment, only to go under.'
Chapala started when she heard these words
And feared, the queen had read her heart.
But boldly declared, 'There is no guile in this,
And doesn't your brother know the good and the right?
Since his eyes' thirst, in dream, hasn't been quenched
He hopes to satiate in the waking state.
Hasn't the Lord of the cosmos created beauty
That the eyes might sanctified be?'
'Then go, inform him,' said the queen,
'I shall send Sairindhri to him:
In a goblet she will carry some drink
And place it near him; then he may see her once.'

Chapala bowed and took her leave
And delivered to Kichaka the message sweet.
'My Lord's honour I upheld,' she beamed,
'Held by the scruff the woman's pride.
She will come with drinks to your noble presence;
Let that charming dame first see your royal face,
And then when she hears you wooing
Would cupid spare her and not bind her feet?'
Kichaka smiled, and praised Chapala's wit;
Floating upon love-waves then he said:
'Let that treasure of loveliness cross my eyes,
Let her appear only once, verily a lightning of the earth,
And may the pupils of my eyes receive
The cascading stream of her nectar-sweet beauty,
And wash away all sin, sorrow and weariness,
And raise soothing waves of fragrant breeze.'
Quickly he bathed and smeared on his body
Sandal-paste with perfumes; then hurriedly dressed,
Got the mansion deck'd, and sat on the balcony high,
On a throne of gold, fervent and eager.

In the front were arranged bouquets
And garlands were hung at the top.
Hoping to cajol the dame and smear on her body
Some sandal-paste, he kept it ready.
His body alone rested on the seat of gold,
The mind was away hearkening for her tinkling steps,
Like the *koko* at dawn, across lotus-fields
Scanning the beloved's path with stilled eyes.

And there in the palace the Virata queen
Sent for Jagnaseni and spoke in honeyed words,
'O gentle one, carry this goblet of wine,
To my brother, and return soon.'
Krushna, hesitating, said, 'I feel scared
To visit your brother's palace;
Merciful lady! please dispel my fear,
Be kind to withdraw the order.'
Soothingly said the queen, 'Dear one, what's the fear?
What makes your mind so tense and restive,
Seeing what do you nurse such terror in your heart?
His palace is neither the sea nor the forest,
No crocodile is there, nor lion;
O you guileless one, why this pretense today?
Krushna said, 'Royal lady! hear me please,
True it is, no lion nor crocodile is there,
But there is cupid of the five-arrows with his alligator-crested flag,
And so I am afraid of going to your brother.'
The queen again comforted, 'Do not fear, friend,
As I am to him, so are you, too, his sister.
Moreover, one who is housed atop Dharma's peak
How does she dread the current of sin?
Dharma ever protects the pious souls
And the Lord is four-armed to shield the virtuous.
Vivacious lightning, the cloud's wife,
On the skiey fields sports with playful limbs,
But darkness that lusts for her and chases the cloud,
Is it ever able to defile her virtue?
O gem of chastity! keep once my troth,
Draw not back your feet.
Have no fear in heart, your soul in virtue strong,
I beseech you, go with the goblet in hand.'

Unable to refuse the queen's request
Goblet in hand stood the fair-limbed one,
Her mind prone to move, yet unwilling,
Her tender feet about to stir, yet unstirring.
Like a flower floating on a strong current
Spurred by the queen helplessly she moved,
But midway she paused, her mind in a whirl,
Her timid heart pounding in natural tremor.

Mused she; 'Since morning I am aware
Evil has roused Kichaka into a vile passion:
For his dark desires to fructify
He has designed this compelling trick;
Strongly tied to her brother's affection,
The queen is trapped in a net of delusion,
In her loving eyes the Kichaka glass-bead
Attains the status of pure diamond.'
Looking up, the chaste one in great distress
Prayed, 'O Dharma! you're the hapless woman's strength.
Give me the courage to obey the command of one,
On whose food and raiment here I live;
Secure I have preserved my gem of chastity
But now I am afraid the thief might steal.
Be my guard then and lead me on,
Hari be there to protect my rear.'
Invoking the Lord she moved forward
With a walk that would seduce a sage's heart.
In slow gait she advanced under the arches,
Verily like Parvati on mountain-paths,
The goblet in hand in charming relief,
Like the nectar-pot in Mohini's* hands.
Or Saraswati carrying the juice of poesy,
Walking the earth for the love of her devotees!
Then she came upon a garden path,
And walked, the noble one, beautifying the earth.
People who saw from afar would think
It was a royal swan moving in lotus fields.
Hidden away behind the trees a moment,
Instantly she flashes again across one's eyes,

* Vishnu took the form of a ravishing enchantress, Mohini, and deprived the demons of their share of nectar.

Like a star hiding behind floating chunks of cloud,
And on their surface shining out again and again.
Soon her feet touched Kichaka's palace-gates
Pausing, like a sage being made to praise a dunce.

Like moon-beams on swings of waves
Slowly climbed the charming one a flight of steps.
Her feet then trod the palace-yard,
Not feet, but goads of Kichaka's doom;
Wild fire it was in the guise of a woman,
That entered the hills of the Kichaka-clan.
The palace-Laxmi there with a smiling face
Greeted Krushna with her love-embrace.
Mutually enhanced they their beauty and grace
As Ganga and Yamuna at the Prayag-confluence.
Seeing a maid along the corridor pass
Accosted her Panchali and asked, 'Where's Kichaka?'
The maid pointed out a building
That housed Kichaka's private chambers.
Draupadi found there the queen's brother,
And with bowed head before him placed the goblet.
Then she retraced her dainty feet,
Seeing which Kichaka's heart fluttered wild,
And jumping from his seat he exclaimed, 'O my dear,
Won't you buy this slave with your favours kind?'
Flustered at his manner the chaste one
Clutched her saree-edge tight, and hurried on.
Kichaka had hoped, savouring the beauty of her face,
He would life-long his sorrow efface.
But like lightning had the face flashed once
And then on his hope had a thunder-bolt struck.
To beg for restoration of his hope's life
Kichaka pursued Krushna with eager speed.
Ahead ran Draupadi faster and faster
Like a terrified doe fleeing a tiger.
The damsel's *anchal* fluttered behind,
On her back were scattered her dishevelled hair,
Swayed her waist, and her arms swung,
And danced the curls on her charming cheeks,

Tight were the lips shut, and her breath was taut,
And on her bosom danced her slackened clothes;
Seen from behind her blood-red soles
Created an illusion of the ground-lotus;
Bending her head under trees she ran,
And straightening, raced on open ground;
The new leaves on the wayside plants
Kissed her feet as she sprinted past.
Kichaka pursed the fleeing Krushna,
Around his neck the noose of passion:
As she ran with rope-end in hand
Kichaka moved en route, drawn behind.
Thus as she reached the garden-end
Draupadi's eyes in fatigue darkened.
By and by her speed declined,
And the strength of her feet too ebbed.
The giant Kichaka's hand on Draupadi's saree
Began brushing from time to time.
His eyes were fixed on Krushna's form,
And as he chased, he looked neither up nor down.
Suddenly his head by a huge tree-branch
Was hit and he sank there on his haunches;
Rubbing his head he sat smouldering at the branch,
Then rose in anger and pulled it apart.
Meantime Draupadi rushed to her quarters
And sat there brooding on her life's woes.
Drenched was her body by streams of sweat –
She wiped it with her anchal and fanned herself.
Relieved she prayed: 'Praised be you, Lord,
Redeemer of sorow; in the same hand you wield,
Mercy and sword, and use them both
To dispel the sorrows of the meek, and the wicked ones' pride.'

CANTO - V

On palace-top roared the Kichaka-lion -
'Who's my peer on earth in heroism?
The world trembles at my arm's might
And enemy hosts are all singed in my heat.
All thro' the world my fame's banner flies,
And at the twang of my bow Yama's* abode shakes.
On my strength is mighty the Virata king
Yet insults me this slave of a Sairindhri!
Great warriors in fear of me show their back
But this mere slave in scorn did turn her back!
I shall surely have her serve my feet as a wife,
Let him who dares fight, and save her from me.
If I can't make her my chariot in the sex-war,
I shall not keep my base life - this I resolve.
If five *gandharvas* are her consorts,
Deer-like will they perish by my line of arrows.'
From ear to ear spread this threat,
Each warning the other: it was a secret.
Whatever had happened the previous day,
Was a hot talk in home and public place.
When impulsively someone discussed it aloud,
Another, counselling caution, sharply reproved.
One said Kichaka's mind was bad,
This was but common to big men, another held.
All that happened inside Kichaka's mansion
At washermen's ghats fell their dark reflection.
Wood-cutters returning with loads on head
Talked about it, trudging home from the forest.
Draupadi heard about Kichaka's evil pledge and grieved
That a new calamity was on her vexations heaped.
Cogitated she, 'On what raft may I
Cross these crisis-waves insuperable?

---

* Yama: The Lord of Death.

The queen cannot prevail on her brother,
And to a vow of silence would the king resort.
If Dharmaraja[1] comes to know of this
Merely his heart's agony will increase;
If the Gandiva-holder [2] gets wind of this
Exposed we shall all be, should he resort to a fight;
The young twins are not equal to the task –
A forest-fire isn't tamed by water in an elephant's trunk.
So I shall report the matter to the great wrestler,[3]
'Tis certain he'ld take some counter-measure.
But he too would seek the nod of the elder,
And wouldn't do anything without his express order.
First let me then report to Dharma Yushisthira
And next with his permission meet Baka's killer.
In the royal presence shall I now submit it to him.
Petition before the king and appeal to husband –
Both tasks would then be together performed.'
Thinking thus, Krushna rushed to the court,
Where the king with Dharmaraja sat dicing.
With bowed head she stood before Virata,
And aiming at her husband spoke in a plaintive voice:
'O crest-jewel of kings, Justice Incarnate,
This maid seeks support of royal power;
Kichaka has nurtured evil in his heart
And transgressing all virtues, grown tyrannical;
On the queen's orders today I carried a jar of wine,
And was returning after placing it by him
When he made lewd passes with flattering words
And chased me when I refused.
He has vowed now, failing to capture me,
He'ld force me to serve as his wife.
Strength of the weak, O King, uphold royal duty
And on Kichaka's liberties impose proper limits.'
When he heard this from Sairindhari Virata said,
'Look you, Kichaka's resolve is of adamant,
And lucky is she who sports on his lap;
What good is it to live ever as an unhappy maid?'

---

1. Yudhistir is known as Dharmaraja, the king of righteousness.
2. Arjuna who could wield the great bow *Gandiva.*
3. Bhima, the second Pandav, was a mighty wrestler. He had killed Baka the demon.

Justice-loving Kanka[1] then spoke in a decisive tone,
'O blown-lotus-eyed, listen:
Only Bhima's might would accomplish here
Feat appropriate to Kichaka'a desire. [2]
In this kingdom you have no other redress;
Resort to the second-husband[3] – that's my advice'.
Virata concurred: 'Kanka is right.
Let gold now be studded with a ruby bright'.
Draupadi thought -'Now dies Kichaka,
As did in Ekachakrapur the evil Baka.'
Making a show of grief and disappointment then,
Jajnaseni returned to her quarters.
Kichaka's maid was already there,
Anxiously waiting, her eyes fixed on the road.
Smiling at Sairindhri she said. 'O beauteous one,
Without you, the jewel of heroes is in sore distress.
He, whose sway is absolute in this land,
In whose palace sports the royal goddess of wealth,
For the sake of whose love princesses turn beggars,
Strange that you hesitate to be his heart's delight.
As I've been ordered by the hero,
In brief let me report his clear message:
"To cure your malady of miserly-love
The proper medicine would be applied today;"
O *Saphari* [4]-eyed! the saphari that sports in water,
Defiant of the cold, can it go on jumping?'
Draupadi said, 'There's nothing to say more –
To whom would one report if the protector turns gobbler?
But give me respite for this day alone,
Tomorrow come, and take back my answer certain.
I know, one who lives among a tribe of fowlers,
Has fruits for repast one day, and meat another.'
Agreed the maid and went back to inform Kichaka.
She reassured him – 'Tomorrow will your desire be fulfilled;
The rein of the damsel's mind-steed, pulled your way,

---

1. Kanka was the assumed name of Yudhistir.
2. The surface-meaning being – 'Perform only acts appropriate to the mightily valiant Kichaka's desire.'
3. Two meanings again – 'Resort to the protection of Bhima' and 'Accept Kichaka as a second husband.'
4. A tiny fish that jumps continually. But in winter its sprightliness is reduced.

Towards you now it trots.'
The tree of Kichaka's hope brust into leaves
And his heartland cooled in the soft smooth shade.

In the spring-night-sky reigned the moon;
Charming moonbeams frolicked in nature's lap
With moonshine-grace was entranced the endless sky,
And entranced were silvery bowers spread dense to the shores.
The nectarous moon-washed leaves of trees
Murmured softly swaying in the spring breeze.
The *chakravaka*-couples' plaintive notes resonated in air,
As did the dry-throated *chataka*'s wails of despair.
Somewhere in the sky flew the *tentoi** calling –
Her heart alone knew whether she sang of joy or grief.
Elsewhere sedately ran a warbling stream
With a young gallant walking by carolling.
Thrilled at the music the river-friendly birds
Through both banks ranged with joyous twitters.
Under the cool moonshine slept fair-limbed Bhima,
In the kitchen-house courtyard bright.
His pearly body smeared with white sandal-paste,
And covered in floral-designed raiment
Appeared like a snow-clad gold mountain
Embraced by the rays of the rising sun.
In deep sleep the hero on a mattress lay
Like a lion asleep on lush soft grass.
Drupada's daughter sneaking thro' a lonely hour
Came, and stood in stark relief by Bhima's side.
She surveyed from head to toe to be sure it was he,
And then tugged at his feet and shook him fast.
Waking with a start the hero rose at once,
And shouted, 'Who're you?' To which she sadly answered:
'Why would you recognize, lord, this unlucky slave,
Misfortune's bait she is always, everywhere.
The poor lotus has on her forehead writ,
The fate of being trampled by elephants' feet.'
Quickly the hero then took her into his lap,
And said, 'Freely speak what ails you, dear;
Risking another exile in the wild forest
I'll finish the one who offers you threat.

---

* A rain bird, here lost in the spring night.

If on the lion's courtyard the jackal prances
How long shall the animal-king show forbearance?
Speak, dear, I can brook delay no more –
Who dares invite on his head the thunderbolt?'
Draupadi complained, 'Lord! the evil Kichaka
Longs to have me for his vile lust.
Hearing what his procuress told me today
I fear, his atrocities would be insufferable.
Kingdom, woman, gem and wealth, when masterless
Naturally tempt other men's hearts;
Only because he thinks I am unprotected
Does the evil-minded Kichaka in lust salivate.
This I have already mentioned to the son of Dharma,
And he has this duty to your share allotted.
To his female pimp I only said this in the end,
"Come tomorrow and have my final say."
On the morrow will she come to pester me
And would surely cause havoc if I decline.'
As he heard this Bhima's body shook in anger
And his fair face at once turned crimson.
His unblinking red eyes expanded wide
And the pupils rolled fearfully wild;
Hot blood in his arteries and veins
Flowing fast flushed him all over.
Thought first the hero in his fury,
He'ld go and wring Kichaka's neck right away.
Then after a stunned moment he stood resolved,
He would kill the villain in a secret spot.
The sinful lust which the sinner cherished
Under the self-same ruse would he be dispatched.
Holding Draupadi's hand he sweetly said,
'Stop worrying now, my darling beloved;
Assure the maid, you'ld go on a visitation –
Let the lecher come to the rendezvous at night
The theatre-house at the city's end,
Fix that as your appointed place.
At the right time I'll be there in your guise
And quickly return after performing the rite.'
At Bhima's words the lady shook off her fear
And returned to her quarters praising her lord.
Turning the past events in her unquiet heart
Lightly she slept through the hours of the night.

CANTO - VI

The night ended, the sun began to climb the sky:
And for an answer promptly arrived the go-between.
To her Krushna said, 'I have no choice;
I cannot but serve the hero's desire.
But I am alarmed at the danger of public scandal;
Take care then that none should know of our secret affair.'
Replied the maid, 'O love-adept
Except for you, him, and me, how would another know?'
'O spotless moon-faced one,' she reassured her again,
'The rendezvous shall be of your choice;
So tell me, where would today that indulgent bee
Kissing your lotus-face fulfilled be?
Draupadi said, 'The dance-hall at city's end
Lovely in the moonlight and fragrant
With the aromatic garden breeze, there,
In the silent night "the mighty one" shall meet me.'
The maid could not guess the pun,
With which Draupadi had called him the "sacrificial animal."
So smiling and jubilant she sped back to Kichaka
And reported the words in happy terms;
Hearing which at once he was immersed in joy,
Like one born poor when he receives a precious gem.
The dance-hall was exquisite like the royal palace,
Yet he decked it again lavishly with assiduous care.
Longing for Draupadi, his mind all absorbed,
He sat alone, keeping watch for the night to come.
With the Moon came his sporting consort Night
And the delighted earth in the guise of jasmine bloom smiled.

Smearing sandal-wood paste on his limbs,
And wearing long garlands on his chest,
Dressed in white muslin and decked in ornaments
In the very first hour of the night, the lustful Kichaka
Impatiently to the dance-hall rushed
But found not there his cherished gem.

Reflected he, perhaps she had come early, and tired of waiting,
Had sadly returned, the one of quick *khanjana*-eyes, feeling betrayed.
Thinking then, she might be strolling in the garden,
He went there to search her out.
When he saw a tree's bosom pierced by moonbeam
He hurried there believing it was the female gem.
Seeing in the distance then a flowered creeper,
Thought it was she, and raced for her athirst in soul.
Moonbeam-brightened water around roots of plants,
Beguiled him as if they were her charming feet.
When he heard some bird calling in disturbed sleep,
He thought she was softly whistling in sleep, and instantly rushed.
Whenever frustration began to enter his heart
Trickstress Hope would drive it out fast.
Searching and searching thus he desperate grew,
While the night advanced into the witching hour.
Bhima, meantime, finishing early his chores,
In the second quarter, disguised as a woman
Arrived at the dance-hall, and full of warth,
Kept intently waiting for Kichaka's visit.
Studded with murk-tearing gems, the hall
Was girt by gardens bursting with flowers,
Carrying whose fragrance blew a gentle breeze,
Under the cool spread of the ambrosial moon.
But none of these engaged his heart nor eyes,
Which remained focussed upon Kichaka's path.

Scouring the garden and finding not Sairindhri
Kichaka again entered the dance-hall to look for her,
And then suddenly as he saw a white figure there,
He ran up, and moaning, 'O my life's mate,' clasped it hard.
Bhima had been waiting like a hungry tiger,
With a roar he now grabbed Kichaka's neck.
'Not woman but foe', hissed out Kichaka,
Like a bamboo-hole* shrill in a gust of wind.
More and more fierce and hard they wrestled
And with the mighty duo's footfalls quaked the city.
The citizens, in dreams by the tremor caused,
Some enjoyed the luxury of riding boats,

---

* Another meaning of the word, 'Kichaka'.

Some others swung on forest-creepers,
And yet others travelled on horse-drawn carriages.
Fist on fist fell with resounding thud
Like thunderbolts striking on a mountain-head.
Rolling, pulling, trampling, crashing,
Louder they bellowed than rumbling clouds.
They yelled, bawled, growled, and snorted,
Like elephants at war and lions battling.
So they fought, in defiance shouting:'Can you survive the day?'
And, 'Fate has granted me my desired fight.'
At Kichaka's challenge, 'Who are you', Bhima shot back,
'No good knowing the enemy; rather pray your deity'.
And thus they fought on.
Unable to bear Bhima's smashing, thunderous fist
Kichaka, at last, on the ground collapsed.
Bellowing dreadfully one last time,
He rolled his eye-balls and gave up the ghost.
Bhima saw the body, listless, dead,
And leaving it there to his kitchen-house sped.

CANTO - VII

Flowers bedecked came the dawn-belle
Of bee-collyriummed lotus-eyes;
Her bird-song anklet-bells rang out tinkling
And the *kunda**-teethed stole all living hearts;
Dainty her aurorean feet
And sparkling her head-piece morning star.

The dance-hall watchman, all tremulous ran,
And with folded hands spoke weeping to the king,
'O royal master, inside the dance-hall
This servant has today seen a shocking thing;
You won't believe till you see -
I know not how to put it to your majesty.'

Anxious, exclaimed the king - 'How strange all this!
Speak, O guard, speak; speak without fear,
Hearing your words, in distress sinks my heart,
And my mind with doubts grows restive;
Hope nothing untoward be,
Speak first, then shall I go and see.'

Said the guard, 'O king, the bolted door is ajar,
The dance-hall is thick with dust,
And a huge shape lies there, broken-jawed, lifeless,
Its nose gory with congealed blood;
In terror as I approached,
To me it looked like Kichaka's corpse.'

---

* Kunda: A small white fragrant flower.

Startled by the words, the king rushed fast,
And royal minions ran alongside;
Citizens on the way saw the king's frantic haste
And groups upon groups followed close;
Entered the hall the king
And cast his eyes on the inert thing.

Disfigured twisted face, white eye-balls with upturned lids,
The tongue protruding between clenched teeth,
Blood that had streamed through nose and mouth,
Spilling over face and neck, had thickened on the floor,
Drinking which the flies
Droned and hovered around in swarms.

Dishevelled dusty hair spread on the ground,
Some strands lying on the faded face –
Was it Providence that waves of horror had reared,
To drown all kin in a current of pain*?
Peered and recognized the king,
But not a shred of belief could admit his mind.

Well is the proverb known of feuding eye and ear
But here in combat were the mind and the eye;
As the conflict raged, courage and patience left
Deserting the hapless heart of the king;
Shaken he went back
And the news through the palace with lightning-speed raced.

The flustered Kichaka brothers, ninety-nine in all,
In despair ran and saw his corpse;
Stunned in disbelief, as if by the thunderbolt hit,
They learnt Sairindhri had caused their elder's loss –
Promptly they resolved
Upon the funeral pyre must she burn with the dead.

---

* Gangadhar here refers to the *karuna* (pathos) and *bibhatsa* (horror) *rasas* (aesthetic emotions).

Some carried the body, some hurried for the rites
Raising a pyre of sandal-wood and rice;
Shaking in grief and anger, the remaining brothers
Rushed to Sairindhri with vengeful hearts -
By the hair as they tried to pull
In dread and anguish sank Draupadi's soul.

The mighty bellied Bhima, trembling in wrath,
Smeared all over in kitchen-soot,
In form terrible, rushed into the group
Like a tusker in ichor among lotus plants -
Some he laid low with fierce kicks,
And killed some others with his awesome fist.

Rotating by the hair some he flung down dead,
By the neck some others he smothered,
Some he lifted by their legs and dashed on the ground,
Into fragments he smashed yet someother's head;
Ran for their lives a few
Far from the carnage at Draupadi's house.

As they fled desperate,he gave them the chase,
A terrible figure in hot pursuit;
With his hair flying, his white teeth fearfully flashing
Faster and faster as he moved,
Wondered the citizens -
Had the god of death come in a vengeful mood?

In panic the men and women, collecting their young ones,
In a flurry bolted themselves in,
Unable to find his son, scurried someone panting,
And another ran home clasping his child.
Stilled was the city in fear
As birds in the forest when the falcon is near.

Over there the pall-bearers, lighting the funeral pyre
Were waiting for the others to drag Sairindhri there,
They saw it wasn't her, but their fleeing brothers
Pursued by a dreadful, dark figure -
As if maddened by hunger
Chases a deer-herd a black panther.

Fleeing all breathless, they reached near the pyre
And shrieked aloud, 'No hope of life now left,
This black thing from somewhere, has many of us slain,
And pursues to post us to death's abode.'
But vainglorious the others,
Vaunted aloud, 'Come, we shall together kill him off.'

'Kill, kill,' shouted someone, 'Pull his rumpled hair and kill;
Another said, 'Heave him by his legs,
Fling his body into the mouth of the roaring flame –
May he there burn and die.'
Hardly had he spoken when
The black one came and devastation began.

One by one he dragged by hair or by hand
And threw them into the blazing pyre
Wriggling all alive inside leaping flames,
Perished the Kichaka-brothers in terrible pain;
Kichaka's corpse too landed
And with plentiful food the fire swelled.

Sizzling, hissing, in malevolent form of flaming red
The fire drank the spurting blood,
Crackling, snapping, it masticated hard
And ate up the corpses all.
Oh, the one thro' the world so famous,
Now in a trice was thus reduced to cinders.

Washing off the black smear, freshened with a bath
Bhima went to resume his kitchen-chores;
Floated Kichaka's house, the palace and the city
On a sea of mourning lashed by waves of tear;
Women inside Kichaka's mansion
Poured out streams of tear from their eye-caverns.

Hair and clothes in disarray, emitting long hot sighs,
Beating their heads and chests, with stricken looks,
They rolled over and over, and slushed the courtyard –
Those women with tear-soiled cheeks and breasts;
Their deep wailing sound
Thickened with the palace-walls echoing round.

With hearts sorrow-laden the widows performed obsequies,
And stayed then reconciled to their fates,
Dreading the *gandharvas*' wrath, appeasing Sairindhri,
Sudesna too kept herself unprotesting and quiet;
The king, the city, the ladies,
With terrified hearts meekly bided all.

Prafulla Kumar Mohanty

INDUMATI

PART - I

Thrilled are the people of Vidarbha today;
The city is agog
Swaying upon waves of a sea of joy.
Princes many from far and wide
Are gathered for a *swayambara** called by the king
Where Vidarbha's princess would choose her consort.
Lofty mansions dressed in white,
Like hillocks of chalk-stones, glisten all around.
The air is filled
With neighing and trumpeting of horses and elephants;
Drums and pipes from various lands
Played in diverse strains
Resound all over, strange and sweet;
The noise of the crowds mingles with music
To overwhelm the ears.
Festive notes of bustling young maids
Fill the palace of the king.
With no room there,
Sorrow has removed herself far.
Maids of honour are astir, all in a flurry
To dress the princess.
One rubs the sandalwood, another musk,
And yet another weaves a garland of flowers.
One has brought out a box of jewellery
And placed near the princess with open lids.
She would choose and wear
The finest pieces, one by one;
Some maid displays a sheaf of *sarees*
Of glossy silk in myriad colours
For her to pick and wear
The one that takes her fancy.

---

* An ancient form of marriage in which a princess would choose her husband from among royal personages congregated for the purpose.

One has with gold combs dressed her dark satin hair
And woven into patterned braids;
Another girl there stands in front,
A gold mirror in her hand.
Out there the royal hall
Is decked out smart and grand,
Exquisite beyond all,
Putting to shame even Sudharma* above.

There arrived the princes one after the other
Like resplendent stars
Appearing on the lap of the goddess of the evening.
They settled on splendid thrones
Of burnished gold.
And it looked as though
Lotuses had bloomed forth suddenly
All over a lotus-pond.
Among them shone the young prince Aja,
Son of Koshal's king.
It seemed Indra among his heavenly host
Had descended upon the earth,
Or the haloed morning son
Had a burst of reflection
In the still, clear water
Of a pond of full-bloomed lilies.
As when the full-moon rises in the sky
The light of the stars goes dim,
So in the glorious presence of Aja
Low ebbed the pride of the princes.
From their mind at once ceased
All hopes of the princess' hand,
As at the arrival of Autumn cease
The rain-clouds upon the sky.

And then came the princess.
Demure, she stood amid the host of seated kings,
Quivering like a flash of lightning fair
Beneath a rainbow,
Or a lamp suddenly lit high

---

* The royal court of Indra, the king of gods.

Inside a quarry of precious stones,
Or the goddess of splendour* in august presence
In a forest of fresh-bloomed lotuses.
She, the charmer of the princes' minds,
With a bridal garland in hand,
Stole the glory
Of a lily-wreathed moonlit autumn night.
In wonder they gazed
At that image of loveliness
Suffused with a grace never seen before.
The beauty-craving hearts of the princes
Instantly dipped like fishes
Plunging deep in the sea of her charm.
The princes sat avid
Coveting the garland in her hand,
Like a whole swarm of hungry bees
At the sight of a single lotus in bloom.
But who would know, from whose garden of fortune
Came the flowers that wove the garland,
Who its possessor was?
The one to whose neck the garland would proceed
Would deem worthless the glory of Indra.

By the side of the princess stood Sunanda, the lady's maid,
Of intelligence keen and a proper age,
Who well knew the lineage, conduct and all,
Of the royal scions assembled there.
She first escorted the princess
To the presence of the Magadha King,
And in a sweet and limpid tongue
Detailed at length his virtues and fame.
'Look, O beautiful one,' she said,
'Here before you is the king of Magadha,
The only moon of the world entire;
A fascinating vermilion mark is he
Adorning the forehead of the noble Lady Earth.
Most caring to his subjects is he,
Deeply devoted to gods above,

---

* Kamala: Laxmi, the goddess of prosperity

Of a rare, exquisite handsomeness,
Irresistible in might,
Tormentor of enemies,
Worthy of his fame as vanquisher of foes.
If you so desire
Accept the noble hand of this great king,
And shine as star Rohini
By the clear autumnal moon.'
At this the princess, of the elephant's graceful gait,
Turned her face and walked up towards the next –
Indeed, has the lotus ever been
Happy with the moon?
Then her dear companion
Conducted her, the gem among maidens,
To the king of Anga,
And in sweet words described clear and full,
The charms of the king:
'Look, O maid of *Khanjana** eyes.
His Majesty here, the lord of all the Anga lands,
Verily another Cupid in grace,
The crowning glory of youth,
Sweet and tender this prince,
Bright with virtues large,
Master of vast wealth, quick of intelligence,
And learned in varied arts;
Scourge of enemy-hordes,
Gracious and gentle with friends;
Wise in codes and laws,
Skilled in warfare, an unfailing archer;
Pleasing to the eyes, of a captivating form,
That would entice heavenly dames;
He is the one upon this earth,
Your proper consort.'
But just as the *ketaki* flower,
Though full of fragrance is served not by the bee,
So, too, the beauty of the young prince
Did not charm her heart.
Her companion then

---

* A small black bird of quick flitting glance.

Led her to the presence
Of the king of Avanti, and excitedly said,
'Look, O dear one of quick sidelong glances,
Look, before you is a lion-king
Of mighty limbs and terrible power,
Bull-shouldered hero
Who blazes like the lion
In the world of tiger-like kings.
The mirror of his noble mien reflects
Enterprise and valour; in him it appears,
All virtues of the warrior-class
Or the heroic sentiment itself
Has taken a beauteous material form.
By the city, his capital, flows
The transparent Shipra of steady current
And surging ripples,
Adorned with flocks of cackling swans.
Upon its bank stands the royal palace,
Sky-scraping, exotic, glistening white;
And Mahakal's temple,
Its top gloriously resplendent
With the beams of the effulgent moon.
Women devotees of Shiva
Bathe in the Shipra at early dawn,
And carol in sweet, low tones
Offering worship to the god.
The temple too joins the chorus
In the form of echoes.
So moving are the hymns,
What to speak of human firmness,
Things even harder than rock
Would melt on hearing them.
Bevies of courtesans there
Fan the god with bejewelled chowries.
Round their slim waists shine
Muslin with gold-embroidered flowers.
If you crave to be adored as Laxmi
In that city of beauties marvellous,
Then take up here
The lotus hand of the king.'

As the night recedes from the morning star
And sails past the sky at dawn,
So did she, of a self-absorbed elephant's gait,
With soft tread glide away.
Approaching then the scion of Pratipa,
Of the line of the famed Kartabirya,
The enchanting one paused,
Flashed like lightning a brief moment
And then flitted past nonchalant.
She held back near the king of Mathura,
That princess non-pareil,
As her cockoo-throated friend spoke aloud:
'O moon-faced one,
'You must have heard of Brindaban,
Rich abode of nature's charms,
Where spot after spot,
Cupid has pitched
Exquisite tents of creeper-bowers.
Oh, the numberless creepers of jasmines there –
malati, madhabi,malli,
That entwine the trees to rise in beautiful bloom,
And fill the quarters with fragrance sweet.
Lovely Lady Nature
Showers upon the feet of the god of love
Handfuls of flowers.
Blossoms in happy cheer the soft morning breeze
Collects for her at dawn, everyday.
Through the woods flows the river Yamuna
In a plum-blue stream
Mocking floats of freshly-laden clouds.
A necklace of emerald it seems
Adorning the breast of the sylvan Laxmi.
The tendril-wavy ripples in their bosom hold
Shoals of fishes
Of molten silver hue, supple in aquatic dance.
Forests of thick-leaved *kadambas* are there
And fascinating groves of mango
Where delightful upon the ears descend
Ceaseless cooing of cuckoo-couples.
There in the forests of *jamun* trees
Flocks of parrots sit in happy repose;

And the environs resonate with
Full-toned notes of joyous dove-couples.
The gallant prince loves to roam those forests.
O charming one of glistening teeth,
Bright as pomegranate seeds,
Accept his hand,
And spend your days in revels sweet.'
She was not impressed,
The discerning elegant princess,
By words such as these;
For how should the swan
That longs to frolic in Manasarovara lake
Delight in ordinary ponds?
Ahead, seated in style, she saw
The king of the south who flaunted a heroic title,
The one who roamed through
The table-lands of Mahendra hills,
Whose land was covered
With the fragrance of flowers on creepers of clove.
But soon he was consigned to disquiet deep,
When the precious one withheld her favour.
Next across her vision appeared
The Lord of Pandya land.
Emperor Pandu,
Whose *Brahmasira**-arrow was a terror to his foes,
The sun of whose virtue and valour
Dazzled the world with its scorching rays,
Before whose might cowered
Even the redoubtable Ravana,
And whose feet were honoured
By plentiful gifts of the Malaya mountains –
Him now Indumati drowned
In a sea of shame.
Like the river Bhagirathi coursed the young princess
Forward, to unite with her own sea,
While like tributaries followed behind
The hearts of all other kings.

---

* Name of a luminous, powerful arrow mentioned in the Puranas.

Then she saw
The jewel among young princes,
His beauty as of a hundred Cupids in one.
Risen from the ocean of the solar race
A lucent moon was he;
From a tender half-smile on whose haloed face
Flowed a stream of nectar.
At his sight melted right away
The moon-stone of the princess' mind,
And in the pond of her heart unfolded
A hundred water-lilies of love.
Her eyes danced,
In ecstatic joy, like a *jivanjiva** in frolic.
She stood there gazing with unblinking eyes
And revelled within in silent joy,
As does the sun-flower at dawn
At the sight of the newly risen sun.
Aja swayed in uncertain thought, wondering
If the charming one would really be his.
Just then his right arm throbbed, and at once,
The good omen dispelled his doubts.
The clever Sunanda fathomed the princess' mind
And elaborated on Aja's glories:
'Here is he, O flawless lotus-eyed princess,
Sun-dynasty's finest jewel.
Oh, what ravishing form,
How gladsome to the eyes!
His arms reaching down to the knees,
And a countenance ever wreathed in cheer,
Well-built and of shapely limbs,
This prince, the young son of emperor Raghu,
Verily a necklace of precious gems
Upon the bosom of the goddess of royalty;
Lying on whose noble frame
Ornaments that are designed to deck
Appear themselves adorned.

---

* The bird '*chakora*' that 'drinks' moonlight.

Of irresistible might is Emperor Raghu,
Peerless wielder of the bow,
Hearing the twang of whose bow-string
Kubera, the god of wealth, was seized with fear;
And rained fast in the night
Countless gold coins for the royal coffer,
With which the Emperor of Kings
Honoured numerous holy men with plentiful gifts.
For the hundredth *Aśwamedha* sacrifice
That his father performed
He followed the sacrificial horse in close guard,
And when the chief of gods stole the animal,
Engaged him in fierce battle.
The unfailing thunderbolt failed
Upon the youthful person of Raghu,
The god then applauded and made peace with him.
Marching out on expeditions
He has made his victory-drum resonate all over.
Upon this vast expansive earth
He alone is the Emperor Supreme;
Kings bow down their royal heads
To pay obeisance at his feet.
The palace of Raghu is filled with
Precious stuff beyond the reach of gods.
Elephants that used to roam
The banana forests by the Himalayan springs,
Pace along his courtyard today
With vermilion designs on their foreheads.
Splendid white chowries of *Chamari*-hair*
Shorn from the animals on the plateau
Of Kailash mountains
Enhance the royal glamour,
Fanning the monarch's head.
Gems that used to dispel the darkness
In the deeps of the caves in Himalayan mountains
Illumine the king's palace in clusters today.
Pearls that were washed over and over again
In high-crested breakers of the sea,

---

* A variety of cows found in the Himalayan range.

Hang now stringed upon countless lines,
Swaying and glistening inside the palace.
His charming capital city
In the mirror of the river Saraju's waters
Surveys her white-painted face,
And vying in splendour and beauty
Mocks at Amaravati, the city of gods.
Charming gardens upon Saraju's banks
In great affection
Smear upon the body of the city-dame
Pollen from fragrant flowers;
And the sound of *mridangams**
Played by delicate fingers
Of merry female musicians
Echoes through the sky-high mansions
Spreading delight all around.
That city is a wondrous hall
Of entertainment for Beauty the Maid, where
Incessant flows a fountain of joy.
'O, you ornament of the earth!
Round the neck of this prince hang
Your betrothal garland.
Then shall you shine on the earth
Like a gold creeper upon an emerald tree.
In fun and frolic various
You will consummate your virgin youth
In the company of this consort dear.
When you loiter across the sands of Saraju,
The trees upon her banks would know,
You be a young bride in bliss,
And so in endearment fresh
Upon your head would handfuls of flowers drop.
Saraju would in the meanwhile keep gazing at you
With fish-eyes, stretching her rippling hands
In eager affection, to wash your feet.'
The princess stood there looking at Aja,
Still as a picture;

---

* A variety of percussion instrument.

Curbed by the force of bashfulness
She couldn't reveal her inner feelings,
Yet natural symptoms of love
Her heart made manifest;
For how can night's darkness
Conceal the scent of the wild jasmine?
Sunanda knew, but feigning innocence, said,
'O princess of the gait of the royal swan,
Let's then proceed to some other prince,
If such be your wish.'
When she heard this, the princess,
Sharp she fixed an angry stare
Upon Sunanda's face,
Like a she-elephant that roamed in the wild
When pierced with a goad.
And then the paragon of maidens
Putting the garland in Sunanda's hands
In a limpid voice intoned:
'Place it round the prince's neck.'
Enjoined thus the maid-in-waiting
Smartly lifted the ambrosial garland
And decked the bosom of the prince.
Drums then rolled and pipes trilled,
Auspicious conches blew,
And the concourse of Brahmins in the court too
Raised a chorus of sacred chant.
Clouds of dejection that darkened
The king-starred sky of the court,
Upon the field of Aja's heart poured
Continuous nectarous showers.
The lucky ones always meet with luck,
And the unlucky afflictions ever,
As when the ocean was churned
Vishnu got Laxmi, and Siva, all the poison.

The kings returned dejected to their tents,
Ruing their misfortune.
And King Bhoja went to the palace
Happily together with the bride and the groom.
Seated on an elephant
Covered with ornamented caparison

The scion of the Sun Dynasty
Shone with his young bride
As the chief of gods with his queen.
The city people knew the royal groom was coming,
And so welcome arches were raised
And filled sacred pitchers placed at their feet.
Mansions in the city wore colourful looks,
With garlands of mango-leaves strung,
Like strands of hair on charming foreheads.
On both sides of the royal path
Lined stood rows of banana trees
Which swayed and danced untiringly
Elegant in the soft breeze.
When on the royal street appeared Aja
In the marriage procession with his followers,
Suddenly there rose a din of joy
Through all the city.
Men and women of the capital,
Eager for a sight of the handsome groom,
Hastened to the place,
Their minds like boats with sails unfurled
Upon a current of curiosity.
Housewives rushed with quick steps
Up the roofs of tall buildings.
A young woman ran clutching
Her loosening saree in her lotus hand,
The sound of the tinkling anklets on her feet
Rang through the insides of the mansion –
It was as if the earth sang
Songs of benediction for the groom.
Another dame ran so eager,
Her braids loosened and the floral bulb came away
As though the moon had been released
From Rahu's mouth.
Slipping from the elegant coiffeur
Of a woman's thick long hair
The flowers fell one by one
Like stars from the lap of a cloudless sky.
The women arrayed in colourful raiments,
Some red, some yellow and some white,
Stood in rows.

Nay, women they were not, but a garland exquisite
Of the Lady-City, woven with
White jasmine, *champak* yellow and oleander red,
That she had sported
To her great delight upon her bosom!
The windows were crowded full
With lotus faces of youthful maids
As though the constellation of *Krittikas**
Shone upon mirrors numberless.

Seeing the peerless groom, his unmatched beauty,
The city-folks were swept
By waves of joy upon a sea of wonder.
The women stood transfixed
Still as statues of gold,
With all their senses and faculties
Crowding upon the margins of their eyes.
They exclaimed to one another,
'O what ravishing form!
Is it Kama, the god who was burnt
In the fire of Siva's anger,
Incarnated in renewed beauty?
How splendid his face,
That excels the rising moon of nectarous sheen
And smears upon the eyes on its own
A blissful unguent!
He is in his juvescence
Sporting a line of whiskers thin,
The lovely flush of his early youth
Brightening all about.
Fortunate is Indumati, blessed be she!
To her good luck was held the *swayambara* –
Were it not for the goddess of fortune
How could she have so noble a consort!
A princess she, naturally wise,
Of intellect superb and judgement calm,
Easily she picked the lone diamond
In a string of beads of quartz.

---

* A particular constellation of stars.

How charming they appear
The young couple upon the tusker's back!
Is it the sun upon the eastern mountains,
His consort on his lap?'

While people kept talking thus
Aja reached the lion-gate of Bhoja's palace.
The spectators fell back there,
Checked by the guards.
Women of the royal household came out then
And in great jubilation
Quickly escorted the couple in
And led them to the inner courtyard.
There they seated them on gem-studded seats
Upon a gold pavilion with decorated arches,
Raising a chorus of auspicious *hulahuli*.
That the heart of the noble maiden
Had been bound in love to the groom's
Was now made manifest for all to see
When their hands were tied with sacred *kusa** grass.
The young bride's coral-purple palm
Resting upon Aja's scarred hand
Looked fascinating as the dawn
Beautified with a sun-beamed cloud-mass.
As their hands were joined together
A sudden thrill warmed and tingled their frames,
Like the tree and its creepers being together in bloom
When the sweet southern wind begins to blow.
Honouring the sacred fire as a witness
The couple went round the sacrificial pit
And made their fealty-pledge,
Never through life to sever their tie of love.
They took a moral lesson,
That as the rising flame enhances
And brightens the fire,
So does the wife raise her husband's glory.
The blaze of the sacred fire
Soaked their faces
And on the sweat shone the flames
Rendering their countenance a deeper red.

---

* A variety of grass used in religious rites.

Precious ornaments and apparel on their bodies,
In that felicitous state,
Fully exhibited their splendours
Radiant in the firelight.
The blush upon the bride's face
And the ruddy swell of joy upon the groom's
Embraced, as it were, in that state,
Each the other's face.
Gazing for long upon the lustrous young couple
The women of the palace filled their hearts
With a new joy, brightened by a light new.
The priests, King Bhoja, and all their favoured friends
Showered on the heads of the bride and the groom
Sacred rice coloured with turmeric.
Then followed the ladies,
Similarly pouring the auspicious grains,
Conveying their jubilation
With the sounds of bracelets and anklets
That tinkled and rang out sweet.
All other wonted rites of wedding
Performed King Bhoja in great ceremony.
At the end of it all the princess,
Emotion-choked, her eyes tear-filled,
Took leave of all in sorrowful strains.
Offering her respect to the elders
She humbly touched their feet,
And lovingly addressing her friends
Held them in tight embrace.
Happy on gaining her husband,
But sad on parting from her kin,
In the heart of the princess commingled,
The *rasa** of joy with that of grief.

King Bhoja bade his sister farewell
Presenting her gifts rich and various;
Rode with the groom's party full three days,
And then took leave to return to his palace.
The prince with his retinue moved on
Seated with his beloved on a chariot grand
Heading for his home, his own kingdom.

---

* Aesthetic emotion as expounded in Indian poetics.

The group of rejected princes
Bereft of the gem, the princess they had sought,
Had lighted up the fire of envy
In the fastnesses of their hearts,
And were feeling scorched within.
They reminded each other in bitter tones
How Raghu in the past had trounced them all,
And planted his feet upon their heads.
Now his son in an open court
Had painted their faces black.
After such humiliation, lamented they,
How would they show their faces back home!
It was hard, they said, to go on living
Weathering such insults time and again.
Born into the noble warrior class, they exclaimed,
If one lived as a coward, and deemed himself alive,
Who else should be branded 'dead while alive'?
'Aja now travels with his bride, and so
Let us,' they proposed, 'throw upon them
The large net of our armies
And catch the two like a pair of wood-pigeons,
Bind hard and carry them away.
The hardest task in the world gets easy
When many unite as one,
As strands of thin jute rolled and woven
Keep on the leash even a rogue elephant.'

So conferring together
Haughtily advanced the kings
And with their vast armies
Launched an assault on the prince.
The young prince saw them charging,
The hostile kings with numerous soldiers,
Rushing as rain clouds terrible,
With their swords and spears as lightning flashes,
Elephants' trumpetings as resonant thunder,
The flags as flying cranes,
And the soldiers' battle-cry,
As a raucous chorus of *dahuka** birds;

---

* Bird associated with the rainy season.

Sharp-edged *ketaki* flowers, the daggers,
Rainbow, the archer's-bow –
Thus rushed the army of massed clouds
To devour the Aja-sun.
Aja knew they would,
On the small retinue of his fiery soldiery,
Rain down unending showers of arrows.
And so he enjoined his minister to guard his beloved,
Then picked his bow and arrows
And himself advanced to the battlefield.
He exhorted his soldiers:
'O Warriors, O you heroes, see,
See how the enemy like a murderous ocean
Rushes at us.
Come, let us boldly cross it
With the ship of our strength of arms.
Where Aja is the helmsman,
Never should you apprehend the ship might drown.
Forward you advance,
Concentrate your beings' might
And destroy the enemy hosts.
Heaven's joys, if killed in battle,
And life of affluence, if victorious;
But a life in hell is certain for him,
Who earns the infamy of retreat.'
Hardly had he finished when
The two armies clashed in fierce struggle.
Warriors in chariots, foot-soldiers,
Fighters on elephants and cavalry-men
Took on each their counterparts,
And engaged in straight combat.
So vast were the strings of arrows
Released into the sky,
The battlefield went dark
With their thick downpour.
Contending warriors could no longer know
Friends from foe; and wrought up so,
Many were immersed in the play of war,
Fighting their own ranks as if in a spell.
Alone did the mighty hero Aja
Fearlessly take on the host of kings,

Riding and crushing his foes
Like a lion among a herd of tuskers.
Now with the bow and then with the sword
And again and again with the mace
He charged and cleared away
The forest of enemies;
Now and then the enemy kings
In a quick move encircled him
And wrathfully rained upon Aja
A continuous shower of arrows.
But with each arrow Aja flung,
He broke those in hundred pieces.
And then himself covered the battlefield
With irresistible arrows flying fast.

Thus with the passing hours
The battle grew fiercer and fiercer.
The sky in all directions became dark,
With the only light that of the flashing arrows.
The battlefield now turned
Into a rousing theatre of music and dance;
The elephants and horses in song,
In a high pitch keeping rhythm,
The archers playing their bow-*veenas*
And the headless torsos at dance,
Which the deities of the quarters watched,
Surveying both the warring ranks.
And then the raging hosts appeared as fearful currents
Terribly perilous, with elephant-formations
Like a maze of huge boulders
Loud with a roar of angry yells,
And streams of thick blood with foamy turbans
Where nimbly played swords and knives
Like shoals of fishes.
Hoping to cross the river with boldness
The warriors sailed through enemy-canyons,
With the aid of their bow-canoes and oars of arrows.
All those belligerent kings again
Showered their shafts on Aja;
But beyond their pale was the heart of the prince –
Not ruffled in the least.

He flung now the powerful *praswapana** arrow,
Which swiftly flew
And made the battle-fatigued armies
Fall into a deep swoon.
Some fell asleep on their chariots,
Some others on the backs of elephants and horses,
Still others freely lay down
On the ground softened by the flow of blood.

Having thus won the battle, the prince
Repeatedly blew a sonorous victory-conch.
His soldiers felt so elated,
They waltzed all over excitedly.
When men do not judge their own strength and that of others,
And are mastered by anger,
They sink into dismal depths
Of the ocean of calamities:
So the royal armies lay there fast asleep.
Had Aja wished, he could have easily then
Killed off the entire lot.
But it's only with the strong
That the strong display their might.
To test one's strength on the weak
Is against the ideal of the warrior-class.
The sleeping, the unarmed, and the ones
Who have come for succour,
Women frail, messengers, and children –
To kill them with one's superior strength
Brings obloquy upon a hero's name.
The righteous one thus stuck to his virtue
And saved the enemy ranks,
Like the waters of the sea
That cross not the shore
Even though obstacle-free.
The kindness of the noble heart
Is equally offered to all,
Like the tree that does not withdraw its shade
Even from the person who comes to raze it down.
The heart of a kindly being
Grows naturally sorrowful when he sees others suffer.

* In the Puranas, the arrow that induces sleep.

So the prince only provided the relief of sleep
To his battle-exhausted enemies.
The mind of the noble one does not grow cruel
Even when tormented by another –
Would the sugarcane yield anything but
Sweet juice when it is crushed?
After adroitly churning the enemy-sea then
The expert warrior Aja
Joyously returned to his wife, emerging
Like an elephant from the lotus-fields.
Seeing her husband at war,
Tears had streamed down
The eyes of the young bride
Like dew from the sky at night's end.
Now she experienced a rare delight
To see her husband thus victorious,
As if the charming lotus-maid
Saw the face of the sun
Released from the cover of the clouds.
Looking at his beloved said the prince:
'O dear one of lovely lips, crimson as the *bimba*-fruit.
Watch, watch the battlefield with a fleeting glance –
How many princes, come for your sake,
In arrogance born of blind anger,
Bereft of far-sight, almost lost their lives
As animals in the sacrifice of war!
Their families when they come to hear of this,
Will all be swept in currents of grief.
So many of the kings, their faces bloody,
Lie prostrate with the corpses, on the ground,
Away from their flower-bedecked downy beds.'
Hearing these words the bashful Indumati
Lowered her head, smiling softly.
Herself shy, she made her friend speak
Words of praise on her husband's prowess.
Thus throwing salt on the slashed noses
Of his enemies, Aja resumed
His royal progress towards his kingdom,
Flying his banner of victory.

PART - II

Anguished at heart with the absence of the prince
The queen of Ayodhya, having had
No news of him for long,
Sorrowfully said to her confidant maid:
'At the end of the night last I saw
A dream, a most wondrous one,
When I recall it now, my body trembles
Like a banana leaf in the wind.
The prince, my son of tender limbs,
Was returning upon an elephant white,
The maid-in-waiting was swaying over his head
A white *chamara.**
On both sides of him flew
White flags and banners fluttering gaily.
On my son's lap shone his bride,
Beautiful in immaculate white.
On his broad chest hung delectably
A garland of milk-white flowers.
In the young bride's hands lay reclined
A long stemmed white lily.
Upon their heads fell flowers
In a shower from the hands of the artists in heaven,
Witnessing which my eyes were afloat
Upon coursing waters of joy.
Next I dreamt that numerous kings
Attacking him from every side
Fought fiercely against my young child;
Pierced by the enemies' deadly arrows
His delicate body was soaked
In blood that ceaselessly streamed.
As I watched utterly helpless,

---

* *Chamara* is a fan, made of the hairy tail of *Chamari* cows

Tall tides rose in a sea of sorrow
And swallowed up quick the vessel of my patience.
Suddenly then my sleep broke,
I sat up on bed and looked around
Trying to find my son.
The hair on my body had stood up on end
Like thorns on a *kadamba* sapling:
And it was soaked in sweat
Like the lotus in dew at night's end;
Not a moment's sleep could I have after –
All night I spent brooding over my son, the prince.
After that strange dream
In a ferment has been my mind.
And my heart gets splits
Thinking of the prince, his body pierced with arrows.
O, that I might see again
The unblemished face
Of my child, the life of my being!
When will the apple of my eye be here
And drive my sorrow away?
Of natural charm ineffable, my son
Has gone to the *swayambar* assembly;
In envy the kings there, may be,
Have wished to do him harm.
He is of such a tender age
And innocent heart, my son,
How would he escape injury
If the kings there hatch an evil plot!
Protector of the helpless, O Lord,
Saviour of the defenceless,
Wielder of the sharp-toothed disc,
Shield my friendless child
In the shadow of your mighty arms.'
Thus spoke the dispirited queen
To her dearest maid-in-waiting,
And sat still like a rock in summer
With all the heat of sorrow embosomed within.
Her oval face on her left palm supported,
She looked like a day-old flower
With its loosened stem which lay
Bent over a tender leaf.

On the royal platform in the court was seated
Emperor Raghu,
With vassal kings many in attendance,
When approached the prince's messenger.
With bowed head and folded hands he advanced
And touched the emperor's lotus-feet in reverence;
Then he narrated the events of Vidarbha city
In accents of uncontainable joy.
'O Noble Lord, king of kings,' he said,
'The *swayambara* was happily done,
And the most beautiful maid in the three worlds
Hung the auspicious bridal garland
Round the neck of our young sweet prince.
So many kings who had come there
Went pale and ashen in their faces
When they did not receive
The light of favour of the beautiful moon
Shining in the Vidarbha sky.
Completing then the wedding ceremony
In great pomp and splendour
The prince was returning home
Bringing with him his peerless bride,
When the jealous kings, blind in envy,
Joined hands together and attacked him
With pluck and insolence high.
They all suffered defeat
At the hands of our single prince.
For how can a herd of goats ever triumph
Over a cub of the king of beasts?
After planting his left foot on their heads,
The prince, the mightily powerful one,
Is returning home; his tents today
Are already pitched on the bank of the Ganga.'
Hearing the news the noble king Raghu
Felt delight deep and intense,
As if some one had suddenly into his ears
Poured a stream of nectar.
Issuing orders to his ministers
To decorate the city, he hastened
To his wife in the inner apartments
To convey her the happy news.

The queen heard,
And the realm of her joy then
Expanded limitless;
It was as if a mountain rill
Had cascaded down a heat-oppressed head.
The news was loudly announced
In the streets of the city,
And the citizens were agog
Thrilled beyond measure.
The city of Ayodhya was drenched
In a pure moonshine of joy.
All were loud in the praise of the prince,
'Glory be to him, glory,' they exclaimed.
Hearing the news all the feudal chiefs
In pomp and splendour went forth
To escort the prince into the city.
Felicitated by all
As the prince rode home in their company,
He narrated the events of the battle,
Imparting the while to the eyes of the people
A joy priceless and rare.
Together then with his bride he went
To touch his parents' feet in great devotion.
Seeing the prince with his young bride
The king and the queen in happiness swelled
Like the sea at the sight of the moon
In a full-moon-embellished night.

A few years later the king
Bestowed on the prince the charge of the kingdom,
Himself embracing the *banaprastha dharma*;* and in due course
Left for the world of the gods.
Aja ruled,
Easily shouldering all the kingdom's burden
That his father had gifted,
With not a trace of vanity tainting
His wisdom-brightened heart.
With filial love he nurtured his subjects,
Impartial ever and attentive to all,

---

* Duties of a renunciate in the third stage of life before *sanyasa* or final renunciation.

And consumed the enemies like blades of grass
In the flames of his scorching might.
Nectar-white moonshine
Of the full-blown moon of justice
Dispelled from his kingdom
All murk of dishonesty and evil.
Not to speak of his heart,
Even into his ears couldn't enter
Scandal and calumny that might be whispered around
By envious rumour-mongers.
But sorrow-laden prayers of the suffering people
Found a passage quick, echoing loud
Through the mansion of his heart
That was filled with precious gems of compassion and mercy.
Aja's treasury served only the people's need;
Not a mite from it was wasted
Misled by anyone's deceptive words.
He craved not any sensuous delight,
But was always keen on the people's welfare.
When he found his subjects happy,
He revelled in joy in his untarnished mind.
Subjects who had enjoyed Raghu's benevolent rule
And were now bereft of his care,
Through Aja's reign
Did not at all feel his absence and loss.
All of them chanted the refrain
Of Aja's immaculate name and fame.
Only the demons of sloth and insolence cavilled,
Finding not any stay.
Low habits like promiscuity and theft,
Even when they put on alluring garbs,
Could never beguile the people's minds
In the great realm of Aja.
Bestowing on Indumati his fast, unwavering love,
Aja passed his days in connubial bliss.
In due time Indumati conceived,
And in due course was born a handsome son.
Wishing that his son's chariot
Should range through all ten directions,
The king declared,
'By name of Dasaratha may my son,
Be famed through the entire world.'

Like the moon in the bright fortnight
The baby grew day by day.
Watching which the parents experienced
Measureless joy.

The season of Spring arrived then,
Intent upon serving the Earth-queen.
First he draped her body in the silk
Of purple-coloured soft young leaves,
On her forehead then carefully arranged
Curls of creepers and vines,
And then decked her hair
With fresh-bloomed, captivating flowers.
At night he hung on her bosom
Strings of the pearls of dew,
Which the sun in the morning everyday
Snatched away stretching his hand (ray).
He sprinkled on her body a perfume
Stolen from the Malaya mountains,
By the cool, soft breeze that blew
From the south sea, wet with the spray of its waves.
Honey-drunk bees sang sweetly,
And forests and gardens were sweetened, too,
With the dulcet notes of the cuckoo.
When Aja, the lord of the earth, saw
The Earth-dame's beauteous form,
He went out to enjoy the pleasures of the garden,
In the company of his beloved wife,
Verily the earth's jewelled necklace.
As the couple roamed in the flower garden,
Lost in entrancing love-talk,
On Indumati's chest fell suddenly
A flower garland from the sky.
The moment she beheld
That celestial garland,
The bird of her life flew off
And her body sank dead on the ground.
Seeing his dear wife sprawled out
Like an uprooted tree,
Into a swoon by her fell the king
Like a shadow beside a body.
Regaining his sense with the tender care

Of his attendants after a while,
Longingly he looked at his wife's body,
But found it was devoid of life.
The body that had the dazzle of burnished gold
Lay now colourless, utterly wan,
As if a statue of gold had suddenly
Changed into mercurial form.
Solemn and cautious, he placed his hand on her chest –
Cold it was, like a stiff iron under the bare sky
At the end of a wintry night.
He saw her face was no longer wreathed
With the habitual soft smile;
Her eyes that trounced the quick-flitting *khanjana*
Were now cold and still,
With her brow and cheeks gone ashen and pale.
He placed his hand at her nostrils, and found
The life-breath did not blow.
Unable to contain his grief then,
He held her in his lap and lamented aloud:
'O, the one of matchless face,
O simple, tender, kind-hearted dear,
What fault of mine did harden your heart,
And made you leave me so?
So often had I caused you offence, dear,
But never had I found you sore,
Not for once did my ears receive
Harsh words from your lips; and now
In your voice that trounced the tinkling *veena*,
You say no word to me,
And have left me drowned in
Grief and fear, awful, insupportable.
O my dearest, your body was
Of the element of compassion and mercy,
Over which the creator Brahma had
Cast a plating of love.
Maybe, you found me hard-hearted,
Felt repelled and have shunned me thus;
But does the lightning ever leave
The thunderbolt however hard?
O lotus-eyed dear, wake up, wake up for once,
Open your eyes and with nectar-sweet looks
Dispel the unbearable pain that assails me.

O dear wife, without you
The world looks plunged in darkness deep,
Much like the newmoon night
Under the darkest clouds, and without a lightning flash.
Memories crowd across the mind's path
And relentlessly rend my heart.
The pathway that cool and pleasant goes
Through thick-leaved mango groves,
On which fall grains of sunlight
And look like stars upon the blue vault;
There where trees are locked in embrace
With the flowering *madhabi* creepers,
Making fragrant the ground in all four directions;
Where the crickets sit and loudly chirp
In unbroken piercing tones,
And mellifluous notes of countless cuckoos
Entrance the mind;
There where squirrels dance in joy
Wagging their tails, and drongoes,
Perched still on branches,
Break into twitter every now and then;
There holding your tender hand
I wandered through the noon, and
We joined in love-talk seated on
The platform roofed with *madhabi* vines,
And gleefully played the game of love
Throwing flowers at each other.
In our palace where the gold lamp
That needs no oil, dispels the darkness,
And which is always filled with
Perfumes of resins and joss sticks,
Where the grand-bed of ivory
With its mattresses covered with sheets
As white as the froth of milk
And kept ready with pillows
Round as the full moon of autumn –
Forswearing all that today
At the cremation ground you will lie on
The laps of the flaming pyre.
That terrible vision will haunt
And blind my pupils for ever.
Is there anything more heart-rending

In all this universe?
Oh shame, that my heart of stone
Has yet not cracked into pieces!
Who would now sing the nectar-sweet
Love song to the trill of the *veena*?
With whom shall I sit in swelling joy
And make sweet music?
You have left,
Throwing me inside the deepest well of grief,
At one go making me, for ever,
Renounce all worldly cheer.
Our little boy,
Sweet and tender as the young moon –
How distressed you used to feel
When separated from him for a moment –
Where, where, my soul-mate,
Have you departed today,
Pushing him off on a river of grief?
Where are you gone?
You did not bid adieu
To your companions whose hearts
Were ever one with yours!'
He paused and looked at the flower garland,
And then continued the plaint again –
'Ah, my strange fate, so unheard of,
That a garland which is pleasing to the neck
Should sever it.
Such a flower-garland had
United me with my beloved,
And this new one today has
Separated us for ever.
And so I think what is deemed
Prosperity at the hour of good fortune,
The very same object when bad time comes
Serves as a source of unending peril.
At one time the beautiful lotus
Spreads fragrance growing in water,
And the vapours of the very same water
In another season, lay it waste.
Ah, to my wife who was a tender princess,
So delicate of limbs,
Was the flower-garland so hard and heavy

That it smothered away her life?'
Seeing the king so disconsolate
The servants and attendants loudly wailed,
And in the form of echoes
The royal garden, too, in resonance moaned.
In a moment was the city of Ayodhya
Drowned in torrents of grief,
And the people, shocked and distressed,
Sent up loud mourning cries.
Hearing of the death of the queen
Friends and relatives of the royal family,
Rushed grieving to the king.
Forcibly they took away from the king's lap
Indumati's lifeless body
And cremated it in the roaring flames
Upon a pyre of sandal-wood.

Staying there in the garden itself,
The king performed her funeral rites
With all due custom, and then
Returned to the palace with a forlorn face.
He kept confined to his living room
Like the hapless serpent that had lost its gem.
His body he roasted and burnt
In the fire of his beloved's separation.
Food, pleasure and royal duties –
He despised all as if they were poison.
To him the world appeared
A dense and desolate jungle.
Maharshi Vasistha, the royal preceptor,
The great soul of perfected penance,
Who, by opening his wisdom-eye,
Could command a view of all three worlds,
On whose lotus hands were pictured clear
Happenings of the periods three,
Soon knew all the events
That had occurred in the royal house.
In order to dispel the darkness of grief
Shrouding the heart of the king,
That sun among the sages sent a disciple –
As though a beam of light of his.
The neophyte came to the king

And was received with respect due.
Then he conveyed to the bereaved king
The sage's message of counsel. He said:
'As the great sage was pledged to a *yajna*,
He couldn't come, and so has sent me to you;
Listen with attention to his message, O king –
"Just as the sky is only itself,
So in the entire world, you,
Possessed of all kingly qualities, are peerless.
Your mind is like the ocean, most deep and calm;
No pain and grief should unsettle it.
Whatever is destined to happen would happen
In this world, and it can never be otherwise;
Only those who are not wise,
Nurse grief in vain in their hearts;
Not to understand what Destiny ordains
And to be ruffled in heart on that count,
As ordinary creatures do, is not
Proper for persons of your eminence.
When the flood comes, no doubt, the trees
On the river banks are swept away,
But does the lofty mountain ever shake
Even as floods upon floods follow?
All beings take birth on the earth
Bearing fruits of action of earlier births;
They partake of those fruits here, and then leave,
Led by the law of *karma*.
The lamp of life keeps burning in the body
For the span that the given oil lasts;
When the oil of years is exhausted,
The flame is forever gone.
The *Purusha*,* Who is beyond all thought,
Alone has the right to supply the oil.
He takes note of the *karma* of different creatures
And justly distributes the oil.
Whoever is born into this world
Would certainly die some day or the other.
The all-devouring Time at every moment
Keeps swallowing lives.

---

* The Primal Being; the Creator.

Many have been monarchs of power measureless,
Only their names we now have, their bodies all gone
To the fearsome cremation ground.
To your race belonged a king,
A crest jewel of royal crown.
His name was Puranjaya, and his fame
Had spread beyond the earth to the land of immortals.
Where on earth is he now, he,
The most glorious one, the hero of heroes?
He could not counter at all
The inexorable might of Time.
King Dilipa, your grandfather
And Raghu your emperor-father,
Whose powers were as those of Indra and Shiva,
Are they to be seen today?
The body-tree is not eternal;
It stands upon the banks of the earthly river,
When *prana*, the soil at its roots,
Is washed off, it floats away
In the swift currents of time.
No one is another's, O King,
Each one from this market of delusion,
Once the money is spent,
Returns along his/her separate way.
She for whom you are mourning so long,
Has already banished you from her mind,
And lives now in great joy in the land of the gods
Assuming an *apsara*'s body.
Once the great *rishi* Trinabindu
Was engaged in penance awesome
Deep in a forest when
A heavenly nymph, Harini by name,
Came at God Indra's behest
And displayed amorous postures
To distract the sage and break his vow,
Seeing which the great *rishi* in anger cursed –
"Be thou born a female on the earth."
At those words of the *rishi* the nymph
Faced terrible hazard, and so humbly prayed
For respite with folded hands.
But whereas words of ordinary men, like the turtle's head,

Issue and get withdrawn off and on,
Words of the noble,
Like the elephant's tusk,
Once out, shrink not back.
Yet the inside of a *rishi*'s heart
Is always and ever naturally soft,
Though the outer demeanour be hard,
Like the shell of a coconut.
The *rishi*'s heart began to melt with pity
At the humble appeal of the nymph.
With a charitable mind he spoke aloud to her
The means of relief from the curse:
"The day your eyes chance to come across
A heavenly garland of flowers,
That very instant will you regain your form,
And the shores of mortal life cross."
She thus grew in the line of Krutha-kaushika,
Like the young water-lily in the pond,
And since you are the moon of the world,
She served your heart's delight.
As you roamed in the garden with your beloved,
Your minds filled with the bliss of love,
The *veena*-playing Narad, the divine-*rishi*
Was moving along the skiey path of gods.
As destined, by the force of the wind,
The flower-garland slipped off the end of his *veena*,
And as it fell on her chest, the celestial maid
At once was freed from the curse.
You won't recognise her if you see her now,
She too will not know you, for how can she?
It does not thus behove you to feel
So bereaved, without reason, at her loss.
O noble king, from your mind erase that past,
For whatever was to happen has happened.
Dwelling on the past and brooding in sadness
Is forbidden by the scriptures.
O benevolent king, apply your mind
To keep your subjects happy;
To the king are his own subjects
The most precious wealth upon the earth."'

Having consoled the king with these words of advice
Vasistha's disciple took leave
And went back to the hermitage.
The lamp of wisdom he had lighted
In the abode of the king's heart
Was put out by the gale of delusion
That was drenched in the water of grief.
For the king, his body in mourning
Getting thinner and thinner,
The burden of the kingdom
Grew insupportable.
To him this world of sorrows and material goods
Appeared as but poison.
After some time he put his worthy son
On the throne and coronated him,
And then he left for the place
Where the rivers Ganga and Saraju meet.
There he gave up his mortal body,
And rose and moved to the world of the gods,
Assuming a divine form.

Soubhagya Kumar Mishra

UTKAL-LAXMI

Glory to you, O Utkal-Laxmi:
A paragon of beauty on earth
In whose limbs, at once, dwell
All natural loveliness.

For your habitation
Enchanting hills have pitched
Towering retreats whose scenes
The poet's power of description baffle.

And on the land there below those tents
Roam herds of deer and doe so dear to you
And elephants excited with ichor
Flowing down their temples.

And for your pleasure
Stand here and there
Many a beautiful garden
Filled with fragrant flowers.

There in the deep forest
At the foothills wander
Merrily in herds
The wild beasts you have reared.

And here on the earth green with
New-grown grass go grazing the cows
And with only a desire to serve you,
Keep moving their chowrie-tails to and fro.

And there lie well-decked
Swings of flowering creepers
While the birds sit and sing,
Eager to send you swinging.

And here for you is laid
A bed of cool white stones,
While there stand in waiting
Trees with leaf-fans in hands.

Angsupa and Chilika are famed as
Your beloved lakes for water-sports
In whose midst stand so many hills
Like charmingly laid out pavilions.

And for you, the beautiful Nature-dame,
Your beloved companion, has,
Preserved with great care,
Ornaments many, at various places.

And at Pradhanpat [1] she has treasured a jewel
Scintillating for your *simanta* [2]
The story of whose beauty has spread
Through lips of men to distant horizons.

How subtly has she set on twilight's head
A piece of glass to reflect an image
Of the celestial gem concealed for you
Deep in the bowels of Gumdarh! [3]

Behold: for you has she spread
A necklace of pearls on the sea-shore,
Whose radiance turns pale
The pride of stars.

1. "The Pradhanpat falls in Bamanda constitute a bewitching sight. Lovely rainbows are formed on it in the sunshine."(Gangadhar's note)
2. Parting of hair in the middle on which married women wear vermilion and a chain.
3. Canyon on Mahanadi near Sambalpur.

On your breast lie the Garjat states
With their rulers bright,
Like a locket radiant,
Studded with mine-dug, dazzling jewels.

Your limbs, with the lustrous twin gems,
Sri Rama and Sudhala,* are suffused
In light; a few other lesser lights, too,
Shine there, twinkling.

Some gems there lie pale
As though they never were,
And some others have been stolen away,
By the cruel thief of time.

With stringed floral ornaments is decked
Your head, the sweet triplet of
The illustrious, the wise, and the poet
Spreading out fragrance enthralling.

Your limbs are well wrapped
In white silk of Benaras, the British rule,
With golden fame embossed, line upon line,
In floral designed embroidery.

In so many ways does the Night,
As your beloved companion,
Decorate you; smears your sweet limbs delicate
With dust of camphor that are the drops of dew.

Smears lovingly now the cool
Soft sandalwood paste of moon-beams,
And now anoints musk in the guise of
Darkness rubbed into paste.

Of your beauty enamoured,
Did Lord Jagannath forswear,
The pleasures of the palace of Dwaraka,
And sports in the forests on the banks of Yamuna;

---

* King of Mayurbhanj and ruler of Bamanda, respectively.

And appears at Nilachal,
Like the rising sun on eastern hills;
Throwing his huge arms
Around you in close embrace.

The Lord of the Three Eyes abandoned the city
Of Kashi, to settle in Ekamra forests.
He is here satiating his eyes three
With your exquisite beauty.

And Ganga came flowing
In the footsteps of Lord Viswanath,
The purifier of the universe,
In the guise of river Chitrotpala;

Who on the way was warmly
Embraced by goddess Samalai,
Under the pressure of whose hands
Her necklace on the bosom snapped.

Frantic for the necklace, the goddess
Dug there deep into the earth.
And the deposit of heaved sand
Hardened as a mound.

That is the place people today
Call Hirakud, the diamond-dune
From where gathering diamonds many
Your children have wealthy grown.

Some way down when Lord Maheswar
Of Huma, charmed by her lovely form,
Fondly beckoned to her,
She was ready to flow out to Him.

Breaking into a separate stream
She crossed forests intractable
Infested with hostile rocks
And went north as the Lord's finger had traced.

The Lord appeased, in the mainstream
She mingled and flowed on fast;
And seeing her approach
Lovingly you took her on your lap.

This union is, that your lovelinesses
Should mutually enhanced be;
Thus Providence has thrown on the neck
Of an entrancing image a chain of sapphire.

The Creator who fits out Autumnal Beauty
With a wreath of lilies and moonbeams,
Who has decked a glittering jewel
On the forehead of the heavenly maiden Dawn,

Who has lent to the faces
Of young maidens world-bewitching grace,
Who has breathed fragrance into the flowers
And calm into the hearts of saints,

Who errs not the slightest in
Joining together the worthy, each with each,
That Providence it is Who has gifted you
This ornament divine.

The seasons, as your gardeners,
Supply in abundance flowers varied.
O noble one of floral array, you are
Peerless in your passion for flowers.

Spring presents *navamalika*,
Madhavi, *kanchan*-flowers that
Lines of bees pursue unremitting
Greedy of their fragrance deep.

Summer offers *champak* flowers
And fresh *baul*-blossoms,
Desired by the gods,
And Monsoon, clusters of tulips and jasmines.

Autumn pleases you with *ketaki* and lilies,
    And Late-Autumn with marigolds a hundred-fold,
While Winter offers you worship,
    With charming *sevatis* and mango-blossoms.

Sitting one summer noon
    In a mango-grove I heard
The crickets for you playing
    In deep tones upon their flutes.

And I saw a wind-god
    Carefully plucking
For your offerings
    Sweet, ripe, golden mangoes.

With a devotee's love I picked
    From the offerings a few,
And returned, O Mother,
    Intoning happily the song of your glory.

One monsoon I noticed
    The sun was about to set
While upon the east gathered
    The darkest mass of clouds.

On the lap of the wet clouds
    Lay a rainbow wondrous;
On her forehead the blue-clad East
    Was decked with the seven jewels,

While the maiden West
    Stood in the opposite direction
Wrapped in robes of golden light,
    And with her head-ornament, the sun.

The two charming damsels before you
    Danced with many a lovely posture,
While birds burst out singing
    In tunes heart-entrancing.

On a certain morning I saw them
    In changed costumes, standing
In front of your lion-gate,
    Their dancing art to display.

Thus do all the Beauties of the universe
    Engage in your service high.
Who can be there on earth, O Mother,
    Whose felicities may compare with yours?

Once in the past on a full-moon night
    In the month of *Margasira**
In my thatched cottage I sat
    Engrossed in thoughts of you.

Climbed the moon into the middle of the sky
    And silent fell the earth
And the jackals at the end of the village
    Declared it was midnight.

At this hour occurred
    An event, most strange,
Which now flashes across my mind
    And makes my hair stand on end.

A goddess, supremely beautiful,
    Appeared before me,
And lovingly said,
    'Rue not my child, rue not:

Pleased with your devotion,
    To kindness moved, I shall
Unfurl before you this night
    A deep secret of Utkal's.'

So saying she led me
    By the hand, into a swift-moving
Divine chariot, and drove me
    In the twinkling of an eye across the skies.

---

* November - December

As we proceeded, the chariot
Entered into a realm strange,
Splendour and beauty of whose kind,
Never had I heard of before.

In the middle stood an imposing
Structure, all silver
Supported by pillars of crystal
Fitted with diamonds.

There on a throne of ivory,
Strewn with white flowers,
Sat a shining young man
In white robe.

The radiance of his limbs
Brightened up all four quarters;
Cleansed were the sins of my eyes
To behold such beauty undreamt of.

On his large breast were visible
Patches of blue
Which, to me, appeared only
Marks of musk lovingly smeared.

To his left sat a lady
Of beauty non-pareil,
Clad in white muslin, through which,
The light of her limbs shone transparent.

And the sweetness of her noble face
The deep poison of grief had drown'd,
Yet it seemed the very source
Of the divine creeper of delight.

I don't know what thoughts
Compelled that peerless lady
To drench the earth
With her ceaseless tears.

With her head down, she sat,
            Her cheek resting on her left palm,
As if a lotus with a broken stalk
            Leaning on a lily in bloom.

Ah, the young one of lovely fish-eyes,
            With a beauty never seen before,
Was she Love-incarnate, embellished,
            With the best of every charming thing?

To find a simile worthy of her
            I pressed my fancy long and hard,
But that peerless lady
            All my similes surpassed.

I tried new hyperboles,
            But the more I struggled,
The more that jewel among maidens
            Turned into a hyperbole beyond all hyperboles.

So lovely she was, yet
            Immersed in a sea of grief,
As though Sita sat overwhelmed,
            With news of Rama's exile;

As though Radha was sitting in sorrow
            To hear Krishna leaving for the city of Kamsa;
As though, a traveller weary,
            Confronting a vast, vast desert.

And my heart lit up with
            Flames of curiosity to know
How the wild fire of grief had
            Spread into the flower-garden of her delight.

Into my ears then whispered *Prajna* *:
            'The young man is the moon
Whose beams ambrosial
            Dispel the darkness of the earth.

---

* Goddess of wisdom.

Wives twenty-seven has this one
Dependent on him, and he,
Residing in each house a day
Keeps them happy.

Now he departs from *Rohini* [1],
To visit *Mrigasira*'s,[2] and so,
A fatal fever of separation
Lies in wait to seize her.'

Alas! that the person is so cruel,
So hard-hearted, he leaves
A new-blown flower
To the withering rays of the sun.

Oh, how ruthless is that one within
Who joins in marriage to so many maids,
Even the thunderbolt would accept defeat
Before a heart such as his.

Maidens, therefore, desire not
A royal consort who has a harem,
But would take joy in a cottage,
Living single with their mates.

'It's time, darling', pleaded the moon,
'I left your quarters,
With a smile now happily,
See me off.

Raise your head and speak to me,
Be not piqued, my dear:
And watch out for me, for I'll return
On the twenty-seventh day, for sure.

Most delightful is reunion,
After a separation.
Entertain not any doubt,
Surely shall I come – I shall come.'

---

1. & 2. Positions in the zodiac.

On the delicate maiden every word
Fell like a stroke of thunder,
As though on the soft *sirisa* flower was
Poured torrent after torrent of water.

'It's my fate,' moaned the maiden,
In a voice choked with grief,
'I can't have happiness more than a day
Through every twenty-seven.

A lot more there are, my lord,
To please your heart.
I wonder then why the world affirms,
I'm the partner for the Moon's revels.

Never could my hunger go,
Though joined to the nectar-yielding Moon;
Amid the joys of heaven, ever I suffer
The pangs of separation, all alone.'

'O fair-eyed one,' exclaimed the handsome Moon,
'To tarry here a moment more
I've no right. Who has the power
The laws of God to transgress?'

'See, see, my Lord,' said the lovely one,
'How the earthlings roam,
In great rejoicing
Absorbed in conjugal bliss.

The king there sits in his palace
Holding the hand of his queen,
And his subject in the leaf-cottage sits
In the company of his lovely wife.

Chakravakas alone spend lonely nights,
Sorrowing in separation,
Anxiously watching for the advent
Of the female messenger, Dawn.

The company of their beloveds,
All other birds excitedly enjoy
In water, on land, on the boughs
Of trees, floating on the waves of love.

See, see upon the forest ground
In delight the stag and the doe
Freely roam, to each other bound
In strings of love.

Let aside the living, dear,
Even the non-moving observe you once,
See how the *madhavi* creeper lies locked
In the embrace of the mango tree.

You are so discerning, my lord,
Be kind, and if you know, tell me,
In what way do I match
The earthlings' felicity.'

'You alone are my life's partner,'
Said the Moon, 'Your love-stream only
Is fit for the sport
Of the swan of my heart.

In the *Nandana** of my heart
You alone are the *parijat*,
The rest to an inferior breed belong
And in me no longing inspire.

To sport with you eternally
Is my deepest wish;
It is only the constraint of Providence
That this desire foils.

Let's descend then together, darling,
Upon the earth; let us go
In human frame, and I'll for a while
Your exclusive company enjoy.

---

* Heavenly garden where the never-fading *Parijata* blooms.

Captivating and holy in *Kaliyuga* [1]
Is the land of Utkal where
In the form of *Darubrahma* [2]
Presides the Lord.

Lord Siva the great ascetic is already settled
Away from meditation and penance;
Where, too, has already gone the divine Ganga
World-sanctifying, lucent stream.

Where, in the temple at Konarka has
Chhaya's lord, the Sun, chosen His abode;
And Brihaspati, preceptor of gods,
Already gone to manifest at Devadurga.

Among the people He would be known
As the ever-kind master Sudhala
Whose effulgence will
Illuminate the whole of Utkal.

Already gone is the Muse herself
To compose poems in Radhanath's name,
Whose songs would make the land of Utkal
Renowned through entire Bharat.

Let's go darling, to that holy land
To sport merrily there where
Beings empyrean and gods are thus
Severally incarnated.

There in Utkal is a state
Beautiful, Mayurbhanj by name,
Where the ruler of the lineage of Sri Ram
Is a jewel of the solar race.

There I'll be born in the palace,
Holy and lovely, where the ruler,
The famous Krushnachandra, righteous and wise,
A crown among the king reigns.

1. Dark Iron Age.
2. The lord of the holy stump - Jagannath.

Born into Rama's dynasty
I'll bear the name, Ramachandra,
And for my handsome look will the people
Name me a second cupid.

Ends of my eyes 'ld faintly bear
Traces of my dark spots,
But in the guise of letters shall *Prabha**
Carry my white light far and wide.'

With joy was I overwhelmed
To hear these words, and
In the sea of my delight were raised
Waves irresistible.

'Glory, glory to you, Mother' Utkal-Laxmi,'
I intoned to myself time and again,
'That gods and goddess are thus born
To adorn your virtuous lap.

Thus do the wise proclaim,
That as saviour of the lowly, Lord Vishnu
Has appeared at Nilachal, carrying
With Him all the sacred places.

Hence has the poet declared in Sanskrit:
Chitrotpala is the Ganga of *Kaliyuga*.
Secretly hence the river of white waves
Is transfigured into waters of blue.'

Lo and behold: before me suddenly then
Appeared a figure colossal,
The queen of queens, Rajarajeswari,
With discus and mace, lotus and conchshell.

The comeliness of her dark-blue,
Smooth, feet-touching, curling tresses,
Created in my mind
The illusion of a wave-tossed sea.

---

* 'Prabha' means 'lustre'. *The Utkal Prabha* was a literary journal.

And on her hand was a crown
Sky-licking and dazzling, so
Beautiful – who wouldn't say
It was by Viswakarma Himself made?

The crown's beauty was thrown into relief
By *mallikadhi*, ear-ornament like the tulip-bud,
Which kissed by the hair on the rims
Has its charm increased manifold.

Magnificent she looked in ornaments
Of Bengal on the right hand
Of Telengana on the left,
And of the Larias on her feet.

On her waist lay in the folds
Of her robes, a girdle of gold
Shining clear, with its jewels set
That burn away the eyes' sins.

A pious devotee who had performed
Her *abhiseka*[1] with water from Saraswati,
Sat engrossed in prayer. To my eyes,
He resembled Radhanath Roy.

He muttered: 'Glory to Lalatakesari,
Wise in the art of monuments
Who has fitted upon the head of
The Goddess' image, a crown grand.

Praised be Langula Narasingha Deva
And King Anangabhima
Who, gifting the *mallikadhi* for the goddess,
Have become monarchs of the land of fame.

Praised be the Buddhist kings
For inscriptions[2] fine on her forehead
Though not of the faith, they too have
Acquired merits to enjoy in after-life.

---

1. Ritual worship by pouring water, milk etc. on the image.
2. Also means dots of *Kumkum* paste on a bride's forehead.

'With what'll I worship you, O Utkal-Laxmi:
    What resources have I of offerings?
With pure water of river Saraswati alone
    Fetched from afar, I've your *abhiseka* done.'

Bewildered I stood, for I heard not
    The names of those who had gifted
The lovely girdle; I thought, though donors be,
    If left unsung, useless was the generosity.

'They're Chauhan rulers,' whispered Prajna,
    'Who'd that fine ornament endow'd,
And, in return, some salvation
    Attained, others the heaven adorned.'

When that devotee supreme
    The mantras chanted,
Back sprang the dead
    Into new life and form.

And illumining the four directions
    And carrying offerings and uttering,
'Glory to Utkal-Laxmi,' came
    The so-called inanimate that cannot move.

With a swelling breast came Yayati,
    Holding the banner of victory
On which was painted the picture
    Of a terrible lion lolling its tongue.

Came then the monarch Purusottama
    With a royal umbrella studded with gems
That had been rubbed to shine
    With the powdered pride of Kanchi.

Came Chodaganga Deva then
    And fanned her with a *chowrie* white,
Which, moving, resembled
    River Bhagirathi's* first flow.

---

* Ganga from heaven, which descended on the earth on King Bhagiratha's supplication.

Came Jayanta, holding
        A fan fashioned with peacock tails
And his jewelled headgear, too,
        With peacock tails decked.

And behind the goddess stood
        Gangeswar Deva, his face down,
Hiding his shame behind
        The bejewelled border of her *saree.*

And then came the maidens, holding
        In their hands plates of offerings
With fine flowers and incense,
        And lighting a jewelled lamp.

Came goddesses Lalita and Vimala,
        Holding each others' hands,
And Padmavati Devi came too,
        Her face sparkling with gems.

O'erwhelmed with her love new-found
        Her feet with shoes of shyness shod,
Down a path of thorns came Nandika,
        With the gem of victory as gift.

In the twinkling of an eye raced in
        Usha, among heroic women foremost,
In one hand her bow, in the other
        A fierce arrow burning as mid-day sun.

Hiding her face with her clothes came Kausalya
        And Parvati, holding a bill-hook,
And with her was Annapurna
        Bright as the venus star.

Her feet gone crimson, crushing
        The young sun's passionful overture
Chandrabhaga, the virtuous maid,
        Hastened to the spot.

Troubled was my mind
Even one of Ramai's dynasty not to find,*
Recalling at that hour Balarama Deva
And Kamala Kumari, his queen.

Meghasana, Gandhamardan, Gonasika hills
Appear'd before the goddess,
Not missing their way in the forest
And holding aloft their torches, sky-kissing.

And with them were Malayagiri
Vara, Saptasajya, Kapilas, Saranda
Charchika, Dvisira, Varuni hills,
Their hearts all filled with joy.

The hillocks of Viswanath and Taradevi
Indeed were smaller than they,
But by the power of mantra they found
In the catalogue of tall hills a place.

And invited by mantras,
Came Mahendra hills, his head with
Dense jungle capp'd. And with him were
Bhaleri, Sileri, Kalijai and many others.

And in their midst appear'd
Manibhadra like a dome of gems
Loud with the notes of parrots and cuckoos
Of nectared sweetness to the ears.

And like a priest royal
There appear'd Pradhanpat with his retinue
Holding in his hands a *jhari* extremely beautiful,
A sprouted jug studded with gems.

And the tall hills not mentioned in the mantra
By themselves came and to the eyes invisible
Stood around like lines of soldiers
Broad-chested, ranging to the horizons.

---

* Among those figures mentioned earlier who had been made famous by Radhanath's narratives.

And the mountain Nimai stood
Appearing the tallest of all,
And o'er it shone the star Agastya
Scintillating like a jewel on its crown.

Bankasama stood like the Nimai hill
With its bosom lightning-brightened,
And beside him was hill Karalapat
Holding countless armed Kandha soldiers.

And Tikiriguda hill stood with
Upturned face, eager to offer
A million *bharas** of oranges,
Alluring and luscious.

And there stood at the gate
Harishankar and Narasinghanath hills
To perform in time the *abhiseka*,
In the holy waterfall, Sahasradhara.

And in their company were forest ranges
Hefty, tall and thick, full of
Fine *nageswar* flowers in full bloom
And *naranga* fruits ripe to the core.

And there stood goddess Patneswari
Patna's deity, holding a pot of incense
In her hands, ringed with silver bracelets,
And her body wrapp'd in yellow silk.

And goddess Ramachandi had carried
In silver plate, sun-dried rice
Which, in the eyes caused an illusion
Of grains of diamond.

And with garlands of wild tulips,
Stood decked in the courtyard
Hills like Sisupal, Barapahar,
Chhelia and Jharaghati and Barapati.

---

* Two balanced loads hanging down either end of a pole carried on the shoulder.

When I saw there Budharaja hills
Holding bouquets of *gangasiuli* jasmine
I gazed again and again
With eyes filled with love intense.

And I saw there standing many
Tall sal trees with gifts of
Motijharan's *amla* fruit
Looking like garlands of pearls.

And to the north there stood
Mankadnacha hill with a corps
Of numberless elephants and his worthy
Brothers three, Badamgarh and all.

And with his kins and an army
Of horned deer well-arrayed
Before them, hill Mana had
Maintained his pride,

And fascinatingly dressed, deck'd
With various ornaments,
And their chignons with flowers adorn'd
The rivers dancing.

Foremost among them was Chitrotpala,
Her braid with diamonds decked,
Pre-eminent as Urvasi
Among the heavenly dancers.

Behind her came river Brahmani
With flowers of gold in her hair
Engrossed in dance she bothered not
About the flowers that fell.

And river Deva with her breast
Adorned with the lovely garland
Of flowers pluck'd from Singhbhum's royal garden
Danced in Koili's company.

And were sweetly singing Vedavyas'
Songs lyrical, while the hillock
Brahmani was throwing on Koili's head
Handfuls of flowers.

And the golden river Suvarnarekha
Came flowing with companions many
Carrying the white flag of fame
Of Singhbhum's kin, embroidered with gold.

And Baitarani had worn lovely forest flowers
Greedy of whose fragrance
Gods and goddesses encircled her
In the guise of bees.

And with a variety of flowers –
Champak, *chhuriana*, *punnaga* –
Were the braids of river Bhargavi
Virupa, Daya and Ratnachira deck'd.

As if only out to witness the festival
Ib in the distance kept dancing within
Concealing her lotus face
In her lovely robe, green and fine.

And while river Ang was rushing on
To join the group of dancers, dissuaded
Chitrotpala, whispering into her ears:
'You ain't yet an expert dancer, beware.'

Tel was there, though out of sight;
She could not gain the fame of
A graceful dancer, yet in her heart
Continued to flow the stream of music sweet.

And in the background both
River Tel and Chitrotpala sang
The songs of Brajraja, Raja
Of Kharial, in tunes enchanting.

And decked were their hair that heaved
In knots, with bunches of flowers from
The forests of Khariar: the maidens two
Captivated men's minds, smelling so sweet.

Rushikulya sang her nectar-sweet songs
In Karnataki, and fixing to the tune
Of Kavisurya she carolled
Enchanting the hearts of all.

Jira, Danta, Jhaun, Ranja
And Khulari rivers, as participants gay,
Contrived for their parties a superb harmony
Of song and music and dance.

And happily clapping, sang
Rivers Bheden and Malati
Anika and Goshali and Uttali,
Simple mellifluous songs.

Stealthily rushing in, river Kharakhari,
Began her dance near the spot,
While river Harad, in the company of *Veena*
Merrily in excitement ran.

And the sea blew loud and deep
A crore of conchshells
And with its sacred water performed
Lord Lokanath's first *abhiseka*.

Narasingnath follow'd pouring
With water from Koilighogar
Clear water that ran down the
Foothills of Kodabagabhumi.

Making their splendid appearance
The Saptamatrikas poured the sacred water
Followed by deities innumerable
Their hearts brimming with joy

Among them was goddess Samalai
In red silk, decked with hibiscus garlands
I knew her from Hirakhand*
That on her forehead glittered.

And on the forehead of Rajarajeswari
Goddess Samalai put a vermillion mark
And her face grew lustrous
Like the sea with the rising sun.

Lake Chilika of garlands of swans
Laid carefully round the goddess' neck
A necklace of pearls she had kept
Skilfully stringed together.

She was followed by maiden Angsupa
Who reverentially laid a wreath
Of a million lotus on the goddess' breast
Raising *hulahuli* with the cackle of ducks.

And Gandhagiri offered handfuls
Of sweet-scented *nageswar* flowers
Whose fragrance overwhelmed
The charming *abhiseka*-ground.

And goddess Sureswari who had come
Brightening with her ornaments all the quarters
Offered her worship, holding in her
Leaf-tender hands a golden lamp.

Goddess Padmasani and Chandrasani
Who had the first row adorn'd
Sang their hymns in soft, sweet tune
And overflowing devotion.

Lord Kedarnath decked with lilies blue
That were ornaments of His lucent ponds,
Raised His hands with trident embellished
And shouted 'Victory to Laxmi.'

---

* Diamond piece.

And great saints with Vyasa and Parasara
And Goutama and Bhargava, too,
Came shouting loudly,
'Victory to Utkal-Laxmi.'

And groups of Buddhists and Jainas
Holding the banners of Ashoka
And Parswanath, rent the skies
With loud shouts of 'Victory to Laxmi.'

Their foreheads bearing holy marks various
Danced there groups of Vaisnavas,
Beating mridangams and cymbals and clapping loud,
And singing, 'Victory, victory to Laxmi'.

And then came showers of flowers
And filled with cheer all directions.
Wondering wherefrom the flowers came,
I then looked up at the sky.

And I saw a number of chariots
Of merry white flowers in full bloom
Floating in the sky
Like autumnal clouds.

A rider each chariot had,
Of radiant form,
Resembling lightning
Transfixed upon a cloud.

On top of the chariots
Were inscribed letters rare and bold
Or, were the letters made
Of pure mined gold?

And delighted were my eyes
And my heart to discover there
Names of Jagannath Das and Balaram Das
And Karana Krushna Charana.

And I read again, and the names
Of Raja Krushna Sing and Sarala Das
A saint among saints, and Dinabandhu Das
And Upendra Bhanja swam into view.

And scribbl'd was the name Abhimanyu
Samanta Singhar, and on his banner
Were drawn paired figures
Of Radha and Krishna.

There were still a number
Of chariots I was eager
To know, but blurred were my eyes
With streams of joyous tears.

Flooded was my bosom with the streaming tears
And my being lay exhilarated,
And from my toe-nail up to my nose it seemed,
I was in bliss immersed.

Pabitra Mohan Nayak

LONG LYRICS

NIGHT OF THE MOON

1

Glancing at the ample moon the night-dame
Upon the full-moon dusk hastened her preening.
She decked her brows with vesper bright,
And her ears with the gleaming Pole star, and *Agastya.*[1]
A smile played on her rubied lips,
And she wore a visage cheerful and pellucid.
Illumining the sky with his robust form,
The moon gathered her into his tender beams;
Sweetness thus compounded honeyed the world –
Felicity as this only a blessed hour upholds.

2

Tender as a flower did the night's body
Thrill at her lover's touch.
Swept through the heart's deep-sea a tide of passion,
And the brows of the sky were suffused in radiant beauty.
Young lovers, when they met,
Brought out their graces opulent in mutual touch.
The earth, the sky, the air and the water
Merged in a cosmic beauty.
Can anything in the world with such a beauty be on par?
Can the pebble ever with the pearl compare?

3

Even the rock's heart, the moonstone, ealted in that beauty,
And forests of water lilies in the ponds revelled,
So did herbs and vegetation on land and hills.
And the sky with the *chakora's*[2] song merrily trilled.
Brightened up hamlets with lamps in every house,

---

1. A star in the southern sky, named after a sage.
2. *Chakora* is a bird that revels in the moonlight.

And with bells and gongs temples in excitement rang.
Myriads of hearts pranced in joy's abandon,
And in joy capered kids in groups.
Joy had taken the world captive–
Acknowledged all over is the power of the mighty.

4

Piping his flute the cowherd followed
The eager homeward cattle lowing in joy.
The frisky calves in the pen flicked their tails,
Impatiently sucking their mothers' teats.
Humming a jocund tune, from the weekly market returned the village swain
And from the *ghat* returned the fisherman wearing a happy mien.
The dancer in the dance-hall waved his arms in grace,
In delightful postures, casting sidelong glances;
All displayed joy in mirthful ways,
And thus the world buzzed loud as a village fete.

5

Happy at the moon's sight broke forth a gallant–
'The limpid moon shining through the autumnal night';
And his dear mate joined recalling the next line–
'Lustrous like the God of Love, as a mirror polished bright.'
'Seeing which the noble youth desperate grew,'
Continued the former;
And the second one in melodious tune completed the quatrain:
'And urgently began an epistle pleading and tender.'
Thus they did roam through the night, lost in moonshine,
Singing the verses of Bhanja, line after line.

6

Soft and pretty as watter lilies, a bevy of maidens,
Intoned in varied styles mellifluous strains.
Flickering their nimble eyes adorned with kohl,
Off they ran, and settled again, rollicking about in several ways;
Lovely jewellery on their arms and feet
Rang tinkling to convey their offer of ardour.
And someone's carelessly tied plait, coming off loose
Was the target of a young maid's sweet rebuke.
In the river of joy that flowed in spate
Merrily the lasses swam about.

7

In the palace played the princess with her mates,
As did noblemen's daughters in their mansions,
And daughters of the citizenry among themselves,
All impelled by the frolicsome, mirthful moonshine.
Sweet words of the soft-voiced dames
Mingling with the nectarous flow of the moon
Brought forth a charm that the insensitive knew not,
But to the connoisseur was delectable fare.
In Vrindaban quavered the magic flute –
But who savoured other than the ardent milk-maids there?

8

His royal duties over, the king stretched his back,
And eagerly walked out to enjoy the moonshine.
A student opened a book and called out to his mate,
And excitedly showed him the letters, so distinct and clear.
Back home from the fields, the farmhand cuddled his young son,
And walking about joyfully kissed the infant's moonlit cheeks.
Out there wailed a baby in the mother's arm,
While she cajoled it with Uncle Moon's charm.
The moon, too, made the child blithe in wonder;
Which heart to its divine beauty wouldn't surrender?

9

Forgetful of his fatigue, the wayfarer walked on his way,
His heart uncannily overflowing in joy.
He moved, as if floating upon a torrent of moonlight,
Singing to himself many soulful ditties.
Broke forth another in spontaneous undertones,
But not having a fine voice, into bashful silence sank.
Elsewhere rose a full-throated cadence,
To which kept rhythm the *veenas* of the damsels of the quarters.
Somewhere the bullocks merrily pulled their cart,
As, the driver being lost in song, the switch in his hand stayed still.

10

Borne upon a stream of joy moved the pilgrims devout,
'Glory to Lord Jagannath,' one among them cried out,
And others joined in a chorus of invocation.
The farmer in the field heard the sound of this holy rejoice,
And joining, 'Glory to Lord Jagannath,' he too raised his ardent voice,

Hearing which the pilgrims with redoubled vigour,
Repeated the self-same chant.
Their voices came sailing from all directions,
Chanting a paean of the Lord's glories,
And making it appear as if the very flora were at prayer.

11

With legs thrust upward slept a little bird[1]
To protect itself perchance if the heavens should fall;
O what vigilance, indeed, against mischance –
No fear now even if the heavens were to crash!
As it flew through the sky, curious to know who the traveller was,
'Who's there? Who's there?' the tattler bird queried.
And the traveller answered,
'Lord Rama's man,' walking away gently.
With the holy name fixed in his heart,
Off flew the bird to the other end of the sky.

12

The black buck, its mate and the young ones
Headed for the fields with lush green crops,
Portraying the great poet's account,[2] as it were,
Casting sweet glances all around, as if spellbound.
Startled and curious, every now and then
They leapt through the sky in graceful patterns.
Did they, familiar with your deer-crested form,
When seized by dread, seek to fly to your shelter?
This be ever the pitiable way with the small,
To rush to the mighty whether it helps or not.

13

Hardly birds,[3] the bats hung from branches with their heads down,
Like Shambuka the low-born doing penance in Rama's kingdom.
But bird-like they winged around as the night fell,
Behaving as brahmins self-content,
Glutting themselves in great relish

---

1. The tattler-bird.
2. Kalidasa's *Shakuntalam*.
3. Pun on *adwija*, which means both 'non-brahmin' and 'non-bird'.

With fruits and leaves fresh, and belching aloud.
Indiscriminately they ate up all alms,
Moving from village to village, house to house.
The lowly, too, may brahminical privilege acquire;
The world cannot dam up a law of nature.

14

The plump moon, gentle and exquisite,
Rose high upon his august seat;
Thinner he grew as he gifted the rays,
But his splendour increased more and more,
As does a saint's when he ascends a higher plane,
Blazing forth more radiance, while in mind growing subtler,
Quailing never at sacrifice for the good of the world.
Thus excels in virtues the saintly moon,
With none to compare with him,
Like the sky that compares with itself alone.

15

The moon was once effete and the sky was dark,
When he lodged himself deep in the sun's zodiac.
Some humans then gave him up as dead,
And an obsequial fast at his death observed.*
But reappear he did and again waxed
As the days rolled and the nights passed.
Full away from that influence, the full-moon
Thus extirpated murk with his mighty refulgence.
A man, however famed, surely declines in grace and honour
If to someone else's house he goes to take shelter.

16

The moon was once crescent-thin;
Brightening the night's face just for a while
He left; and in the pangs of separation did the night
Spend her days in silent sorrow.
But the stars joined with the lily,
And dispelled all her grief.
Co-wives though they were, bearing no ill-will,
They displayed their generous nature.

---

* On the new-moon night some people keep a fast.

When someone in the family falls into distress,
The kinsmen always act as his buttress.

17

Demure, like Indian women inside the apartments,
The stars concealed their faces from their consort,
While like an English wife jubilant,
Arm-in-arm with her husband strolled Night.
The stars remained stationed at their house,
With no right to take a turn with their spouses;
But nothing is forbidden in Night's code–
Neither distant lands, hills, rills, nor towns and bazaars.
They think high of themselves, the stars,
But only in night's domain are their faces lustrous.

18

The Moon to the Night owed all his grace;
In her hands lay all his affluence.
Heavens's constellations at her doorstep toiled,
Dancing in varied measures for her pleasure.
Most powerful is Night, the *Yogini*–
The Supreme Giver, day and night, of knowledge and vision.
Blessed by her the firefly
Shines like a star of the sky.
She the Night, giver of peace to fear-seized mortals,
The secret source that inspires impossible victories.

19

The Seven Sages[1] watched eagerly
For a sight of Night's beauteous form;
In the northern sky's hands they placed lamps seven
And accorded the guest a luminous reception,
Seeing which Arundhati [2] hid her face
Bashfully, and softly smiled in suggestive irony.
She extolled Night, saying, 'Well done, O maiden,
The empyrean sages you have enthralled,
Thy charm the cosmos binds, O Dark Goddess,[3] incarnation of Time,
All be thy votaries – human, demonic and divine.'

1. Constellation of seven stars – The Great Bear.
2. A tiny star close to the seventh one in the constellation.
3. Kali.

20

Mercury, the Moon's son, lovely and most tender,
With frolic and fun Night's courtyard he adorned;
Enjoyed the stars his playful manner
And cuddled him with affection by quick turns.
This sage* again ran back to Night's loving lap;
She fondled her child's comely face,
And beside herself with the thrill of love,
She hugged him close and kissed his joy-wreathed cheeks.
No child ever heeds the mother's reproof;
But would play upon the laps of whoever loves –

21

Serving forever at Night's feet
The poet attained divine bliss,
And revealed a celestial vision, nectar-steeped,
Unaffected by mundane din and care.
The Night-dame, beloved of the nectarous moon,
Threw open for her devotee a treasure-house of ambrosia,
Which saw not the unpoetic ones, knocking about
As they did in their dreams in the world of sleep.
Only the poet, whose genius the car of imagination drives,
He alone has sway in the world of emotions.

22

Ascetic or sybarite she delighted all;
Revealing unto the *yogi* the world-vision prophetic,
And offering the pleasure-seeker a face enchanting,
Of sumptuous beauty, honeyed and soft.
To the *yogi*, Night's abode shone bright
With truth transcendent, in galaxies of well-cut, resplendent gems.
Night, for the man of earthly pleasure was the mother's soft bed –
Where he drowned his senses and thoughts.
Lamplight, moonlight, lightning-flash – lights, lights everywhere!
Charmed were the mortals in the world of Night, enjoying their fulgent fare.

---

* In Indian mythology, Mercury is revered as a learned planet-deity

23

Who are you, woeful one, sitting by yourself, desolate?
Why do you so piteously cry?
Why are you bereft of your lover, poor thing?
Why all this plaintive note that so shakes the forest?
Aren't you the shelduck, darling of your mate,
Who through the day used to kiss his most adored face?
At your dalliance had throbbed the freshly bloomed lotus,
Sending into agitation the waters of the pond.
But what is ordained by Destiny can never be altered –
On the heels of joy would sorrow follow ever.

24

The lotus, the mother of Brahma who ordains, and darling of the sun,
Kept in great sorrow, wearing a visage woebegone,
For Laxmi,[1] beloved of Hari,
Had left vacant her bosom's throne.
Heedless of His mother's feelings, Brahma with His ruthless pen
Did inscribe a line of misery following one of delight;
Would grief now release the lotus,
Which it pounced upon, coming so close behind joy?
Good or bad, conduct is the seed that man sows,
From which later a similar crop in his lot grows.

25

Unmindful for a while of the rabbit's saying
In Visnusharma's fable,[2] so well-known,
Sported the elephants in a tank, with their ponderous trunks swaying,
Among tangled lotuses, sending the moon's image tremulous.
Thin and tender the lotus-stalks, like the moon of the second digit,
Which they pulled from the roots to eat, violently dashing against the water.
The plight of poor Lotus had gone from bad to worse,
No defence did she have from any quarters at all.
Shame on Providence, shame on its thoughtless way –
That it should grant such license to a block-headed brute.

1. Laxmi, the divine consort of Hari (Vishnu), Goddess of prosperity, sits on a lotus.
2. Vishnusharma is the celebrated author of the fables, *Hitopadesha*.

26

At the zenith held his court the moon,
The emperor of beauteous supernal realm,
The delight of all eyes, among lustrous stars supreme;
Only a few blazing luminaries he chose for his retinue.
The ones fittest to keep his company
Had been cordially offered seats lofty,
But the lesser stars who could not vie with those
Retired to obscure quarters with faces bedimmed.
In the company of an exalted peer, the worthy in his glory shines.
While ill-matched to a superior, the worthless at his fate repines.

27

Pouring in though the orifice inside the cavern
The moonbeam dazzled as a diamond on velvet dark;
The moon had shot a luminous dart, as it were,
At the newborn Rahu* in the lying-in-room.
Spots of moonlight, lying scattered over the forest deep,
Looked like myriad arrows from the moon's agile bow
That had pierced through the back of Darkness in flight
When the moon pursued him like a hunter.
Dew drops streamed down like blood from his wounds, as it were;
And Darkness on the ground lay, flat on his face.

28

In the world of nature, saw the moon, peace had sovereign sway;
A cool zephyr glided gently through the realm,
The humans all blissfully rested in the lap of peace,
And fire in their hearths slumbered peacefully.
Enjoying the bounty of peace the forest flowers
With beaming faces diffused their fragrance sweet;
The cool streams of the mountains into silence froze,
And the earth became an abode for peace to dwell.
The cricket struck a note, which was long and sustained,
And in all four quarters the presence of peace it proclaimed.

---

* Rahu is the demon of darkness, born of a lioness. Cavern is the place of his nativity.

29

A song of peace droned the concourse of bees,
Ranging through the land, the waters, woods and gardens;
Streams and lakes played the music of peace,
And the foliage upon trees in a low tone hummed.
The gentle waves on the water kept a liquid rhythm,
And the fish joined merrily in the aquatic dance.
The green grass softly swayed on the earth's bosom,
And swinging and twirling, vines decked the sky.
And moon and the stellar bodies were immersed in the *Santa*,[1]
And as reflections danced upon the bosom of water.

30

The moon heard in the west the ocean's awesome roar
And saw the high tides surging towards the shore;
To restore order in the briny realm,
With his troop of guards he then proceeded thither.
The western walls of Varuna's[2] city he crossed
And was received into a realm of priceless gems.
He sunggled in the father's gentle, loving lap
And sank into immeasurable bliss.
Hills, cities, land or water – wherever the worthies visit,
At each place does cordial welcome greet their revered feet.

Ashok Kumar Mohapatra

1. Reference to *Santa rasa*, state of serene joy.
2. Sea-god, mythical father of moon.

SPRING-DAY

The night ended, the earth looked bright,
And the sky above glowed, bathed in light.
All that had been visible in the dark, in the light vanished –
Rose a new spectacle, instead, to greet the light.
In the deep darkness when we were lost,
The planet-friends had stood by us.
Though small in size, that their courtesy was great,
This, of course, we must readily acknowledge.
The larger, kindly planets, too, that remained afar
Served their good as best as they could;
But beyond them still, the friendly community of stars
Persisted in goodwill with genial hearts.
For friends however away still act friendly,
With a feeling heart, in times of distress.
In the sky those stars were no longer seen,
Setting out of view wherever they had been.
Some in the east, in mid-sky had some others dwelled,
Many in the western quarters had lain in recumbent state;
In the north and the south had been harboured many more,
But all just melted away at their respective sites:
From the east billowed a tide of blaze
And engulfed at once the heavenly realm.
Bearing the onslaughts of the havoc-wreaking waves
A planet or two that had still lingered,
Caught nose-deep in the torrents, began to lose their hold,
And defenseless at last, their heads sank.
Light advanced to extirpate the sources of light
Like the axe-handle of forest-wood hacking away the forest.
A new young cousin was thus born in Indra's abode,
And the fire in the lying-in-room was seen flaming up in the sky.

In no time arrived the Friend[1] of the day
And the chill of winter mitigated with gentle rays.
He revealed himself in a form mighty and grand,
And imparting joy, stole heart and mind.
Caressing with warm hands (rays) the heads of hills and trees,
He wiped away tears from Nature's eyes.
With reddened lips of *palasa* the earth then did smile,
And the silk-cotton tree got busy, showering scarlet flowers many,
The sylvan goddess amused herself in various sports,
And *kamalagundi*, the powder of saffron and red, in the air was blown.
Dhataki blossoms and the leaves freshly sprouted
Smeared the forest's limbs with a colour of red.
Blood-red lotuses in the water, and on land the valley-lotuses
Reddened the earth in their myriad throngs.
Masses of algae in water and the *doob* grass on land
The sky above and its reflection below,
Coated the world with a blue hue deep.
In the spray of cataracts and the waves of the sea
Sported the rainbow with its spectrum of colours.
In the distance stood a mountain donned in apparels blue,
While another nearby appeared in rosy garbs.
Mansion upon mansion ranged in a mantle white,
And jasmines and *nialis* caught the reflection.
Leaving their nests settled bids on tree branches
With the bowstring-wings drawn taut for the battle of life;
Their feathers (armour) by the bills they carefully arrayed
And formed a battle order in the lotus-shape.
Humans under the siege of the monster Sloth had overpowered lain,
On their faces poured Consciousness the nectar of animation.
With difficulty were the eyes opening slowly when
The new friend with his hands (rays) offered them an ambrosial unguent.
Awakened to a new life, strength and mind all fresh,
Through the world, a perilous forest, began to wander humankind.
Perching on the wall-tops [2] the sparrows in flocks
Watched the first sunrays on the brow of the east,
And puffed joyously the feathers in habitual style,
While the sun's limbs grew full-blown, slowly.

1. The sun.
2. The next eight lines contain a series of pun-words carrying double meanings: *prachira* means 'wall' and 'the east'; *bihanga* means 'bird' and 'the sun'; *patanga* means 'the sun' and 'locust'; and *nabaranga* means 'fresh red colour' and 'frolic'.

Basking in the sunshine a swarm of fleas
Swam in the air up and down.
With the sunrise rose butterflies in droves
Frolicking around in the crimson rays.
From their slumber awoke the animals,
And yawning, straightened their backs, to rise.
Monkeys in sport from branch to branch kept jumping –
Ambrosial *laddus* did they in *kendu* berries find?

At this time did the lotus, looking at her husband's face,
With eyes suffused with tears present her heart's sorrow,
But speechless she stayed with her half-blown visage,
Whereupon the bee came forward to divulge all.
Humbly did he submit: 'O God of gods, King of planets,
Of the conduct of humans, how should I narrate?
A poor beggar am I, going about daily
I beg from door to door with a pouch slung by my side.
On the lotus have I pinned a large hope,
For a fistful of her honeyed alms can fill my pouch.
But thinking that people feel put off
By a daily scrounger, I set out for abroad once;
And their brutality did then I witness myself.
They care not for *dharma* being in pursuit of selfish ends.
Honeybees of my kind had through begging
Stocked up the honey-wealth in their stores,
Which the human-vandals set to fire,
And driving the bees away, they made off with the loot.

Flying back to this pond yesterday,
I saw a huge banyan tree on the way,
And people pouring water at its roots
Rendering its cool shade cooler yet.
Never since my birth have I seen it in bloom,
Though I did notice some young shoots colourful,
In which the tree stood charmingly draped.
Thinking that they must be the trees' flowers,
I quickly settled upon them and greedily sucked,
But finding not an iota of honey, I turned back dejected.
Your royal power this tree does not fear,
And stands firm on its countless feet.
But I believe accursed my luck must be
That such a mighty tree failed to satiate me.

When an elephant came thither to pull off
A branch from this tree, a crowd of people did prevent him.
Thereupon he headed for the pond
And saucily invading her watery abode,
He began to molest her, the delicate lotus-dame.
Unable to stand such outrage thus, I stung him
On the forehead, but he being undaunted, I flew away
To the city, wailing and complaining in every home.
The humans had flowers tucked on their ears;
In every ear did I drone my tearful plaint,
Angered at which they shooed me away,
So to Your Highness have I come to report this matter.
In loads the humans carry away lotuses in their need,
But such is their manner when the same lotus in distress is,
And for the banyan that never flowers their respect is so high!
O *Dharma* Incarnate, dispense your justice as you might please.'

The young sun who rose tall in a slender frame
Had extended to the earth rays pleasant and mild,
But in a fiercely bright form from then on
He ruled the earth in a ruthless order.
From us he withdrew the friendly bearing,
And manifesting a power mighty, proclaimed his rule.
Sovereign monarch, He, the sun god thus
Enforced a rigorous code of rules.
Wielding the sceptre of imperial power
He mounted the gigantic elephant, the sky;
More remorseless grew his power in time,
And he scorched the earth more and more.
The vital fluid from the earth he sucked up deep,
Not realising, this could nurture the opponent.
He saw his wife Shade, offering respite to the earth –
On her too he grew harsh, forswearing the love of the spouse.
All the land Shade had covered did he wrest back
With his outstretched hands (rays) bit by bit.
Finding her husband relentless, she withdrew
And held on to the base of trees for shelter.
Rising overhead the sun in fiery blaze
Knocked the earthly beings with pounding rays.
Shaken by the fear of the sun's ire,
The people ran to Shade, the queen, for succour.

Bouncing back from mirrors and penetrating glasses
The sun broke into her chambers to slash her body;
Irate in his pursuit and to apprehend her,
He searched for apertures and chinks, to thrust his hands (rays).
The earth grew desperate by the heat of the angry sun,
The dogs ran for shady cover with lolling tongues.
The bird on the tree branch kept its mouth open
Emitting a faint, weak cry only now and then.
Hardly did it fly from one tree to another,
Tormented by the heat it soon settled on a branch.
Pigeons announced through their cooing
That the hard days had now come.
Limp and effete already, with heads drooping,
New shoots of leaves looked for shaded shelter.
Cattle took refuge under umbrageous trees
Lying still, only chewing the cud.
Some humans to the cool haven of mansions retired,
While some others kept inside their huts;
But the wayfarers walked their ways,
Raising umbrellas overhead, for they had no option else.
In the hope of respite from scorching heat
Buffaloes squatted in ponds and tanks.
A herd of boars in swampy bogs
Wallowed in the soft, hot mud.
In the waters of gurgling springs
Sported the wild elephants in joy.
But all-enduring mother-earth bore
The brunt of their pounding feet,
Thinking it would work for the good of all.
Futile it isn't to proffer precious life-drops (moisture),
For the selfsame drops make a stream of nectar (water);
Countless drops that have been sucked away
Will in time form clouds to swallow the sun,
Little fearing *Yama*'s father.[1]
The month of Cancer[2] will surely pester the sun,
And in the avatar of *Kalika*[3] riding Leo
Will the clouds just wipe off his glory.

---

1. In Indian mythology the Sun is the father of Yama, the god of death,.
2. *Shravan* and *Bhadrab*, monsoon months in India, come under the zodiac signs of Cancer and Leo.
3. Pun on *Kalika*: clouds and Goddess *Kali*.

Soon from the high skies did the sun decline,
With his heart dimmed and shorn of force.
In the same measure as he had scaled high, fell now he low,
Whereupon arose a buzz of joy that he at last had set.
The streets and markets began to bustle
With crowds of humans and herds of cattle.
Flocks of birds upon the trees twittered
Frolicking about in diverse ways.
Off they flew and settled again
With the shrill cries still in their throats –
For what that clamour was all about,
And from what fear they did, flapping their wings, suddenly take off
And fly to the safety of another tree – all this was hard to guess.
Evening advanced upon the earth as soon as the sun had set
And darkness gradually deepened;
From infancy to youth had grown the sun, and yet unwise:
That he would grow old had never occurred to him.
But dotage took more and more a toll of his lustre,
Until at the end his body vanished altogether.
The sun is dead, his power and glory all over,
And the dame lotus now sits there grieving and sad –
All these were but appearances.

Neither does the sun rise nor ever set, in truth;
What we call 'sunrise' is but our first view of his light,
And 'sunset,' when he gets shut out of our sight.
An abode of radiance is this flaming orb, and eternal,
Although, each for a different mien, his names are several.
Never was he an infant, not young nor old does he grow;
Of unchanging age is he, the benefactor of the earth.
The sun that set today would forsooth rise tomorrow,
Belike only Brahman in his diurnal scheme:
When manifested, assumes Brahman a bodily life,
And whenever withdrawn, the creature's life-force ends.
The sun's exit is but the end of the day,
At which his heart neither rejoices, nor grieves.
Clouds that cover the sky only swallow up daylight,
But they cannot ever reach the sun, scaling his height;
Sickness, sorrow and illusions that seize the mortal beings
Affect not Brahman in the least.
Day is there where the sun is to be seen,
So absorbed in Brahman, the being from grief is freed.

O heart, be therefore one with Supreme Brahman,
And the world for you will be an abode of bliss.
Though billions of suns in His hands are playthings,
The wise one through love makes Him as a locket on the breast;
He imparts a bounty of peace, stealing away the heart's anguish,
Sorrows and delusions stay away in fear of Him.
He alone is one's soul-mate all one's life,
And all world's affluence issue from Him.
He watches over the earthly beings, be they wakeful or asleep,
And forgives their countless wrongs.
Whenever and whatever injuries one sustains,
He hastens to eagerly heal the wounds.
Such be His ways with each earthly creature;
Every moment serves He for the world's welfare.
Summer, Rain and Autumn, each a gainful season,
Rotates in His system through the cycle of time.
Thus the seasons of cold and dew came and bade adieu,
And now has come the Spring-Day for the general good.
Into new life reviving the desiccated plants,
Instilling fresh blood in the veins of humans,
And bringing in draughts of cool breeze at dusk, and dawn,
It helps human-life into new foliage burgeon.
Fresh lotuses in water, jasmines in gardens
And the blooming, wild creepers of forest in nature's lap,
All are thrilled, awakened to a new life;
And so should you, o heart, brighten in their company.
Recalling the glory of the Most Exalted Almighty,
Seek refuge at His auspicious feet.

Ashok Kumar Mohapatra

SHORTER POEMS

ADORATION

O Lord, Life of the Universe,
Unwilling is my heart to call you
An Ocean of Mercy, for only a drop
Of your mercy makes the ocean.

In my prayers to you, O Lord,
Let me not be forced to count a rosary,
For with billions of stars in each bead,
Who can perform the count?

You have not given me strength to bear
The dust of your feet on my head,
For countless suns roll
As dust at your holy feet.

You have infinite power
To discern the ways of the heart,
So in the same measure accept my reverence
As my heart, in fine, holds.

There is no space in my little heart
To enshrine your image,
For how can the Himalayas lie
In the womb of a mustard seed?

When all I see are your own kind gift
With what offerings can I worship you?
For to offer back a gift to the One
Who gave it, would be a gross offence!

That this ego is mine alone
In no way can I disown,
This, I offer from afar, O Emperor of the Universe,
As a gift at your sacred feet.

Madhusudan Pati & Jayanta Mahapatra

AMBROSIAL

The fragrance of newly opened buds,
The rhythm of new verse, delicious,
The melodious call of birds in the wild,
The flowing music of children's prattle,
The forest of blissful virgin lotuses
And the tender face of the new-born child:

Ambrosia all, all flowing nectar,
Carries away life in ecstatic flow.

The gentle breath of the cool breeze,
The lily's beloved, beautiful ever, the moon,
Moonbeams in their milk-white gossamer,
Masses of cloud pregnant with rains,
The graceful, delicate light of dawn
And the dew on first-green leaves:

Ambrosia all, all flowing nectar,
Enthrals the world.

The twinkle and glimmer of stars,
The drip drip of falling rain,
The sun charging forward to dispel the murk*
The exulting earth from darkness freed,
And the sounds of waterfalls leaping long:

Ambrosia all, all flowing nectar,
Drenches this life to bliss.

---

* A variant reading: 'The lightning racing to annihilate murk'.

A drop from the ocean of nectar am I,
Who had quit the sea and ascended the sky,
Descending then, mingling with the nectar-stream,
Should the heat of sin wither me on the way,
I shall turn into dew and come down again;

Ambrosia all, all flowing nectar,
Shall merge with the sea.

Jayanta Mahapatra & Madhusudan Pati

HONEYED

Look, O Life, honeyed is this universe,
Look, how full of honey it is!
The stream of honey will erase
Your sins and mortal fears!

A mother's affection, a wife's love,
Righteous talk with friends and the wise,
And a father's fondness; each one, O Life,
Is a stream that drives away the heat!

New deeds, new meanings,
Ever new paths to knowledge,
Reveal on this earth in newer light
Countless streams of honey, O Life!

In honey-filled forests with honeyed voices
The birds burst into honeyed song
Filling the ears, O Life,
Pouring out the sweetness day after day!

The Lord of day in daytime, the night's stars,
And the moon, the lily's companion,
Wander the skies, bestowing on the universe
The honey of light, O Life!

Earth, earth's bracing hills, lakes and seas,
Woods and gardens, hosts of flowers
And rippling foliage; look, O Life,
How thickly are smeared with honey!

The stream of honey is born in the cavern
Of compassion of the Lord of the Universe,
If you strike upwards, your eye on the stream,
You will gain the Mount of Mercy, O Life!

Insignificant you are, but an inhabitant
Of the kingdom of the Merciful High,
If you only stretch your hands, you'll never fail
To win the touch of His holy feet, O Life!

Put salt in the mouth of one snake-bitten – he'ld call it clay.
If honey doesn't taste sweet when you stray
From wisdom, then drink of a venom-killing potion
Ground from the seed of knowledge, O Life!

Jayanta Mahapatra & Madhusudan Pati

SO SPEAKS THE ORIYA MUSE

Dress me, dear, in such fabric soft
    That my limbs do not get sore,
And give, if you must, only ornaments such
    That put me not to the blush.

Present good apparel that fits my body,
    Prune not my frame for a dress to fit;
Such surgery would surely be fatal to life –
    Spare your mother that ardour.

Pare those nails that are overgrown
    Brighten them with *alta* red,
But to slice my nose if you think it is big
    Wouldn't that leave me pitifully deformed?

Treat with medicines if my body has ailments,
    Let me have the relief of a cure,
But if you paint my limbs in exotic colours,
    That would be rank horror!

In whatever style you deck me out
    That would the people note;
And should you rub my body spotless clean
    Pure and bright through the world 'ld I shine.

While applying collyrium to my eyes,
    If perchance the cheeks are smudged,
Torment me not, but only wipe off the blot –
    A charming colour would then at once appear.

Give me the English flowers you have discovered,
If they have fragrance any;
Or if they are at least of some pleasing hue,
They might my charms improve.

Do not, my dears, force a hat on my head
Nor remove my bangles of gold;
And remember ever to keep on my forehead
This spot of vermilion aglow.

Brothers you are, give up your quarrels
Else your wrangles would vitiate my life;
Strive you together to garner gems precious,
And deck me in strings of those.

Do not be delirious with a fevered ego –
Weeps my heart to hear you so jabber;
Intent on wisdom, join in virtuous talk
And may your good words enhance my cheer.

Collect with care many exquisite things
And furnish my temple rich,
And bravely paint all wooden columns
Washing them with liquid gold.

Bring from many lands plants and vines,
And plant them at the heart of my orchard,
A rich harvest of fruits would it yield –
And happily, my children, you 'ld savour all.

Cleanse my house if filth there be
Repair and renovate as you need,
Move around freely, but in a civil manner –
Do not run riot inside.

Don't you trust your prosperity is real,
Till I be positioned high;
A tree can help just a few under it; but a hill
Gifts fruits and water for all a-plenty

The fields of your country cannot be watered
By countless streams upon the Andes –
Who will dispel the heat in your bosom
If my sacred rill does not flow?

In one voice, in one mind all,
Sing aloud, 'Hail, holy muse,'
Raise aloft the banners of glory –
May the sky be filled with immaculate white.

Madhusudan Pati

ANGUISH OF THE FIRE-FLY

Bewails the firefly sorrowing –
Such a slight creature am I,
Why did fate fit me with such tiny wings!
For fear of ridicule
I fly concealed at night,
Or crouch at a distance
Upon the leaf of some tree.

I do not know that I carry
Splendour upon my limbs
And do not wish
To be counted among the stars.

And yet men deride and scoff, saying,
How can a firefly equal the moon!
How, indeed, should I compare with the moon,
With him that gets his lustre from the sun,
While my spark of light is my puny being's own!

I haven't learnt to boast on others' wealth.
Why should I then vie with the moon?

O you men, laugh not at humble things,
Bring forth rather your inner light.

Madhusudan Pati

LAMP ACCOSTING THE SUN

You are true to your name of *Bhaskar*, O Sun,
Illumining all that moves and moves not;
But why turned you hostile against me,
And robbed me of the little light I had?
Darkness, your foe, you annihilate all over,
I, too, efface it the best I can.
Rightly then should you be pleased with me;
So I marvel, what pleasure do you derive
To see my brightness overwhelmed?
You treated my light at par with murk;
Bravo O *Pravakar*,[1]
Bravo that you should be named *Mitra* [2]
O you deity of sight, how strange is it,
You couldn't yourself distinguish darkness from light?
In this your conduct you stand exposed –
You are no god, but some matter gross.

Chandra Sekhar Rath

---

1. One who brightens
2. Friend.

GANESHA'S SOLILOQUY

They worship me as ruler of *Bighnas*,*
And with much sycophancy incite me
To slay the host of Adversities.
Their cajolery – no words of flattery those
But abuse unbearable,
That no human could endure; but I
Manage to tolerate with my divine forbearance.
Elephant-headed some call,
And some call me single-toothed,
Some describe me as a child of mothers two,
Yet others name me – the one of bulging tummy.
If of Adversities I am King, they are my own subjects;
Why should I decimate my people
And unfurl for myself a banner of infamy?
The king of beasts with his animal nature
Might kill off his subject, the deer,
But how should I, a god,
Perform such an unholy, cruel deed?
That one being god should yet destroy his dependents –
This is utterly unheard of, and never seen:
If I exterminate those in my keeping,
Why should then the earth's people adore me?
After they came to know,
The humans were intent upon the death of *bighnas*,
The latter are wreaking their vengeance on men.
But those who befriend them and with cordiality please
The *bighnas* gift them courage and make them happy,
Revealing the path to success.

---

* Impediments

The *bighnas* are ever the guardians
Keeping watch over my storehouse of success –
Success that never comes within the grasp of those
Who keep away from them in fear.

Chandra Sekhar Rath

HE TOO IS CALLED A *DHARMA -AVATARA**

He who yearns ever to usurp from all
Whose wealth gets trampled under harlots' feet,
Whose life is a burden to millions of men,
He too is called a *dharma-avatara.*

Whose knowledge serves to wring the neck of ethics
Whose intellect grinds a hundred truths to dust,
Whose judgement gets bought out with lucre mean,
He too is called a *dharma-avatara.*

Stealing in gold who offers charity in coppers,
Keeps his superior pleased with bribes,
Offers gifts various to shroud his faults,
He too is called a *dharma-avatara.*

Gets his allowance for expenses on tours
Yet eats of the life of the innocent poor,
Bold in the misuse of official power,
He too is called a *dharma-avatara.*

Goes forth from home with empty hands
And returns with cartloads of things,
The same that are put up for sale thereafter,
He too is called a *dharma-avatara.*

Madhusudan Pati

---

* Justice Incarnate.

INVOKING THE VERNAL BREEZE

Welcome, sweet breath of spring,
Blow in tenderly and pass softly by;
Enrapture the natives of Utkal
Conveying them auspicious tidings.
With a gift of burgeoning mangoes, we welcome you;
Smiling out in ripples soft, graciously accept our offer.
Among good men a friend's offering is esteemed high,
So in your hands its merit would surely swell.
Laving in Rushikulya your feet, you relax atop Mahendra,
Take then a dip in Chitrotpala, and drink deep
From the sweet Subarnarekha.
Offering from Mahanadi your oblations, as you roam from wood to wood,
Awhile pause, and feel entranced by
Nrusinghanath's leaping cascade.
The realm, since you left, has suffered debacles many;
First hear from me, friend!
For your sharing have I carefully stored them in mind.
'Tis a relief as you know to unburden before a friend,
So is the cuckoo eloquent when Spring is around.
You had budded the blossoms and reared
The sprouts to smoothly ripen,
But a violent gale came and scattered them dead.
Flowers you had made to bloom and trees to wear foliage;
It destroyed the blossoms, snapped branches and uprooted the trees.
The soft sun you accompanied had showered pleasant rays,
But after you left it grew harsher day by day.
So scorching, it made life vexed and insufferable,
Made blood ooze away as sweat, and sapped the strength of bones.
When the wind hung suspended, tormenting our beings,
We poor creatures fondly then recalled your sweetness.
For some nights vanished the stars and the moon
And days were in darkness palled

Shook the sky with roaring thunder and then poured in torrents;
The streams you see so limpid and crystal clear
Coursed furious then – turgid, overflowing,
Wearing as ornaments all the dirt that had littered the earth,
Bellowing and dancing upon mighty rocks in tumultuous fury.
Sands of this river in summer noons were granules of fire
And in wintry nights turned into icicles cold.
Biting winter surpassed the horrors of summer
The sun himself terrified, ran to the nitch of *Agni* at South-east.
Bodies that in wet-clothes we had covered in the agony of heat,
Eager were we now to bury them under quilts and blankets heavy.
Moonbeams of nectar seemed venom in the coils of winter,
Like the milk of coconut turning poisonous, when mixed with camphor.
Doubtless we had been lavished then with many a fruit and flower,
But the scar of its ravages still in our hearts we bear.
In hot summer we pined for rains and winter, which when we had,
Such their tyranny, again we longed for summer.
All that is subdued now, quietened by your happy advent;
Come along friend, freely gift new joys from your bulging bag.
We are told, your touch transforms many a plant into sandalwood –
What fault then makes our trees here unworthy of the luck?
But no matter if they fail to be sandalwood, they do burst into flowers,
And all the gardens and woods are made fragrant in your embrace.
Open soon the lotus-limpid, jasmine-sweet casket of perfumes,
Dispense your brightening pills, so that all gloom ends.
Lend love to our eyes, and extending your arms, hug us in affection.
Scatter the grains over fields for colourful birds to pick –
In flocks would they fly in the sky absorbed in singing your glory,
And down below in villages, kids overwhelmed in glee
Would cheer the birds to keep their chorus on.
Where had you been so long, dear friend,
In that world too, do they have such heat, gale and cold?
Won't you open the stores of sweetness you have brought for us this year?
Be gracious, give a favourable answer, and quickly enhance our cheer.

Chandra Sekhar Rath

MOTHERLAND

Only when through his neighbours' houses
He toddles, does the child know,
They be the dwellings of friends.
Later when he frequents nearby streets
He takes them, too, as his own.
And then when he leaves his village
To visit another, he knows,
The one where his home is,
That alone is his own.
He speaks of its river, its ponds,
Its orchards and all,
Everything there as his own
And cherishes them as the most wholesome.
Growing up, when he visits another kingdom
He sings the paean of his king,
And of his kingdom, as surpassing all.
Elephants and horses, nay, even sheep and goats,
Everything of his country he terms excellent;
And claims, the kingdom he lives in alone is
An abode complete in felicities.
If someone, having grown bigger yet,
Chances to travel far abroad
Then he comes to feel,
Greater than heaven is the land that holds his home.
Grown wiser, when he appreciates
The Master of the Universe is the father of all,
He views himself as a brother
To all mankind upon the earth.
He then knows,
The more the human beings one serves
The more worthy does he grow as a son
To the Master in His cosmic home.

Thus is the story of the village, the state,
The country, and the world,
Imaged forth everywhere in human life.
If one in whose heart hasn't sprouted yet
Love of the motherland and mother tongue,
If such a one be counted among the wise,
Who then would be deemed as ignorant ones?

Chandra Sekhar Rath

EXHORTATION

Upon this new dawn of a new year
With a new splendour shines a new sun of good fortune.
The new proclamation of the new Emperor
Brings into being a province new.
New strength flows into Utkal's life
And brightens a new path of hope.
For the sun of Utkal, a barrister grown,
Has returned to adore the Mother's feet.
All around reverberates the cry: 'Arise, arise,
Tighten your girdles and work begin.'
Work's steam-engine blowing her conch-like whistle
Waits at the station but, dear me,
You're still lying asleep, and a ticket not yet booked!
See how with eager and urgent steps
Travellers are clambering in.
Dazed, if you merely keep watching the sight
You'ld, my dear, perish in hunger under the tree.
That for which you have traversed thus far,
If you fall behind now, it will come to nought.
The lotus blooms in the light of the new sun
And flocks of birds rise up ebullient.
How long and far they fly from their nests
In search of food and mirth!
The bee, too, greedy for a store of honey
Wanders through forests and mountains far.
No one who has some strength left in him still,
Remains dumb, and into abjectness sinks.
A sleeping lion has no food in its mouth,
But with toil even the ant has its store filled whole.
If you just lie under the tree with an open mouth
The fruits that drop wouldn't by themselves enter.
The elephant, the tiger, the lion of enormous strength
Are all easily trapped by the skill of man.

It is knowledge that fathers skill,
But knowledge cannot be if language is not;
It is only through the power of language that
Man subdues all creatures and reigns in the universe.
An imbecile he whose language is feeble,
For how can he compete with the others?
Those of superior speech slight him as unworthy,
And themselves become leaders in societies high.
Is not that man just an animal
Who knows not the difference between honour and insult?
How can one of weakened tongue acquire knowledge high?
And what honour can he have in the royal court?
If, then, you aspire to elevate yourself
Elevate first your mother-tongue.
And if ambition there be none in your heart,
Enjoy your days upon the royal bed of pleasures.
But then, you must cherish as your necklace,
Your neighbour's kick-marks that you receive on your breast.
If the ruler gives out a call for higher stations
How many of you would be worthy of those?
Confer together and judge, after
You have matched yourselves against your neighbours.
Then you'ld know how pitiable you are,
And know again how lowly you've rendered
Your own mother-tongue.
Is there any other nation on the earth
That experiences shame
To touch a book in the native language?
Arise, breathren, arise:
In this new light if you keep on sleeping
People would watch and in derision laugh.
There is no time even to rub your eyes;
Rise, and on the auspicious path of duties advance.
Make an offering of your wealth, devotion and mind,
And render refulgent
The face of your mother-tongue and land.
The Lord, upon that auspicious path,
Would grant you good fortune,
And your life will be fruitful
In blessed endeavour.

Tapas Kumar Chakrabarty

GLORY

Noble souls observe the vow of serving all,
Like the earth and the sun offering a harvest of sunshine and crops.
Scorched by others the noble ones yet bring them cheer
Like the Himalayas, warmed by the sun, gifting its sweet cool water.
Humble are the great though on lofty heights stationed –
How lofty the sun, the moon and the stars, but all with faces lowered!
When harmed by others a good turn the noble one does,
The sun whom the clouds swallow up, draws moisture to saturate the clouds.
Noble beings, to save the drowning ones, into deeps of danger plunge,
Thus in the desert stands the water-plant to appease the traveller's thirst.
Thrills the noble one's heart to watch others prosper,
Like the lotus, bride of the day's maker, blossoming to see the day larger.
Anxious keeps the noble one to return good to his benefactor,
As the pond, filled by clouds, is ever busy sending up moisture.
Even his life he may lay down for the good of the world,
Like the fireworks, burning himself away, to brighten the face of the earth.
With the noble lie things precious, and with the petty things mean,
In Himalaya you meet the white tusker, and in Barapahad* only the boar.
Seeking support of another noble, the noble one loses not honour –
Knowing this the king of animals, only in the great woods takes his shelter,
A nature's law this – the lowly thrive under noble ones' grace;
Look how the fleeces of cloud, in the sun's light brightly blaze.
With power drawn from the great, even more imperious becomes the petty one,
As sands heated by the sun prove hotter than the sun.
Not unlikely it is, a noble one may spring from a lowly womb,
As lotus from the mud, and pearl from the oyster are born.
Adversity shakes not his fortitude strong –
Gold is ever gold though hammered, or in fire burnt.
Equanimous in weal and woe he preserves his nature noble,
As the vast ocean swells, alike in the new moon and the full.

---

* A small hill-range.

The noble are untarnished in the company of evil,
Like blossoms amid thorns exuding fragrance sweet.
Even if he lives in a den, goodness from the noble doesn't part –
Does *Tulsi* lose its smell when it grows in the cremation ground?
The ignoble one, though highborn, cannot himself sustain high –
Born of lightning, plunges the thunderbolt low.
The evil one's harsh tongue ruffles not the noble heart,
How can the hunter's venomous dart affect the body of adamant?
The deluded know not the value of the noble one's words,
As mere candles they count the sun-like stars.
To tarnish the noble is the nature of the wicked,
But nothing is then lost of his lustre of greatness.
The moon wouldn't lose a whit of its fullness
If purblind eyes of ignorance see it wane.
The noble ones sink not, though to common eyes they may so seem –
Our sun when it sets here, on the American sky is rising.
To be jealous of the great would cause mere heartburn,
To stare hard at the sun would only rob one's vision.
Merrily the good go round singing the noble one's fame,
As the soft breeze spreads around the sandal-wood's perfume.
Noble ones impart cheer, but on that too the evil ones cavil –
As boiling oil flares up when water is sprinkled.
Of a sweet-tongue is the noble one, but the evil one ever talks bitter:
The honeycomb brims with nectar, the comet spits only fire.
At the misery of others wrings the noble heart in pain,
As at the peal of thunder resounds louder the rock-cavern.
Under the wings of the great ones, none for calamities cares –
The wind-powered galleon peacefully sails through the seas.
Good of others is served by the noble one's aid alone,
See how helped by the wind the ship ferries cargo and men.
The world enjoys the happy fruits of the noble one's deeds:
It's by his skill that electricity as a hand-maid serves.
Shrewdly he makes the sky-coursing vapour work as an earthly charioteer,
That conveys horseless carriages at the speed of wind.
Humility shows greatness, as the dawn the advent of the sun –
The cuckoo's dulcet call the approach of spring heralds.
A hundred times more welcome is reprimand from the great –
What worth a low one's praise – a cock's crest to the peacock' tail?
The great is greater in death than in life,
The withered flower yields perfumes more fragrant than in bloom.
Courage, the wish-fulfilling tree, from his exalted heart sprouts –

An essential plant, that feeds all mankind ambrosial fruits.
Praise be to courage that defeats the dread of death
And makes all imperial glories attend as servitors.
The courageous attain the unattainable, the unobtainable obtain –
Thus did Columbus the American shores find by this virtue alone.
Mankind upon his endless journey holds fast the hand of courage
And can by it from the deeps of sorrow gems of joy retrieve.
Man inhabits the abode of gods, the Himalayan peaks,
And trusting his courage rules Lanka, the mythical city of demons.
The noble crave not fame; it is fame that pursues them,
As unsought grows the pearl inside the tusker's head.*
A natural harvest is fame in the field of genius,
Thus with lightning on a mass of cloud, the thunder reverberates.
Uninvited to his abode comes Laxmi, and there luxuriates –
Who, after all, calls the rainbow to frolic upon cataracts?
Only the pomp of robes and ornament makes not a noble man,
Can a multicoloured bead of glass be prized as diamond?
Noble is he, the great among men, who in nature's laws is learned,
And cultivating the love of God, in the holy gem of *dharma* is decked.
The heart of man is a fertile field for the huge tree of *dharma* to grow,
Oh, till it by the plough of learning, and the seed of piety sow.
It needs to be watered by good conduct, and fenced by the company of the true,
Then would issue forth its branches – humility, mercy, geniality and good deeds.
Beautified by the green leaves of devotion to God and service to man,
It unfurls a pure, white, divine flower of eternal fragrance;
Drawn by its aroma the Lord comes flying to kiss it as a bee,
And it bears fruits of undying fame – ambrosia that makes man immortal.
The great alone can know the great, but the blind would remain petty,
Beholding the sunrise smiles out nature, but shuts the owl his eyelids tight.

Chandra Sekhar Rath

---

* A mythical supposition.

MUSINGS OF MOTHER BHARAT [1]

[Manipulating an extended poetic conceit Gangadhar in this poem indicts the British, insightfully relating the political, bureaucratic, cultural and economic insidiousness of colonialism. On the surface, the poem is a love-complaint on behalf of the milkmaids of Vrindaban, conveying the bitterness of the betrayed lasses. The Muse of Poetry takes up the cause of the innocent milkmaids and narrates parts of the history of Krishna's activities as a young boy of Gopa (Vrindaban), making him out as a cheat, a thief, a sorcerer, and a cruel, selfish being. The real thrust of the poem, however, is different. With dexterous use of puns the British colonizers in India are deplored for their guile, hypocrisy, misrule, selfish exploitation, cruelty, ingratitude and evil ways.

This is the last poem by Gangadhar, composed after he had retired from service in 1922. Ed.]

1

In the empyrean of the Golak [2] complained to the Lord the maiden Muse,
All that you have done on the Indian soil the mind cannot efface;
O Lord of Gopa,[3] you defiled our class and clan by deceit
And on whatever was our own imposed your lordship.

2

You subjugated all, by might vanquishing and by evil deeds scaring,
We couldn't even spend our nuptial night without first massaging your feet;
And in that you showed off your generosity -
Guzzling up all our wealth, our mind and pride, to teach us slavery.

---

1. Other variants: Musings of the Muse of Poetry; Anxieties of Lady Bharat.
2. Abode of Vishnu / On the globe of the earth.
3. Krushna (also spelt Krishna)/ the British.

3

After you we laughed, after you talked, with all our mind at your feet
Except for you and yours, we upon this world had no other future;
Lord of Gopa, we danced to your tune and were ever at your beck and call,
Obsessed with your vanity,[1] with our own we trampled our pride and glory.

4

Eating, dressing, sleeping, dreaming, your feet had we ever in mind,
Cupid-stirred, [2] even a moment's separation scorched our inner being.
Lord of Gopa, you're the master of all guile and trick;
Your cups, cushions, coughing – to us you made everything bewitching.

5

In your words lay all sweetness; easily you gauged our minds,
And all things we deemed insipid till in their favour pronounced your lips;
Lord of Gopa, we abhorred like poison our homes and garments,
You held us in spell, and at your looms [3] we paid our honour's coins.

6

Watching your strength grown on our cream and butter
The enemy-warriors [4] took fright, and couldn't do battle;
Lord of Gopa, all that you had then declared,
Did you, when filled with pride of victory, redeem a single pledge?

7

From the day that Akrura [5] an upheaval caused, the bond of affection slackened
And thence was revealed what you really were, and what you had become;
The one whose identity was disclosed in Panchal,
One who was the seed of conflict, his glory you enhanced.

---

1. Also 'wine'.
2. On seeing Cupid / When not finding liquor.
3. Manchester cloth-mills
4. The Germans.
5. *Gandhinija* : Akrura / Mahatma Gandhi, his own.

8

Akrura offered you worship and ignoring his pains to Gopa [1] went,
And, far away, you cared not for our anguished cries and lament;
The banner of fame fluttered the whole world over
That by skill you could douse all fire,[2] and so Ugrasena [3] grew happier.

9

Eventually was revealed our difference, you, a native of Dwaraka,[4]
Had come in infancy to be nurtured upon our wealth;
Lord of Gopa, soon after through the world grew you famous,
But now you feel ashamed to live as friends with us.

10

We didn't visit you to invite you here, you came in pursuit of profit,
We thought you were simple-hearted, and so kept you lovingly at home.
Lord of Gopa, you might claim you did us a favour; but no,
You did it all for your own – we had no need of you.

11

Preceding you, Balaram of the famed mace[5] came too,
Inflammable in nature he was but didn't rob us whole,
He never stole garments like you
Nor did he send fabrics in pity of Drupada's daughter. [6]

12

You toddled along holding our hand, and slowly grew stronger,
And now tell us, without you, we are helpless altogether.
Into your hands we surrendered our life and living,
Aspired for your service, and daily now die in the agony of tears.

---

1. Gandhi went to prison.
2. British Parliament.
3. The joy of the violent army-men increased – reference to General Dyer and the Amritsar massacre.
4. Island abroad.
5. *Mussalman*; Balaram, Krushna's older brother.
6. Cotton export / Protecting Draupadi's honour in the Kaurava court.

13

You butcher the bull[1] as a duty, and drink deadly poison,[2]
Your fame as Putana's killer enlarges the glory of women;[3]
Impossible it is to fathom your womb – those whom as friend
You offered your army,[4] you saw them perishing one and all.

14

The war of Bharat around Krushnā and Krushna[5] rose from deceitful dice
And a faith grew strong – wherever was Krushna, there victory was;
People blamed Duhshasana[6] as the cause of it all
But who could avert it? The decree of Fate was inexorable.

15

The vast fortunes of Virata,[7] enjoyed shrewdly the sons of Pandu,
The masters stepped back, and ended up worshipping their feet;
The answer[8] finally came, and uncovered the guile and force:
Now they were fated to live only as revenue-payers.

16

Great warriors fed on the Kauravas, but wished the Pandavas' victory
Grieving on your insult they held only Duryodhan guilty.
Both camps had nurtured their devotion to you,
Yet your goodwill never helped any foe of the Pandavas.

---

1. Krushna had killed a bull-demon / The British love beef.
2. Krushna had sucked the poison-tipped nipples of Putana / the British love biscuits.
3. Snide remark against promiscuous British women.
4. The Kauravas / Allies whom the British destroyed.
5. Blacks and non-blacks (white).; Krishnā : Draupadi, the Pandava queen.
6. Brother of Duryodhana in the *Mahabharata* / bad governance.
7. Where the exiled Pandavas took shelter, incognito, during the last year of their exile / Vast land which the British usurped.
8. Prince of Virata, Uttara.

17

Fault not the letters; add the right sibilant to get at the meaning,
Light and heavy, long and short, contrive as needed,
Dear reader, that duty rests in your hands;
With bowed head submits the composer – you be the adjudicator.

Chandra Sekhar Rath

THE SAFE HARBOUR

Unwavering refuge have I taken
At your feet, O Lord mine,
Sure that, someday, in life or in death
Your mercy would descend on me.

Your feet are the refuge of the world,
And whether they adore those or not,
Can you, indeed, inflict
Endless grief, and bear to see
The poor things struggling through the sea of life?

Passing fast are days and nights
Passing fast months and years,
And it defies my understanding
That this my afflicted state should never change.

How can you spurn
That which you yourself have made!
Your punishment I'ld deem my glory –
How then wouldn't you soften towards me?

Yes, redeem you may or destroy
You may surely do as you please,
And knowing that all be your wish
This my self'ld quietly bide his time.

A secret truth have I heard, O Lord,
And continually do ponder –
However great the sin, you can't
Force one out of your world, ever.

Tapas Kumar Chakrabarty

CONSECRATION

Hail, O Lord of the universe!
Hail, O Lord of all things!
The source of my life, oh hail!
Why don't you prevent,
When my mind strays wayward?
And when I offer it at your feet
In worshipful adoration,
Why do you, in contempt of the sin,
Fling it away –
You who are famed as
Saviour of all?

I have taken refuge at your feet
For you alone are in the world
Redeemer of terrible sins.
How then would they be absolved
If you take fright and remove yourself away?

If you call this my delusion
And the sins only what my deeds have earned,
Then I offer here all my life's earning–
Be merciful, O Lord, to accept them.

Is not the mind your own gift?
And isn't it paramount in life?
What justice is it then –
You demur at accepting what you yourself have given?

Tapas Kumar Chakrabarty

THE BEE'S PRAYER FOR HONEY*

Glory be to you, O Lord
From whom bodies forth the honeyed moon
In the honeyed sky; you
Have made this universe all honeyed, O Lord:
Grant us nectarous fame.

By day the sun, and planets and stars by night,
Through them is manifest your honeyed effulgence,
And the mountains and the winds,
The world entire is
The home of your honeyed presence.

With the honey you have sweetened
The cuckoo's song and the music of the harp,
With honey have you sprayed
The flowering garden and faces of children.

Flowers, fruits, stems, trees,
Sticks of sugarcane,
They carry your nectar all
Which fills too the rivers and fountains
The lakes and clouds of rain.

You have squeezed honeyed drops, and smeared
The eyes of love and wise discourse,
And so for honey does this beggar bee
Pray at your lotus feet ceaselessly.

Tapas Kumar Chakrabarty

---

* *The Utkal Madhup* (The Bee of Utkal) was a monthly journal. Gangadhar composed this poem on request on the occasion of its commemoration.

WRITTEN ON THE ANNIVERSARY OF *THE UTKAL SEVAK*

With a new gift and renewed zest in the New Year,
O You five-year *sevak** move from door to door.
Speak close into each ear
News from abroad, and beneficent things for the country;
Failing once repeat, till the message sinks deep,
Tire not ever, for this your obligation is, this your sacred duty.
In return of rude rebuffs always words of sweetness speak
Visit all households as a guest, but look not for welcome,
View not as an alien one who treats you not well nor offers a fare.

A few days hence shall come the full-moon of Paus;
In the morning you'll see urchins, shivering in the cold-wind
Going round collecting fistfuls of rice, singing the *chher chera* songs,
Holding a small basket in the left hand and a stick in the right.
One would be naked, another with his mother's old *saree*
Wrapped around the body with a knot behind the neck,
The long piece in several folds.
Someone might be in his father's ancient, tattered clothes
Half of it worn loose, and the other half slung as a bag from the neck.
Another might have worn a towel, held in many knots,
And yet keep a small length free for gifts of *chher chera.*
Delighted they'll move in groups from door to door
And return with their pigmy satchels and baskets full of rice;
Every hamlet would resound to the cries of *chher chera*
And the tapping of sticks - you'll watch it amused.
Till the household offers them some rice,
They'd continue their loud chorus to the tapping of sticks.

---

* Serving person.

A five-year old *sevak* yourself, have an initiation from those kids,
Go to people of note, from home to home, seeking their favour;
Keep on pleading and imploring till your suit is granted,
For none would mind your persistence, nor take offence.
Forget not, till every child has a cover and a shelter,
Your goal is not achieved, your satchel not filled.

Chandra Sekhar Rath